KAREN BROWN'S

Germany

Charming Inns & Itineraries

Dedicated to Astrid

May you soon walk through the Brandenburg Gate

Contents

Introduction

From the sand dunes of the North Friesian Islands to the snow-capped Alps, Germany has a great variety of destinations. To help you choose what to visit we have designed seven driving itineraries, each highlighting the beauty of a particular region. Whether you want to explore the restored baroque city of Dresden, marvel at Ludwig of Bavaria's fantasy palaces, or go hiking in the Black Forest, we have an itinerary to suit you. To further help you in choosing where to go, we have listed outstanding sights beginning on page 12. Sightseeing that you will want to go out of your way to visit is highlighted in the itineraries with an asterisk (*). Because we believe that where you lay your head each night makes the difference between a good and a great vacation we have included a section on wonderful little hotels that we enjoy throughout Germany—you'll find lots of fluffy down comforters and gargantuan breakfast buffets.

The Brandenburg Gate

About Germany

The following pointers are given in alphabetical order, not in order of importance.

BEER AND WINE

BEER: Germany's national drink, beer, is served at beer halls and taverns, particularly in the southern part of the country. Munich is the capital of beer drinking and a visit would not be complete without taking in the Hofbrauhaus beer hall and, in summer, visiting a German beer garden such as the one in the Englischer Garten. Brewed across the nation, the beers vary from light (*helles*) to dark (*dunkles*). From bottled beer served in glasses to foaming steins filled straight from the barrel, beer is consumed in copious quantities.

WINE: Eleven different wine-growing regions producing mostly white wine stretch from Bonn south to Lake Constance, with each region's wines having a very distinctive flavor. The wine regions often have a signposted route that combines sights and wineries in such a way that you work up a proper thirst. You can sample wines by the glass in taverns—*weinstube* and *weinhaus*–while restaurants offer house wines served in pottery jugs and bottles from a wine list. However, the most appealing way to celebrate German wines is to attend one of the more than 500 wine festivals that take place in the wine regions from July to late October—the Tourist Office can give you details about festivals and tours.

When looking at German wine lists, selecting an appropriate bottle often seems a daunting task. If you can see the wine labels, your job is made much easier since the label tells you the district, producer, type of grape used, and the year it was bottled. In addition, look for labels with yellow borders or backgrounds denoting dry wine, and those with lime green denoting semi-dry. Sometimes the labels are not color-coded and the word *trocken* indicates dry and *halbtrocken* semi-dry. Labels grade the wine into *tafelwein*—tablewine, *qualitatswein*—quality wine, and *qualitatswein mit pradikt*—quality wine with special attributes. Some of the wine regions also have special glasses "just for their wine" such as the green-colored wine glass of the Mosel.

CURRENCY

The unit of currency in Germany is the Deutsche Mark, abbreviated to DM. One DM is equivalent to 100 Pfennigs. Banking hours vary, but banks are usually open weekdays from 9 am to noon and again from 2 to 3 pm. Currency exchange offices are located at airports and railway stations in large cities. As a convenience to their guests and clients, hotels and department stores will also often convert foreign currency to Deutsche Marks.

EATING

Hearty appetites are catered for—you will certainly not starve.

Breakfast (*Frühstück*) consists of a copious assortment of delicious rolls, wurst or sausages, patés, cheeses, homemade jams, country butter, and often cereals, yoghurt, or fresh cream.

Lunch (*Mittagessen*) is often the main meal in Germany. Served customarily from noon to 2 pm, it generally consists of soup, meat, and vegetables. However, when traveling, you might opt to save valuable afternoon time by stopping at a brewery (*brähaus*) or beer hall (*bierkeller* or *biergarten* in the parks) for simpler fare of hot sausage, sauerkraut, and fried potatoes accompanied by a glass of cold beer.

Another popular daytime dining option is the pastry shop (*konditorei*) where you can enjoy the treat of having your pastries and cakes served *mit schlag*, a thick helping of cream that makes any regional specialty a delight (albeit a calorific one).

Dinner (*Abendessen*) is usually enjoyed between 6 and 9 pm. When served at home it is usually a light meal, but in restaurants you will find the same types of meals as at midday. Except in tourist centers, the menus are printed only in German, so take your dictionary to dinner with you.

ELECTRICITY

The voltage is 240. Most hotels have American-style razor points for 110 volts. If you want to take your favorite hairdryer, make certain it has dual voltage and purchase a kit of electrical plugs in various sizes and shapes.

ENGLISH

Many Germans speak some English. In large cities, airports, major hotels, and most tourist destinations you will have no problem communicating in English, but in eastern Germany, small towns, cafés, rural railway stations, and the like, you may find that very little English is spoken.

FESTIVALS AND FOLKLORE

With claim to such legends as Snow White and The Pied Piper of Hamelin and with a colorful history, the Germans can find numerous occasions for festivals and celebrations honoring everything from children saving a town from destruction to the completion of the grape harvest. Since these are staged over the course of the year, it would be impossible to experience them all when on a limited holiday, but it might prove rewarding to plan your travel dates to coincide with a particular festival. Some of the possibilities are the following, listed by town:

Bad Durkheim: Second and third Sundays in September—Germany's largest wine and sausage festival.

Bad Harzburg: April 30—*Walpurgisfeier*, the night the witches come to life for one night of merry celebration.

Bad Tolz: November 6—*Leonhardiritt*, a fun-filled parade to honor the patron saint of animals.

Dinkelsbühl: Third Monday in July—*Kinderzeche*, a reenactment of the children saving the town during the Thirty Years' War.

Hamelin: Sundays in July and August—a reenactment of the Pied Piper spiriting away the town's children.

Heidelberg: First Saturday in June, July, and September—the castle is illuminated and fireworks are fired over the river.

Koblenz–Braubach: Second Saturday in August—*The Rhine in Flames*, the Rhine valley between the towns of Koblenz and Braubach is lit by bonfires and floodlights.

Munich: Late September and early October—*Oktoberfest*, the world's biggest beer festival.

Rothenburg: One Sunday a month in summer—*Maistertruk*, a reenactment of the drinking feat that saved the town from destruction during the Thirty Years' War.

GETTING AROUND

BOATS and RIVER CRUISES: Köln-Düsseldorfer German Rhine Line (known as KD for short) operates cruises and day excursion services on the Rhine, Mosel, Main, Danube, and Elbe rivers from April to the end of October. These excursions vary in duration from several hours to a week. No reservation is needed for day-ferry boat services—you buy your ticket from the pier before departure. The most popular excursions are the half-day trip through the Rhine gorge between Koblenz and Mainz; along the Mosel river between Koblenz and Cochem; and the Elbe river between Wittenberg (Luther's town) and Prague. For brochures contact KD River Cruises, 2500 Westchester Avenue, Purchase, NY 10577, tel: (914) 696-3600 or (800) 346-6525, fax: (914) 696-0833, or KD River Cruises, 323 Geary Street, Suite 603, San Francisco, CA 94102, tel: (415) 392-8817 or (800) 858-8587, fax: (415) 392-8868.

BUSES: In conjunction with the German Railroad, buses make the trip along the Romantic Road between Füssen and Würzburg. Principal stops include Rothenburg and Dinkelsbühl. Additional service connects Mannheim, Heidelberg, and Rothenburg. If you have a German Flexipass or a Eurailpass, the price of the bus ticket is included and you do not need to pay a supplement. The buses operate on a seasonal basis. Schedules are available from the German Tourist Office and are published in the Thomas Cook European Timetable.

CAR RENTAL: All major car rental companies are represented throughout Germany at airports and in the city areas. There is a definite price advantage to reserving and pre-paying for a car rental, but remember you will have to pay taxes and insurance locally. Also, depending on the policies and locations of a particular company, there are often surcharges for returning a car to a place other than the originating rental location. Gasoline is very expensive, so budget this as part of your trip if you are driving and be aware that small service stations in the countryside often do not accept payment by credit card. Your local driver's license is accepted in Germany where the minimum driving age is 18. Automatic transmission is usually available only in larger, more expensive vehicles. Lead-free fuel is *bleifrei.*

DRIVING: The German road network consists of autobahns (freeways/motorways marked with blue signs) and secondary roads (also excellent highways). Traffic moves fast on the autobahns where, unless signposted, there is no speed limit. On the secondary highways the speed limit is 100 kilometers (62 miles) per hour. The speed limit within city and town boundaries is usually 50 kilometers (31 miles) per hour. There are a few toll roads, usually over secondary mountain passes, but these are not always open.

While most road signs are international symbols, a few very important ones are usually written: *einbahnstrasse*—one-way street, *links fahren*—keep left, *parken verboten*—no parking, and *umleitung*—detour.

TRAINS: From the high-speed ICE train to the local trains that stop in every little village, Germany has a rail system which is easy to use, operates on time, and embraces over 30,000 kilometers of track, enabling the tourist to criss-cross the nation with ease. Trains arrive and depart with clockwork-like precision. The cars are marked on the outside with their destination and first or second class, and within each there are seating areas for smoking and no smoking. Most trains of substantial size have a dining car, while those that do not often have a vendor who sells snacks and drinks from a cart. In each train station there is usually an information desk where someone speaks English to assist you with schedules. Other services at large stations include currency exchange, accommodation information, shops, and restaurants. Baggage carts are free.

For trains within Germany you can buy point-to-point tickets or a German Flexipass, or use a Eurailpass. We highly recommend the Flexipass that permits unlimited rail travel in all of Germany for five, ten, or fifteen days within the period of one month. Travel does not have to be on consecutive days. The super-high-speed ICE trains that link many of the major cities in Germany (such as Hamburg to Munich, Hamburg to Frankfurt, and Berlin to Munich) are covered by the Flexipass, but reservations are necessary. The Flexipass also allows free travel on buses along the Romantic Road and reductions on river steamers on the Rhine and Mosel rivers. In the USA you can purchase these tickets from DER Tours, 9501 West Devon, 4th floor, Rosemont, IL 60018, tel: (708) 692-6300. For Eurailpasses or Flexipasses you can phone (800) 782-2424 or fax (800) 282-7474. For point-to-point reservations and general information you can fax (800) 282-7474. In addition to being the agent in the United States for the German Flexipass and train tickets, DER offers several short tours that include transportation and accommodation.

HISTORY

Germany has always been a country of shifting frontiers. Since Roman times the country was continually subdivided in an ever-changing mosaic of "units" of different degrees of political importance. These "units" comprised states, kingdoms, Hanseatic cities, free towns, principalities, and ecclesiastical fiefs. Held together by leagues, reichs, confederations, and empires, Germany fills vast volumes of European history. In 1871 Germany became a united country and this unity lasted until 1945 when the country was occupied by Britain, France, America, and Russia (the Allies) at the conclusion of World War II. In 1949 the British, French, and American sectors were linked as the German Federal Republic—West Germany. The Russian sector developed into the German Democratic Republic (East Germany). In November 1989, the Berlin Wall came crashing down, astounding and inspiring the entire world. It took only until the fall of 1990 for Germany to become officially once again a single nation.

This nation has been home to some of the world's most influential leaders: Charlemagne, Frederick Barbarossa, Otto the Great, Martin Luther, Frederick the Great, Bismarck, and Adolf Hitler. Although there has been an impressive list of German leaders who have shaped world history, it is Ludwig II, King of Bavaria, who is most often remembered by tourists. Ruling Bavaria between 1864 and 1886, Ludwig II is fondly known as Mad King Ludwig. A notable patron of art and music, he idolized and subsidized the composer Richard Wagner. Lonely, eccentric, cut off from the mainstream of world politics and obsessed by the glories of the past, Ludwig sought solace in a fanciful building scheme—his Bavarian castles of Neuschwanstein, Herrenchiemsee, and Linderhof. His building extravaganzas brought Bavaria to the brink of bankruptcy and, before he could begin on further palaces, he was declared unfit to rule by reason of insanity. Within a week of his deposition, Ludwig drowned in Lake Starnberg (under circumstances always shaded with mystery).

Your travels will be enriched if you do some reading before your departure to comprehend and associate all that you will see.

HOLIDAY ROUTES

The Goose Girl–Gottingen

Germany has a network of holiday routes that allow visitors to follow special interest, scenic, and historical paths. All are signposted and indicated on most maps. A sampling of the more popular routes are:

Burgenstrasse—The Castle Highway between Mannheim and Nürnberg.

Alpenstrasse—The German Alpine Way between Berchtesgaden and Lindau.

Marchenstrasse—The German Fairy-Tale Route between Hanau and Bremen.

Weinstrasse—The German Wine Road between Schweigen and Bockenheim.

Moselweinstrasse—The Mosel River Wine Route between Trier and Koblenz.

Romantische Strasse—The Romantic Road between Würzburg and Füssen.

Schwarzwald Hochstrasse—The Black Forest High Road between Baden-Baden and Freudenstadt.

INFORMATION

Within Germany, a big blue "I" denotes the location of the tourist information booths in all major towns, train stations, airports, and tourist centers. Before you go, information can be obtained from the German National Tourist Offices.

German National Tourist Office, 122 East 42nd Street, 52nd Floor
New York, NY 10168, USA, tel: (212) 661-7200, fax: (212) 661-7174.

German National Tourist Office, 11766 Wilshire Blvd., Suite 750
Los Angeles, CA 90025, USA, tel: (310) 575-9799, fax: (310) 575-1565.

German National Tourist Office, Nightingale House, 65 Curzon Street
London W1Y 7PE, England, tel: (0171) 495-3990, fax: (0171) 495-6129.

German National Tourist Office, 175 Bloor Street, North Tower, 6th Floor
Toronto, Ontario M4W 3R8, Canada, tel: (416) 968-1570, fax: (416) 968-1986.

German National Tourist Office, Lufthansa House, 143 Macquarie Street, 9th Floor
Sydney 2000, Australia, tel: (021) 367-3890, fax: (021) 367-3895.

SHOPPING

Most shops are open Monday through Friday from 9 am to 6 pm and Saturday until noon
or 2 pm. Many small shops close for an hour or two in the middle of the day when the
shopkeeper goes home for lunch. In resort areas, some of the shops are open seven days
a week.

You will discover the same consistently high standard of products throughout Germany
as a group of well-known manufacturers distribute their products nationwide. Price
variations are minimal. Department stores are large and display a magnificent assortment
of items. In the cities some of Germany's larger department store chains to watch for are
Kaufhof, Hertie, Karstadt, and Horten, as they usually have excellent souvenir
departments and competitive prices.

SALES TAX: If you buy goods and have the store ship them out of the country, you will
not be charged Germany's 15% Value Added Tax. If you plan to carry your purchases
home with you, you can be reimbursed the tax you paid by one of two methods. The first
is to show all your receipts and merchandise at the Tax Check Service at the airport as
you leave the country and they will reimburse you immediately, less a small
commission. The more time-consuming process involves asking for a tax refund form at

the time of purchase or saving all receipts and getting forms from the customs office. When you leave the country or cross a border, be sure to have these forms stamped by the German customs official. If you are leaving by train, you must get off the train at the border and have the customs inspector stamp the form. Keep your purchases together because the customs agent will probably want to see what you have bought. After your trip, mail the forms back to the stores from which you made your purchases and they will reimburse the tax you paid in Deutsche Marks to your home address.

TELEPHONES

Calls made from your hotel room can be exceedingly expensive due to a surcharge system. The easiest and least expensive method to call the USA is to use telephone calling cards that are issued by AT&T, MCI, and Sprint. With these cards, you dial a number that connects you into the American phone system and charges your call to your card.

WEATHER

Rainfall occurs at all times of year. Autumn is mild and long, spring chilly and late, winter often snowy and cold, and summer can vary from cloudless and balmy through hot and muggy to cold and wet. Bring a woolen sweater, a fold-up umbrella, and a raincoat that can be taken off as the day warms, and you will be all set to enjoy Germany rain or shine, cold or warm.

About Itineraries

The second section of this guide outlines driving itineraries throughout Germany. At the beginning of each itinerary we suggest our recommended pacing to help you decide the amount of time to allocate to each region. Most sightseeing venues operate a summer and winter opening schedule with the changeovers occurring around late March/early April and late October. If you happen to be visiting at the changeover times, be sure to check whether your chosen venue is open before making plans. While we try to give an accurate indication of opening times, there is every possibility that these will have changed by the time you plan your trip so before you embark on an excursion check the days (lots of places are closed on Mondays) and hours of opening. We indicate outstanding sightseeing spots by preceding them with an asterisk (e.g., ***Burg Eltz**).

HIGHLIGHTS

To help you decide where to go and what to see, here are the highlights of our itineraries.

Bavaria

Munich, a delightful city whose major sights are: **Marienplatz**, the lively town center; **Hofbräuhaus**, a world-famous beer hall; **Englischer Garten**, a most attractive park; **Alte Pinakothek**, a spectacular art museum; **Residenz Museum** an outstanding museum; and in its suburbs **Dachau**, a concentration camp with the motto "Never Again."

Berchtesgaden, a pretty mountain resort ringed by the Alps. On the edge of town visit the **Salzbergwerk** (salt mine). Drive to the nearby **Königssee**, a picturesque, high Alpine lake. Tour along the **Alpenstrasse**, a narrow road that winds along just below the Alpine peaks. The most photographed place along the Alpenstrasse is **Ramsau church.**

Garmisch-Partenkirchen, a larger, picturesque Alpine resort perfect for hiking, walking, and sightseeing.

Linderhof, Ludwig's oh-so-fanciful home totally over the top in design and decor. In the garden you find the **Venus Grotto,** a man-made cave complete with lake and shell-shaped boat even more fanciful than the house.

Neuschwanstein, Ludwig's early Disney castle, a riot of turrets with a fantasy interior set in a magnificent location.

Wieskirche, a simple countryside church with a magnificent painted interior.

Lindau, a quaint walled town on an island in the Bodensee.

Meersburg, a quaint walled town with a castle that is fun to explore on the banks of the Bodensee. From here take a day trip to **Mainau,** an island in the Bodensee with magnificent sub-tropical gardens.

Highways and Byways of the Black Forest

Take to the quieter side roads to enjoy picture-book scenery.

Schwarzwälder Freilichtermuseum, a collection of old Black-Forest farmhouses.

Baden-Baden, a resort town famous for its casino and health spas: **Friedrichsbad,** the suits-off spa and **Caracalla Therme,** the suits-on spa.

Castles of the Rhine and Mosel

The **Rhine gorge** between Koblenz and Mainz is the most scenic section of this powerful river. Visit the castle **Burg Rheinfels.**

River Mosel, a meandering river in a steep-banked valley covered in terraced vineyards. Picturesque villages include **Beilstein, Zell,** and **Bernkastel-Kues.**

Burg Eltz, the most wonderful fairy-tale castle I have ever seen, is still a family home.

The Romantic Road and the Neckar Valley

Würzburg is not a particularly interesting city but if you enjoy baroque architecture, you will adore the magnificent **Residenz** (palace).

Creglingen, a not-too-interesting village on the Romantic Road with the most superb altarpiece in its nearby church, **Herrgottskirche**.

Rothenburg, the justifiably world-famous, medieval walled town with lots of interesting sightseeing and a **nightwatchman** to point you in the right direction.

Deutsche Greifenwarte, the Raptor Research Center in Schloss Guttenberg, where the talons of eagles in flight almost brush the top of your head.

Highlights of the Harz Mountains

The **Harz mountains,** with their tumbling streams, green forests, and cool blue lakes.

Goslar, a quaint town at the northern foot of the mountains with lots of attractions. On the edge of the town you can tour a mine, the **Rammelsberger Bergbaumuseum**.

Wernigerode, a quaint town of half-timbered houses and an exquisite town hall. Visit the homey castle **Schloss Wernigerode** rising above the town and ride a steam train, the **Harzquerbahn,** into the mountains.

Quedlinburg, a magnificent city with a great many unrestored medieval houses—it's like talking a walk back in time, though some may find it shabby. An interesting castle and church overlook the town.

Exploring Eastern Germany

Eisenach, a not-very-interesting city, has Bach's home (**Bachhaus**) and **Wartburg castle** on its outskirts.

Weimar has an attractive town center and Goethe's home (**Goethehaus**).

Dresden, the city of culture, was badly damaged in the closing days of World War II. Cranes dot the skyline and restoration is well under way. Stroll by the **Parade of Princes,** a porcelain mural. Spend a week museum-hopping in the **Zwinger Palace**. Include the **Gemäldegalerie Alte Meister** (European paintings) and **Porzellansammlung** (porcelain museum). Visit nearby **Meissen** where you can see the famous porcelain being produced at the **Staatliche Porzellanmanufaktur** (porcelain factory).

Spreewald, an agricultural area where you travel on quiet canals that connect traditional Sorb villages.

Potsdam, not a town with lots to see, but on its outskirts the magnificent palaces of **Sanssouci** will astound you.

Berlin, a large city perfect for city lovers. Tour the bullet-riddled **Reichstag** (parliament building). Walk beneath the **Brandenburg Gate**. Marvel in the **Pergamon Museum** at the Pergamon Altar and Babylonian Street. Be amazed at how folks escaped across the wall at **Haus Am Checkpoint Charlie**. Visit everlasting beauty Nefertiti at the **Ägyptisches Museum**. Stroll amongst the gardens of the Hohenzollerns' grand palace, **Schloss Charlottenburg**.

Schleswig Holstein–the land between the seas

Hamburg, a lively city where a large body of water, the **Aussenalster,** stretches from the city to the suburbs.

Lübeck, an attractive, walled, red-brick town.

Sylt, the jewel of the Frisian Islands whose capital **Keitum** is the island's prettiest village.

MAPS

At the beginning of each itinerary a map shows the itinerary's routing, places of interest along the way, and towns with recommended hotels. These itinerary maps are an artist's drawings, not to exact scale, and should be considered as no more than an overview. To supplement them, you will need a set of detailed maps that will indicate all the highway numbers, autobahns, autobahn access points, alternative little roads, and exact distances. Our suggestion is to purchase a road atlas with a scale of 1:300,000 or the Hallwag regional maps that come with an index. Mark your itinerary route with a highlight pen. Driving into cities without the aid of a detailed street map (obtainable from German Tourist Offices) is not recommended.

About Hotels

This guide does not cover the many modern hotels in Germany with their look-alike bedrooms, televisions, and direct-dial phones. Rather, it offers a selection of personally recommended hotels that might be a splendid 12th-century castle crowning a mountain top or a simple vintner's house perched on the banks of the Mosel. But there is a common denominator—they all have charm. Therefore, if you too prefer to travel spending your nights in romantic wine houses, appealing little chalets, dramatic castles, thatched cottages, and 14th-century post stations, we are kindred souls.

For some of you, cost will not be a factor if the hotel is outstanding. For others, budget will guide your choices. The appeal of a simple little inn with rustic wooden furniture will beckon some, while the glamour of ornate ballrooms dressed with crystal chandeliers and gilded mirrors will appeal to others. What we have tried to do is to indicate what each hotel has to offer and describe the setting, so that you can make the choice to suit your own preferences. We feel that if you know what to expect, you will not be disappointed, so we have tried to be candid in our appraisals.

Our goal is to recommend hotels that we think are outstanding. All of the hotels featured have been visited and selected solely on their merits. Our judgments are made on the charm of the hotel, its setting, cleanliness, and, above all, the warmth of welcome. No hotel ever pays to be included in our guide. However, no matter how careful we are, sometimes we misjudge a hotel's merits, or the ownership changes, or unfortunately sometimes hotels just do not maintain their standards. If you find a hotel is not as we have indicated, please let us know, and accept our sincere apologies.

Introduction–About Hotels

AFFILIATIONS

GAST IM SCHLOSS: Many of the castle-like hotels have the notation *Gast im Schloss* ("Guest in a Castle") which indicates that the hotel belongs to an affiliation of historical castle hotels. Most of these accommodations are in proper castles, although some are in charming old mills or romantic manor houses—the common denominator is that they must be in an old structure of historical charm.

RELAIS & CHATEAUX: Without a doubt this is the most prestigious, expensive hotel affiliation. Dress up smartly in the evenings to enjoy formal dinners in luxurious, elegant surroundings.

ROMANTIK HOTELS: Many hotels in this guide are prefaced by the name "Romantik." This designates the hotel as belonging to a group of owner-managed hotels that have a similar standard of historic charm. Almost all the Romantik hotels that we recommend are historic (often folksy), old-world hotels in delightful small towns.

CREDIT CARDS

Whether or not a hotel accepts payment by credit card is indicated using the terms: none accepted, AX–American Express, MC–MasterCard, VS–Visa, or simply, all major.

FINDING HOTELS

At the back of the book is a key map of the whole of Germany plus four regional maps showing each recommended hotel's location. The pertinent regional map number is given at the right on the *top line* of each hotel's description. To make it easier for you, we have divided each location map into a grid of four parts, a, b, c, and d, as indicated on each map's key. To assist you in finding towns where we have hotels, we give some indication of their location on the bottom or next-to-bottom line of the hotel description.

RATES

Rates are those quoted to us for the 1996 summer season. The rates, in Deutsche Marks (DM), are for two people sharing a room, including tax, service, and breakfast. Some hotels have suites at higher prices, which we also include. Be aware that throughout Germany, during festivals, conferences, or special market fairs, room prices increase. Please use the rates we give as a guideline and be certain to ask what the rate is at the time of booking.

RESERVATIONS

Reservations can be confining and usually must be guaranteed by a deposit. However, if you have your heart set on a particular hotel, avoid disappointment and make a reservation. Reservations should always be made in advance for the major tourist cities and resorts during the peak season of June through September, and also during certain special events such as Oktoberfest in Munich. Space in the countryside is a little easier. There are several options for making hotel reservations:

FAX: If you have access to a fax machine, this is a very quick way to reach a hotel. With a fax there is less of a chance for a misunderstanding because you have your response in "black and white."

LETTER: If you start early, you can write directly to the hotels and request exactly what you need. Clearly state the following: number of people in your party; how many rooms you desire; whether you want a private bathroom; date of arrival and date of departure. Ask the rate per night and if a deposit is needed. When you receive a reply, send the deposit requested and ask for a receipt. NOTE: When corresponding with Germany, be sure to spell out the month. Do not use numbers since in Europe they reverse the format used in the United States—for example, 6/9 means September 6, not June 9. Allow four weeks for an answer. Although most hotels can understand a letter written in English, opposite we have provided a reservation request letter in German and English.

Introduction–About Hotels

RESERVATION REQUEST LETTER

HOTEL NAME & ADDRESS
Ich mochte anfragen: I would like to request:

Number of rooms with private bath/shower
Wieviele zimmer mit bad oder douche

Number of rooms without private bath/shower
Wieviele zimmer ohne bad oder douche

Number of persons in our party
Die anzahl der person unsere groupe

Arrival date (spell out month)   Departure date (spell out month)
Wir kommen an _____   *Wir fahren ab*_____

Please let me know as soon as possible the following: *Bitte lassen sie mich bald wie moglich*:

Can you reserve the space requested?   Yes   No
Ob sie die angefragten zimmer haben?   *Ja* _____   *Nein*

Rate per night?
Der preis per nacht?

Are meals included in your rate?   Yes   No
Sind die mahlzeit in diesem preis einschliesslich?   *Ja* ___   *Nein*

Do you need a deposit?   Yes   No
Benotigen sie eine anzahlung?   *Ja* ____   *Nein*

How much deposit do you need?
Wenn ja, wie hoch?

Thank you, and Best Regards,   *In voraus, herzlichen dank, mit Freundlichen Grussen,*

YOUR NAME & ADDRESS

RESERVATION SERVICE: Travel agents and members of the general public in the United States can make reservations at all of the hotels in this guide through **Euro-Connection**, 7500 212th Street SW #103, Edmonds, WA 98026, tel: (800) 645-3876 or (206) 670-1140, fax: (206) 775-7561. In addition to making hotel reservations, Euro-Connection can rent cars, purchase rail tickets, book private cars and drivers, and plan custom itineraries. Often it will cost you the same price to book through Euro-Connection as it would to make reservations yourself, though in some instances a fee for service will be built into the price you pay. We have always found Euro-Connection to be reliable and their staff knowledgeable but we are not in any way affiliated with them and cannot be responsible for any reservations made through them nor money sent as deposits or prepayments. Details of their services follow the index.

TELEPHONE: If you speak German, telephone for your reservation and you can have your answer immediately. If space is not available, you can then choose an alternative. Consider what time it is in Germany when you call (even the most gracious of owners are sometimes a bit grouchy when awakened at 3 am). Basically, the system from the United States is to dial 011 (the international code), 49 (Germany's code), then the city number (dropping the 0 in front of the city code), then the telephone number. If you are calling WITHIN Germany, do not drop the 0 before the city code. Most of the hotels have someone who speaks English. The best chance of finding the owner or manager who speaks English is to call when it is late afternoon in Germany.

TRAVEL CONSULTANT: A knowledgeable agent will handle all of the details of your holiday and "tie" them together for you in a neat package including hotel reservations, airline tickets, and car reservation. Discuss what the charges will be for such a service.

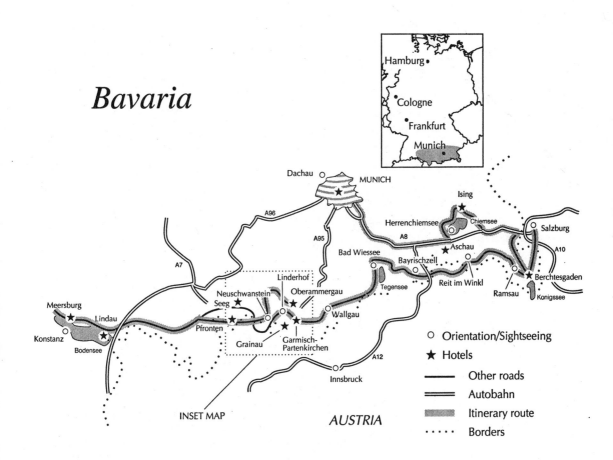

Bavaria

Inset map (Germany):
Hamburg •
•Cologne
•Frankfurt
Munich

Dachau ○
MUNICH
Ising ★
Herrenchiemsee ○ Chiemsee
Salzburg ○
A96
A95
A8
A10
A7
Bad Wiessee
Aschau ★
Bayrischzell
A12
Linderhof
Oberammergau
Tegensee
Reit im Winkl
Berchtesgaden ★
Ramsau ★
Konigssee
Neuschwanstein ★
Seeg ★
Wallgau ○
Meersburg ★
Lindau
Pfronten ★
Konstanz ○
Bodensee ★
Grainau
Garmisch-Partenkirchen ★
Innsbruck ○
INSET MAP
AUSTRIA

○ Orientation/Sightseeing
★ Hotels
—— Other roads
══ Autobahn
▨ Itinerary route
····· Borders

21

Bavaria

It is no wonder that Bavaria is a favorite destination for so many travelers. This southeastern corner of Germany proudly maintains the reputation of having the friendliest people, the most breathtaking mountains, the quaintest villages, the prettiest lakes, and the most famous castles in Germany. Summertime paints Bavaria's valleys and hillsides with edelweiss, Alpine roses, and orchids. Winter gently softens the landscape in a carpet of snow. This is a region where traditional costumes of lederhosen and dirndls are worn with pride. This itinerary traces a route that begins in Munich, Germany's "secret capital city," dips briefly into Austria to visit Salzburg, winds through the high Bavarian Alps, visits the resort towns of Garmisch-Partenkirchen and Oberammergau, highlights Ludwig II's fairy-tale castles, and concludes at the Bodensee (Lake Constance) at the lovely towns of Lindau and Meersburg.

Linderhof

Recommended Pacing: Spend two full days in Munich, giving you time to visit one or two museums, explore the city center, experience one or two beer gardens, and make a half-day trip to Dachau. A half-day drive (including sightseeing) brings you to Berchtesgaden which merits a three-night stay (two if you do not visit Salzburg). The drive along the Alpenstrasse takes a complete day (with sightseeing and lunch). Base yourself in the Garmisch-Partenkirchen area (we offer places to stay in Grainau, Pfronten, Oberammergau, and Seeg, any of which make an excellent base for your explorations of the area). If you cover all of our sightseeing suggestions here, you will need four nights (three will probably suffice). A half-day drive will find you in Lindau or Meersburg where we recommend a one-night stay.

*Munich, the "gateway to Bavaria," stars as one of Europe's most beautiful cities. Locals refer to Munich as "the village" because it is compact and easily explored on foot with the aid of short trips on the clean and efficient U-bahn and S-bahn underground railway systems. Munich, a wonderful beer-drinking, music-loving city, rivals Paris and London with its excellent shopping, museums, cultural events, and plethora of things to see and do. You do not need a car during your stay here, so if Munich is your first German destination and you are arriving by plane, leave your large pieces of luggage at the luggage office at the airport and travel downtown via the S-bahn, returning to pick up your car and bags as you depart. Purchase a pass for the subway system: it's a great deal and allows two adults, up to three children, and a dog unlimited U-bahn, S-bahn, bus, and tram travel for 24 hours (DM 20).

A logical place to begin a tour is the **Hautbahnhof** (main train station), a dynamic, lively place with tourist information, Burger King, bookstore, bus terminal, and the convergence of many of the U-bahn and S-bahn lines. Walk out the front door of the station and head for the first square, the **Stachus**, whose official name is the Karlsplatz, after Elector Karl Theodor—the townspeople, however, had such a high regard for Foderl Stachus that they named the square after him in 1730. Leaving the Stachus, wander under **Karlstor Gate** (past McDonalds and Burger King) and into the pedestrian

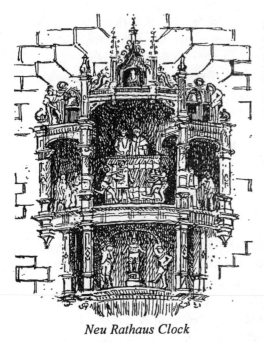
Neu Rathaus Clock

zone of the old city that is alive with fountains, fruit stands, ballad singers, and lay preachers. Off to the left, notice the Renaissance façade of **St. Michael's** and ahead the twin turrets (square with rounded domes) of the **Frauenkirche** (cathedral), both a landmark and symbol of the city. ***Marienplatz**, the beautiful square that serves as the heart of Munich, is just a short distance farther. Tables and chairs spill from cafés well into the square dominated by the ornate, lacy-wedding-cake, golden-sandstone exterior of the ***Neu Rathaus** (town hall). When the clock on the town hall strikes 11 am, noon, or 5 pm, colorful figures emerge from around the clock to perform a jousting tournament. Awaiting the hour is a perfect excuse to frequent one of the little cafés in the square.

Take a short walk off the square to Munich's oldest parish church, **Alter Peter**, with its impressive 11th-century interior. Climb its tower for a panoramic view which on a clear day extends to the Alps. Close by the Alter Peter church is the **Viktualienmarkt**, a permanent marketplace/beer garden full of stalls providing excellent, inexpensive things to eat. Head back towards the Marienplatz past the **Speilzeugmuseum**, a toy museum with lots of dolls and soldiers, along with a vast array of cars, planes, and trains, and onto the Tal (jutting into the street in the distance you see the **Hotel Torbräu**). Munich is famous for its beer halls which serve well priced food as well as huge quantities of beer and at Tal 7 you find **Weisses Brähaus** with a sophisticated, pub-like atmosphere. If you are looking for oomp-pa-pa music, singing, joviality, and fellow tourists, the famous Hofbräuhaus is just a five-minute walk away. Head down the Tal, turn left on Hochbruchstrasse, turn left as you face **Hotel Rafael**, and you arrive at the enormous barn of a building that houses the ***Hofbräuhaus**. Row after row of rough-hewn tables and benches surround the musicians and in summer the merriment spills out to the tables and chairs set beneath the trees on the large patio. (Our favorite beer garden for a warm summer evening is found in the vast park ***Englischer Garten** near the Chinese pagoda.)

There are three outstanding museums to visit: the Alte Pinakothek, the Residenz Museum, and the Deutsches Museum. The ***Alte Pinakothek** is closed at the moment for renovation. Hopefully it will be open by the time you visit as it has an incredible collection of works by 14th- to 18th-century masters such as Raphael, Michelangelo, Van Dyck, Rembrandt, Brueghel, Goya, and Titian. During renovations the major works are being displayed next door at the **Neue Pinakothek**. (*Alte Pinakothek, Barer Strasse 27, U-bahn 2; Neue Pinakothek, Barer Strasse 29, U-bahn 2, 10 am–5 pm, closed Mondays.*) The **Deutsches Museum**, often referred to as "Germany's Smithsonian," has a vast array of displays where you push buttons, turn wheels, and pull levers, making the serious subject of science and technology great fun. There are over 19 kilometers of displays, so you need to be very selective. The lack of explanation in English makes it frustrating for non-German-speakers though you can purchase a guide book in English. (*Located on its own island in the River Isar, S-bahn to Isartorplatz, 9 am–5 pm.*) The ***Residenz Museum** is so huge (over 100 rooms) that different tours are offered on alternating days. This was the enormous gilded home of the Wittelsbachs, who ruled Bavaria for more than 700 years. A separate ticket admits you to the **Schatzkammer**, a treasure house filled with the Wittelsbachs' glittering crowns, jewelry, and knickknacks. (*Located on Max-Joseph Platz, 3 blocks from Marienplatz, 10 am–4:30 pm, closed Mondays.*)

An easily accessible half-day trip from Munich is Hitler's first concentration camp, ***Dachau** (1933). The barracks are gone but reconstructions give an idea of the conditions prisoners had to endure. Around the perimeter fence the watchtowers still stand and a museum (unsuitable for children) exhibits without compromise what life was like here. You can view the crematorium ovens where over 31,000 people lost their lives, even though this was not primarily an extermination camp. A visit here is a very powerful experience and the camp's motto, "Never Again," strikes home. Dachau is 45 minutes northwest of Munich. Take the S-Bahn 2 towards Peterhausen to Dachau and the 220 bus from outside the station. The driver knows where you are going and indicates when to alight. From here it is a ten-minute walk following signposts for *Konzentrationslager.* Leaving the camp, bus 222 takes you from just outside the camp gates back to Dachau's train station. (*9 am–5 pm, closed Mondays.*)

Fall, of course, translates as the **Oktoberfest** and many from all over the world congregate in Munich to participate in the festivities. This happy, noisy celebration of the sausage and the hops begins in September and concludes on the first Sunday in October. The festival confines itself to a meadow in the southwestern part of Munich called the Theresienwiese.

Leave Munich on autobahn 8 in the direction of Salzburg. About an hour's drive brings you to **Prien** (just a few kilometers north of the autobahn) where you turn right for the **Chiemsee,** Bavaria's largest lake set against a backdrop of distant mountain peaks. Although not as beautiful as some of Germany's other lakes that are tucked into mountain pockets, the lake is a draw for sports enthusiasts and has two very interesting islands: **Herreninsel**, the lake's largest island, where Ludwig II built his imitation of Versailles, **Schloss Herrenchiemsee**, and the adjacent picturesque little island **Fraueninsel**, crowded with a Benedictine convent and fishing community.

Park by the lake and buy your ferry ticket (you can include either or both islands). A 20-minute ride across the lake brings you to Herreninsel where, after a 20-minute stroll through woodlands, you reach Schloss Herrenchiemsee set in a clearing facing magnificent fountains with lawns running down to the lake. If you prefer, you can take a horse-drawn carriage between the dock and the front steps of the palace. **King Ludwig II** of Bavaria had two idols, Louis XIV of France and the composer Richard Wagner.

Herrenchiemsee was his recreation of Versailles, complete with the magnificent hall of mirrors. While Louis XIV used Versailles to dazzle the world, Ludwig used his Versailles as the backdrop for his exuberant fantasy—during his numerous visits he ordered thousands of candles to be lit at night and he wandered the decadent rooms enacting his fantasy of absolute monarchy secluded from the real world on his isolated island. Tours leave every 20 minutes and last half an hour—English tours are available. The **König Ludwig Museum** that occupies the ground floor of the south wing gives a summary of the king's life and outlines his building projects: Herrenchiemsee, Neuschwanstein, and Linderhof are the only projects that were partially completed before his death at age 40 in 1886. Raised in isolation at Hohenschwangau, Ludwig began his reign with great promise at the young age of 18. Before long, though, his interest in politics diminished and, in a vain pursuit of happiness, he embarked on his monumental building spree of fairy-tale castles. The expense of the program and Ludwig's erratic behavior alarmed the government, who feared (probably justifiably) that Ludwig might bankrupt the country with his wildly extravagant projects, so they declared Ludwig unfit to rule by reason of insanity. Four days later Ludwig was found drowned under mysterious circumstances—supposedly suicide, but the world still wonders, "Who done it?" Whatever the truth of the matter, today the tourist benefits, as all of Ludwig's palaces are now museums. (*9 am–5 pm April to September, 10 am–4 pm October to March.*)

Leaving the Chiemsee, continue east along the scenic autobahn to exit 115 at **Bad Reichenhall**, following signposts to the mountain town of *Berchtesgaden. Set in a crescent of towering mountains, Berchtesgaden, an ancient market town, is a very popular tourist destination. Explore the **Schlossplatz** (the picturesque castle square) with its ancient granary, accounting house, and **Residenz** that was transformed from an Augustinian monastery and is now an interesting museum full of weapons, tapestries, paintings, and porcelain. (*10 am–1 pm, 2–5 pm, last admission 4 pm, closed Saturdays Easter to September and weekends October to Easter.*) Berchtesgaden is a lively town that is packed with visitors in summer. Confine your sightseeing (Königssee, Salzbergwerk [salt mines], and Kehlstein [Eagle's Nest]), to early mornings and spend your afternoons on the well marked walking paths.

Located 4 kilometers south of Berchtesgaden, *Königssee's setting and beauty are comparable to some of the world's most magnificent fjords. Steep walls enclose this idyllically beautiful Alpine lake that is accessible from the tip of its one small resort village. It is a popular excursion and overhead signs direct you to the huge parking lots (paying, of course). Traffic on the lake is restricted to electric boats that glide on a half-hour journey around the bend of the glass-like green lake where the picturesque 18th-century chapel and settlement at **St. Bartholomae** are built on a pocket of land near the lake's edge. A backdrop of maple trees and mountains completes the idyllic scene. There are cafés, restaurants, and walking paths to explore before the return boat journey. (*Sailing every 10 to 20 minutes 7:15 am–5:30 pm June to mid-August, tel: (08652) 4027 for rest of the year.*)

Salt was the principal source of Berchtesgaden's prosperity in the 16th century and now the *Salzbergwerk (salt mines) are one of the town's principal tourist attractions. Don miners' garb, sit astride a mining wagon, and travel through tunnels of gleaming salt crystal. On the hour-long tour you'll raft across an illuminated subterranean lake, slide down two long, slick, wooden banisters, and learn how they mined salt long ago. (*8:30 am–5 pm May to mid-October, 12:30–3:30 pm mid-October to April, closed Sundays. Tours can be booked in advance, tel: [08652] 60020, fax: [08652] 600260.*)

Hitler's Alpine retreat **Kehlstein (Eagle's Nest)** is overrated and should be visited only for its view, not for its associations with Hitler who visited there only five times (go only on clear, sunny days). The road from Berchtesgaden to **Obersalzberg** winds two-thirds of the way to the summit where the parking lot is crowded in summer. A shuttle bus takes you on the narrow, winding road with its hair-raising hairpin bend over the Scharitkehlamn gorge. An elevator whisks you the last 125 meters to the foreboding, granite-walled structure. (*8 am–4 pm May to end of October, weather permitting.*)

Bavaria

SIDE TRIP TO SALZBURG

The proximity of **Salzburg** (25 kilometers) makes this Austrian city made famous by *The Sound of Music* just too exciting a proposition to pass by (allow a day, and be warned that it is very crowded in summer). Cross the border at Markt Schnellenberg and you know you are in Salzburg when you see McDonalds and car dealerships. As in all cities, parking is the problem—watch for a small blue signpost "P Altstadt" (for parking), indicated to the left. Follow signposts for Altstadt Mitte leading you beneath the castle and through suburbs to a parking garage carved into the rocky promontory beside the Altstadt (old town). Take your parking ticket with you as you pay at the booth (German currency accepted) before returning to your car.

Getreidegasse

Salzburg Cathedral with its three massive bronze doors was built about 1630 and modeled after St. Peters in Rome. There are over 4,000 pipes in its organ.

You can tour the adjacent **Residenz**, the grandiose palace commissioned by Archbishop Wolf Dietrich. It's an impressive baroque edifice. You can tour only with a group—tours in English are given only in July and August. (*10 am–3 pm daily.*)

Getreidegasse is the old town's colorful main street famous for its many old wrought-iron signs looking much as they did in 1756 when Mozart was born at number 9. **Mozart's Birthplace (Geburthaus 1756)** filled with portraits, musical scores, old keyboard instruments, and violins is a popular Mozart shrine. (*9 am–5 pm in summer, shorter hours off season.*)

The **Hohensalzburg Fortress** dominates the skyline. While it is not worth touring the interior, the basic entry fee gives you access to the view and the courtyard. The funicular from the edge of town near the cathedral which runs every ten minutes whisks you up to the castle. (*8 am–4 pm daily.*) Just across the pedestrian bridge from the heart of Old Salzburg are **Schloss Mirabell and Gardens**, built by Archbishop Wolf Dietrich for his mistress Salome Alt. There is no charge to wander through the lovely terraced lawns.

Returning to Berchtesgaden from Salzburg, follow signposts for Munich and the autobahn. When Munich signposts disappear, keep following those for the autobahn which you take in the direction of Villach (E55). Once on the autobahn, follow signposts for Berchtesgaden (exit 160).

Ramsau Church

Bavaria

It's a five-hour drive from Berchtesgaden to Garmisch-Partenkirchen, much of it along the *Alpenstrasse (Alpine Road). Adding in time for sightseeing and lunch along the way, allow a day for the journey. Hope for sunny weather as the Alps are incredible against a backdrop of blue sky. Mark your route on a detailed map as oftentimes you follow signposts for towns without ever going there.

Leave Berchtesgaden in the direction of Ramsau (9 kilometers, road 305). At **Ramsau** turn left for Hintersee, which takes you into the village past the world-famous *Ramsau Church** with its backdrop of towering Alpine peaks and brings you to a small Alpine lake, the **Hintersee**, whose crystal-clear waters reflect the hotels on its far shore. Drive around the lake and continue on the narrow road that takes you through pine forests to an Alpine meadow dotted with farmhouses. Turn left (signposted Alpenstrasse), following a country road which returns you to the 305 at the head of the pass.

Descend to **Unterjettenberg**, a cluster of houses in a green meadow with the high Alpine peaks as a backdrop and cross the River Saalach (signposted Traunstein). The 305 descends through woodlands and just as it opens up to a broad valley makes a sharp, left-hand turn (signposted Reit am Winkl) and climbs the pass high above the village of Ruhpolding. Passing high Alpine lakes, isolated farms, clusters of chalets, hiking trails, and breathtaking vistas, it's a 21-kilometer drive to *Reit im Winkl**. This attractive village provides the perfect excuse to leave your car and explore its quaint shops and restaurants. On the outskirts of Reit im Winkl you cross the border into Austria and the 305 becomes the 172 which follows a tumbling mountain river for the 5-kilometer drive into **Kössen**.

Just 7 kilometers away lies **Walchsee**, a small lake with a beautiful setting where the pastures rise steeply from the lake to forests and the craggy gray mountains. Pass through the town of **Durchholzen** before crossing back into Germany. Cross the busy autobahn (E45) into **Oberaudorf** and wind through the town's busy main street following signposts for Niederaudorf (2 kilometers). Before reaching the village, turn left on a narrow country road for Bayrischzell (20 kilometers): en route the road climbs steeply to the little village of **Wall** that clings to the hillside with spectacular, rolling valley vistas below and rocky, snow-covered peaks above. Passing through hamlets of two or three chalets, the road crests the pass and winds down to the enticing ski village of **Bayrischzell**. Detour into the village and browse through the shops and cafés around the little square that sits beside the church.

A 15-kilometer drive (on the 307) brings you to the **Schliersee** lake where **Neuhaus** nestles at one end and the town of **Schliersee** clusters at the other. The more industrial town of **Hausham** lies just 1 kilometer away and from here you follow signposts to the **Tegernsee**. At the lake turn right into the attractive town of **Gmund**, skirt the lake on its northern shore then turn left for the resort town of **Bad Wiessee** (road 318). At the southern end of the lake turn right towards Achensee. The road soon leaves the Alpine pastures and travels through wooded forests toward the Austrian border (if you arrive at the Austrian border post, you have gone too far). Turn right at the signpost for Bad Tolz, following the 13 as it travels beside a large dam where Alpine peaks are reflected in the deep aquamarine waters. Take the first left (Wallgau) and follow the 307 to **Vordereiss** where you leave the main road and cross the river to follow a narrower toll road through rugged countryside to **Wallgau**. Between Wallgau and **Kryn** the green pastures are strewn with picture-postcard barns. From Kryn follow the E533 into Garmisch-Partenkirchen.

Our suggestion is to base yourself in the Garmisch-Partenkirchen area. We suggest hotels in Garmisch-Partenkirchen, nearby Grainau and Oberammergau, and just a little farther away at Pfronten and Seeg. Any of these towns makes an excellent hub for exploring this lovely area.

Framed by some of Germany's most dramatic, jagged peaks, ***Garmisch-Partenkirchen** is backed up against her highest—the towering Zugspitze. At one time two villages, Garmisch and Partenkirchen merged to meet the demands of accommodating the 1936 winter Olympic Games but the distinction between what were once two communities is still apparent. Garmisch is a bustle of activity, with broader, newer streets lined by larger stores and hotels. Partenkirchen, with narrow, winding streets and timbered buildings, preserves more old-world charm.

Garmisch-Partenkirchen is a skiers' delight in winter and a walkers' paradise in summer and fall. One of the loveliest well-marked trails takes you through the **Partnachklamm Gorge** (behind the Olympic ski stadium) where you walk along a rocky ledge with a guardrail between you and the tumbling river, sometimes passing through rock tunnels and behind cascading waterfalls. You get a little wet (take a raincoat) and the gorge is chilly even in summer, but the experience is breathtaking.

Pretty walks can by taken by riding the cable car up the **Wank** mountain and walking down to the valley floor. (*Summer service 8:30 am–5 pm.*) Additional scenic views are found by taking the Osterfedbahn to **Osterfeldkopt** (2050 meters).

For some it's a must to travel to the top of Germany's highest mountain, the **Zugspitze** (2966 meters)—remember to take warm sweaters for this excursion. The Zugspitze cog railway departs from the Zugspitzebahnhof, next to the main railway station, almost every hour on the hour (also from Grainau). The train ascends through the valley and brings you out below the summit of the Zugspitze—a cable car departs about every half hour and whisks you the last 3 kilometers up the mountain. Enjoy the view, soak up the high Alpine sunshine, and return to the valley on the other cable car for the ten-minute descent to the **Eibsee Lake**. From here the train returns you to Garmisch or Grainau. (*Departs hourly 7:35 am–3:35 pm in summer, last return approximately 5 pm.*)

CIRCULAR TOUR FROM GARMISCH-PARTENKIRCHEN

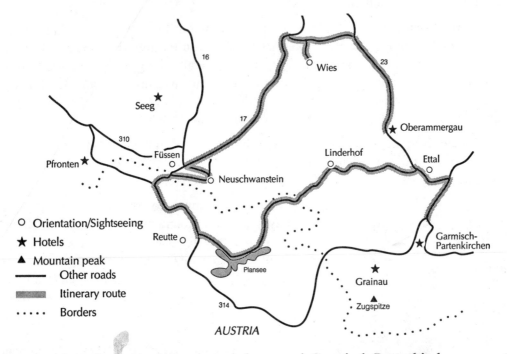

Because there is so much to see and do around Garmisch-Partenkirchen we outline a circular tour, but be aware that there is so much sightseeing that you cannot accomplish everything in one day. Leave Garmisch-Partenkirchen in the direction of Munich for a short distance then follow signposts for Augsburg and Oberammergau which brings you to the little village of **Ettal**. You cannot miss your sightseeing destination here for overshadowing the village is the **Klosterkirch** (monastery) where Benedictine monks distill liqueur, although you see not a monk nor a sign of their commercial operation. The church is an exquisite baroque riot of colorful paintings and gilded woodwork.

Klosterkirch, Ettal

Continue for a very short distance in the direction of Oberammergau and turn left on a country road that quickly brings you to ***Linderhof,** the smallest and most homey of Ludwig II's palaces. Be sure to buy an English guidebook at the entrance, as there aren't always enough English-speaking guests to warrant a guided tour in English. A ten-minute stroll through park-like grounds brings you to the squat little palace with its fountains and Italian-style gardens. The guided tour leads you from one outrageous room to another, including the decadent state room and the dining room where Ludwig ate solitary meals at a table which was lowered, like a dumb waiter, below the floor so that meals were served without Ludwig being disturbed by servants.

Walk up the hill to the ***Venus Grotto.** Ludwig commissioned the building of this cavernous grotto hung with stalactites and festooned with garlands where a conch-shell boat floats in the middle of an illuminated lake and the jeweled Lorelei cliff glitters with crystals. A short distance farther along the woodland path you come to the **Moorish Kiosk** where Ludwig dressed up as a Turkish sultan and smoked his hookah surrounded by young boys dressed up as palace eunuchs. Small wonder that the Bavarian government questioned his sanity! (*Allow for a wait in summer, 9 am–5:30 pm April to September, 10 am–4 pm October to March.*)

Continue across the Austrian border through wooded countryside on a road that quickly brings you to the **Plansee** whose rocky shore seems to rise almost directly from the glassy lake. As the valley opens up to the rooftops of Reutte take a right-hand turn signposted Deutschland (Germany). This takes you around the town and brings you onto the road for Füssen and Könnigsschlösser (King's Castles). **Füssen's Hohes Schloss** standing high above the river is usually overlooked in favor of its more famous neighbors.

Many recognize ***Neuschwanstein**, located high above the valley atop a rocky ledge, as being the inspiration for Walt Disney's Sleeping Beauty's castles at Disneyland and Disneyworld. You begin to appreciate the effort that went into building this castle as you walk up the steep path to the fortress high above. The only way to decrease a half-hour uphill hike to a ten-minute one is to take a shuttle bus or horse-drawn wagon part-way to the castle. This is one of Germany's most popular sightseeing attractions and the only way to avoid summer crowds (and long lines) is to arrive early in the morning. If you just cannot schedule the first tour of the day, our advice is to admire Neuschwanstein from afar and tour Linderhof (less crowded) to get the picture on Ludwig's taste in interior design. The castle's fanciful interior, designed by a theater-set designer and an eccentric king, is a romantic flight of fancy whose rooms afford spectacular views of Alpine lakes and snowy peaks. Ludwig greatly admired Richard Wagner and scenes from his operas are found throughout the decor. At the end of the castle tour, walk up the Pollat gorge to the Marienbrucke that spans the ravine above the castle: you will be rewarded with a spectacular view. (*Allow for a long wait in summer, 9:30 am–5:30 pm April to October, 10 am–4 pm November to March.*)

From the road at the foot of the castle, it is a short walk to King Ludwig's childhood home, **Hohenschwangau**. Though the interior is somewhat heavy, it has a homey quality to it. It was here that Ludwig met his adored Wagner, and here that the young king lived while he kept a watchful eye on the building progress at Neuschwanstein. (*8:30 am–5:30 pm April to October, 10 am–4 pm November to March.*)

Leave the castles in the direction of Augsburg and travel up the ever-broadening valley through rolling green farmland to the large village of **Steingaden** where you leave the 17 and turn right onto a country road signposted Weis and Oberammergau (29 kilometers). Detour to **Wies** to visit the ***Wieskirche**, a pilgrimage church whose simple exterior belies the most exquisitely beautiful interior. It's a popular excursion so there are cafés and paid parking but once you step into the beautiful interior all the surrounding commercialism is forgotten. (*8 am–5 pm and till 7 pm April to September.*)

Neuschwanstein

As you drive from the Wieskirche to Oberammergau you cross the **Echelsbacher Bridge** that spans a deep, wooded ravine with the rushing River Ammer far below. To appreciate the fabulous view, park at one of the car parks (found at both ends of the bridge) and take a few minutes to walk back and forth across the bridge.

Detour off the main road into the famous village of **Oberammergau** where many of the homes have ornate murals and seemingly all the shops sell very expensive carvings. Every ten years the *Passion Spiel* (Passion Play), a religious play, is performed here. All the residents in town are involved in the production and performance of this play that celebrates the end of the misery and death associated with the Black Plague. In between plays it seems that everyone in the village carves. While it's a bustling spot during the day, in the evening it's very serene. The church has a very attractive interior. From Oberammergau a half-hour drive through Ettal returns you to Garmisch-Partenkirchen.

When it is time to leave the Garmisch-Partenkirchen area a two- to three-hour drive will take you to the most westerly part of Bavaria, the lovely island of Lindau. Along the way there is much to see. Leave Füssen following the 310 towards Kempten. As you near **Pfronten,** study the nearby hilltops and locate the ruined medieval fortress of Schloss Falkenstein where Ludwig planned to build his next castle. His death put an end to his fanciful building program, so instead of a grandiose castle you now find two lovely hotels, **Burghotel Schlossanger Alp** and **Burghotel Falkenstein**, on the mountain.

Just as you leave the village of **Nesselwang** take a left-hand turn down a lane for Wertach, which gives you an opportunity to travel a quiet country road for a short distance. Regaining the 310 at **Wertach**, turn towards Sonhhofen. The road climbs steeply to **Oberjoch**, a ski resort spread across the summit, and opens up to vistas of the valley as it winds down past **Hindelang** where you pick up signposts for Lindau. Join a dual carriageway for several kilometers at **Sonthofen** and on to **Immenstadt** whose narrow streets are clogged with traffic as you follow signposts for the 308 and Lindau. Leaving Immenstadt, you also leave the soaring granite peaks of the Alps behind and travel beside a lake and along a green valley bordered with green hills. The valley opens up at **Oberstaufen**, a small town that steps down the hillside where seemingly every home has a fabulous view of the far side of the valley whose green pastureland is dotted with farmhouses.

Meersburg

Traversing rolling green hills, you arrive at the **Bodensee** (Lake Constance), the nearest thing to an inland sea in Germany. The problem with the Bodensee is that it is impossible to appreciate its beauty from the shoreline. There are not many places where you can actually get beside the lake and the traffic-clogged road (31) that parallels its shoreline runs slightly inland. A solution to this is to tackle the traffic-crowded 31 only to reach your base in the Bodensee at Lindau or beside the Bodensee at Meersburg and do your sightseeing by boat.

Arriving at the Bodensee, follow the well signposted route through the suburbs to Lindau Insel. If you are not staying on the island, park your car in the large car park just before the road bridge to the island of ***Lindau**. The island's main thoroughfare, Maximilianstrasse, is bordered with lovely old houses and the **Altes Rathaus** (old town hall) on Bismarckplatz dates from the 15th century and is famous for the brightly colored frescoes that decorate its façade. The harbor is guarded by the Lion of Bavaria and the Mangturm, a tower that was once part of the town's medieval ramparts. All along the harborside promenade restaurants and cafés spill out onto the pavement. During the summer months regular ferry service connects Lindau to Konstanz (Constance), Meersburg (2½ hours), Mainau island, Bregenz (Austria), and Rorschach (Switzerland).

Another base for explorations of the Bodensee, *Meersburg, lies an hour's drive (two hours' in heavy traffic) beyond the geographic bounds of Bavaria towards the other end of the lake. We include it in this itinerary because it is such an adorable little medieval town, offers charming accommodation, and is perfect for boat trips on the Bodensee. Arriving in Meersburg, follow signposts for the Altstadt (on your left). (If you cannot find parking at the top of the hill, follow signs for the ferry and park in the large car park beside the ferry terminal.) During the summer months regular ferry service connects Meersburg to nearby Konstanz (Constance) and Mainau island, and farther afield to Lindau and Bregenz (Austria).

Wander amongst the little narrow, cobbled streets lined with half-timbered houses along the Steigstrasse. Atop a rocky promontory overlooking the lake, the **Altes Schloss** (old castle) dates back to 628 when a longhouse and tower fortress were built by King Dagobert. The castle was enlarged over the years and by 1510 the structure you see today, complete with drawbridge and moat, was in place. The castle was bought in the 19th century by Baron von Lassburg as a storage place for his vast collection of books and weapons. His sister-in-law, Annette von Droste-Hülshoff, wrote some of her most famous poems here and her little rooms are very much as they were when she lived here. (You can also visit her little house in a nearby vineyard.) The Lassburgs went bankrupt and the castle was bought by the Furstenberg family (as in the beer). They sold the books to buyers in the United States but kept much of the weaponry. Tour the castle at your own pace with the aid of a typed sheet (in English) and enjoy the various rooms that are furnished to illustrate what life was like in the castle's different eras. (*9 am–5 pm.*)

In 1520 the nearby town of Konstanz (Constance) became Protestant so the bishop moved from Konstanz to the castle in Meersburg. It was decided that the castle was not grand enough for a resident bishop, so the **Neu Schloss** (new castle) was built between 1750 and 1802 to suit the bishop's palatial tastes. No sooner was the bishop installed than his bishopric was moved (furniture and all) to Freiburg. Happily, they were not able to move the magnificent ceiling paintings and the grand rooms are a perfect venue for changing art exhibits and musical concerts.

Garden lovers will not want to miss taking the boat excursion to the tiny island of ***Mainau**. Lovely, fragrant gardens bloom from March to October in the grounds of an 18th-century castle owned by a Swedish count. From Mainau you can return directly to Meersburg or take the ferry to **Uhldingen** to tour the prehistoric lake-dwellers' village reconstruction before either taking the bus (every half hour) or walking 5 kilometers beside the lake back to Meersburg.

From Meersburg a two-hour drive takes you to Freiburg where you can join the *Highways and Byways of the Black Forest* itinerary.

Castle above the Rhine River

Castles of the Rhine and Mosel

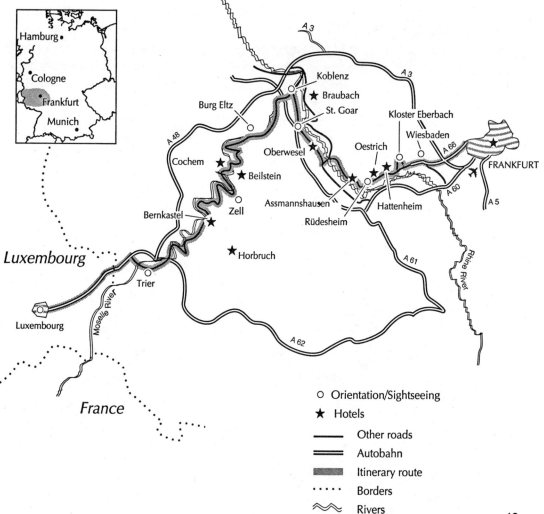

Orientation/Sightseeing ○
Hotels ★
Other roads ——
Autobahn ══
Itinerary route ▨
Borders ·····
Rivers ≈≈

Castles of the Rhine and Mosel

This itinerary covers two of Germany's most magical destinations—the Rhine and the Mosel wine regions. Powerful and broad, the River Rhine rushes towards the sea. High above the river, castles guard the heights or lie on islands amidst the churning flow. The river narrows to swirl past the legendary Lorelei rock whose muse dashed unwary sailors and their boats onto jagged rocks. A procession of famous villages and towns hug the river's banks. At Koblenz "Father Rhine" is joined by his loveliest daughter, the Mosel river. The Mosel's path is gentler, looping lazily back and forth as it passes tiny ribbon villages of half-timbered houses. Steep vineyards line her banks while castles stand guard from the hilltops above. The beauty of these rivers is enough to fill a rich chapter in your vacation, but if this is not sufficient to tempt you, be reminded that this itinerary offers the opportunity to alternate excursions with sampling the fine wines of the Rheingau, Mittelrhein, and Mosel wine regions.

Cochem

Castles of the Rhine and Mosel

Recommended Pacing: Spend one night along the Rhine (Hattenheim, Assmannshausen, Oestrich-Winkel, Oberwesel, Braubach) and one along the Mosel (Cochem, Beilstein, Bernkastel, Horbruch). If you include Trier and Luxembourg in your sightseeing, allow two nights along the Mosel.

This itinerary begins in **Frankfurt**, conveniently reached by direct flights from cities throughout the world. If you arrive at the Frankfurt airport, you can easily begin your journey immediately by picking up a rental car at the airport and starting on your way (without heavy traffic it is less than a 45-minute drive to **Eltville** [listed as Hattenheim-Eltville] where we recommend the **Kronen Schlösschen** and **Weinhaus "Zum Krug"** as places to stay). If you choose to visit the pleasant, modern heart of the city, be aware that a couple of historic gems have been restored: **Goethehaus** where Johann Wolfgang von Goethe was born in 1749, is open as a museum showing how a well-to-do family lived in the 18th century and nearby you find the **Romerberg** a square of old restored gabled buildings. If you want to spend a night in the city, the **Hotel Westend** is an excellent choice.

Follow the autobahn 66 west from Frankfurt through **Wiesbaden**. In a few kilometers the autobahn ends and continues as road 42: this main road and the busy inter-city railway trace the river's bank. The first part of this itinerary loops back and forth from this main artery, exploring the gently sloping, vineyard-covered hillsides that line the bank of the River Rhine. Known as the **Rheingau,** this small wine area is especially famous for its Riesling wines.

A short drive brings you to the wine town of **Eltville** where in medieval times the archbishops of Mainz had their summer palaces. Here you leave the busy river road and climb through the vineyards to **Kiedrich**. Drive into the little village and visit its pretty pink church with its elaborate interior before continuing up the hill to **Kloster Eberbach**. Set in a snug little hollow at the upper reaches of the vineyards, this former Cistercian monastery enjoyed 700 years of prosperity thanks to the production of wine.

The Cistercian monks led an austere, silent life of prayer and hard work, allotting only a few hours a night for sleep on hard, narrow wooden pallets. Stroll through the quiet cloisters and cool halls with their graceful fan-vaulted ceilings to the refectory that now houses an impressive collection of enormous old wine presses. The severe architecture, plain plaster walls, and lack of embellishments mirror the austere lifestyle led by the monks. (*10 am–6 pm April to September, 11 am–4 pm October to March.*)

Leaving the monastery grounds, turn to the right and follow the country road as it dips down through the vineyards back to the river at **Hattenheim**. Drive through the old town center to the adjacent village of **Oestrich**. Turn left down one of the winding village streets and you emerge back on the busy Rhineside road for the short drive to **Winkel**.

Turn right in Winkel and follow the road up through the vineyards to the bright-yellow castle on the hill, the **Schloss Johannisberg**. This famous castle is the emblem of wines produced in this area and its name, Johannisberg, is synonymous with the production of Riesling wine. From April to December you can enjoy a meal at their country-style restaurant (*closed Tuesdays*) and visit the wine shop. On a fine day the castle terrace affords a panoramic view across the vineyards to the river below. The palace cellars contain century-old wines of fabulous value. You can arrange for a tour of the cellars and wine-tasting (on weekdays only) by writing to Schloss Johannisberg, 65366 Geisenheim-Johannisberg, Germany.

Returning to the river road, it is a short distance to the most famous wine town of this area, **Rüdesheim**. Park you car and walk by the river, bypassing the many tourist shops selling gaudy souvenirs, and turn into the narrow, cobbled **Drosselgrasse**, the town's most attractive street. Here, on what is reputed to be the jolliest street in the world, one wine tavern props up another and, even if you do not partake of the wine, it is fun to wander along this festive street. A short stroll along the river brings you to the more serious side of wine production, the **Wein Museum Brömserburg** (Bromserburg Castle). Ask for a leaflet in English that guides you from room to room up turret stairways to see the artifacts pertaining to the production and consumption of wine from the earliest days. (*February to November, closed Mondays.*) If the weather is fine, consider taking the **Seilbahn** (cable car) to **Niederwald** high above the town where you find a huge statue of Germania erected to celebrate victory over the French in 1871.

Leaving Rüdesheim, the river road winds below steeply terraced vineyards as the Rhine forsakes its gently sloping banks and turns north into a rocky gorge. Passing below the ruins of **Ehrenfels Castle**, the **Mauseturm** (Mouse Tower) comes into view on an island near the opposite bank. Legend has it that Archbishop Hatto II was a cruel master who paid a terrible price for his sins: he was driven into the mouse tower by mice who then proceeded to eat him alive.

The river valley narrows as you near the town of **Assmannshausen** and the first of the famous castles that overlook the river comes into view on the opposite bank— **Rheinstein Castle**. Take time to drive into Assmannshausen and explore its poky, narrow streets full of charming little old houses. The wisteria-covered terrace of the **Hotel Krone** provides you with a refreshment stop (or excellent place to stay) and fine views of the passing river life.

As you drive north along the riverbank, as fast as one castle disappears from view, another comes into sight perched high above the rocky river valley. The Rheingau wine region ends in the little town of **Lorch**, where you take the small chugging car ferry which fights the strong river currents and slowly transports you across the river to **Rheindiebach**. As you enter the **Mittelrhein** wine district, you see verdant vineyards gently sloping to the river replaced by steep river terraces occupying every southern-facing slope, where the grapes can soak up the warm summer sun. Between the vineyards, the high riverbanks are thickly wooded.

It is just a few minutes' drive from the ferry to **Bacharach**. Park your car by the river and walk into the town to discover that the plain river-front façade conceals a picturesque village of half-timbered medieval houses around a market square. As you leave Bacharach, a much photographed castle, the **Pfalz,** comes into view marooned on an island amidst the swirling flow.

The Pfalz

As you drive into **Oberwesel** turn left before the brick-red church, the **Liebfrauenkirche,** and pause to see its interior. Gothic in style, the church is noted for its many beautiful altarpieces, the oldest built in 1506. Follow the winding road upwards to the **Auf Schönburg** castle, perched high above Oberwesel. Park your car beneath the castle walls, cross the wooden bridge spanning the gully that isolates the Auf Schönburg on its rocky bluff, and climb the well-worn cobbles which wind you through the castle to the hotel at the summit. The façade is out of a fairy tale—towers, turrets, and crumbling battlements. If you are lucky enough to be staying at the hotel, you can explore the interior of the castle. However, if you are not staying at the castle, you can enjoy the view from the terrace below the hotel.

Leaving the Auf Schönburg, glance to the river where it swirls and eddies amongst the rocks on the opposite bank. Legend has it that these rocks are the seven maidens of Oberwesel Castle who were so cold-hearted towards their suitors that the river overturned their boat and turned them into stone.

Around the first river bend, the fabled **Lorelei** rock comes into view. The currents around the rock, which juts out sharply into the river, are so dangerous that the legend arose of an enchantress sitting high on top of the rock combing her golden tresses and so entrancing the sailors with her singing that the rules of navigation were forgotten and their boats were dashed onto the rocks.

The Rhine landscape is splendid when viewed from the river but even finer views await you from the ramparts of the castle, **Burg Rheinfels**, located high above **St. Goar**. Below flows the mighty Rhine dotted with chugging barges and on the opposite bank are the whimsically named **Burg Mauz** (Mouse Castle) and the adjacent larger **Burg Katz** (Cat Castle). Built in 1245, the Rheinfels castle was reduced to the crumbling ruin you see today by the French in 1797. With map and English explanation in hand, you tour the castle, climb the ramparts, and get a feeling for what the fortress must have been like in its heyday. A model in the museum shows just what a grand edifice this was. (*9 am–5 pm April to October.*)

Keeping the river close company, about a 20-minute drive brings you to the outskirts of **Koblenz** where you bid the Rhine farewell and, by following signposts for Cochem (49), navigate through town to the banks of the **River Mosel**.

The pageant of the riverbank marches steadily on, but how different the Mosel is to the Rhine. The Mosel is narrower, moving more slowly—gracefully looping back and forth. The road too is narrower, with thankfully less traffic and no busy adjacent railway track. The Mosel's steep banks are uniformly covered with vines—for this is wine country and every little ribbon village, with the terraced vineyards rising steeply behind it, is involved in the production of wine. The villages are often no more than a cluster of houses, yet they all have their own famous brand of wine.

Pass beneath the 61 autobahn that bridges the river valley high above you and cross the Mosel to the village of **Lof**. A few minutes' drives bring you to the edge of **Niederfell** where you turn right, signposted Burg Eltz P & R. (Look specifically for this sign: it leads you to parking that involves the least amount of uphill walking.) After several signposts Burg Eltz P & R signs become Burg Eltz and the route winds you uphill out of the river valley, through rolling farmland to the village of **Munstermaifeld**, where you turn left to arrive at the parking for ***Burg Eltz**. A 1-kilometer (15-minute) walks downhill means that you have a 1-kilometer walk uphill to return to your car. The walk is worth it for this is, in our estimation, the loveliest of castles in Europe. High upon a rocky outcrop encircled by woodland, the picturesque Burg Eltz is a fairy-tale castle of turrets and towers piled one upon the other between the 12th and 16th century. It's still the home of the Count and Countess of Eltz and the Countess designs the lovely flower arrangements in each of the rooms. Tours are rarely given in English but with the aid of an English fact sheet this is not a problem. Your guide leads you from one magnificent historic room to another and you learn that, at a time when many castles contained only one fireplace and one toilet, this castle contained forty fireplaces and twenty toilets. While waiting for your tour to begin be sure to visit the Treasury (*additional charge*) where you will be rewarded by displays of absolutely elegant china, silverware, and jewelry. (*9:30 am–6 pm April to end of October.*)

Leaving the castle, take the first right-hand turn signposted Mozelkurn that drops you back to the river and quickly brings you into **Cochem**. Park your car and explore the pedestrian center of this small town. Turn a blind eye to the souvenir shops and let yourself be tempted inside a coffee shop for some mouthwatering pastries and a cup of coffee. Thus fortified, wander through the narrow streets and follow the well-signposted walk to the castle (Burg), **Reichsburg Cochem**, sitting atop a hill above the town. The trek is worth it, for while the valley is beautiful when viewed from below, the view from above is even more impressive. Touring the castle is not recommended: too many gloomy rooms full of heavy, ornately carved furniture. (*9 am–5 pm mid-March to mid-November.*)

Beilstein

Cross the river at Cochem (signposted Beilstein) and the prettiest stretch of the Mosel river valley opens up before you as the loops of the river almost double back on themselves. Soon *Beilstein comes into view, a little picture-postcard village hugging the riverbank below the vineyards. Walk up to the tiny, cobbled square crowded by centuries-old houses. Stroll up the quiet, cobbled streets to the church and the little **castle** (*9 am–6 pm April to end of October*) and return to the square to tour the little **Weingut Museum** which is full of winemaking artifacts before going into the cool, deep cellars of Joachim Lipmann to sample his wines. Across the square is the lovely **Hotel Haus Lipmann**. If the weather is warm, settle on the hotel's terrace to watch the little ferry as it shuttles cars back and forth across the river while long river barges chug slowly by.

Winding down to Bernkastel-Kues, as you go through one little village another appears on the opposite bank, each with little houses fronting the river, a large church, and a backdrop of steeply sloping vineyards. Amongst the many villages **Zell** stands out as being one of the larger ones, famous for the production of Black Cat wine: you see a black cat on murals throughout the village.

Bernkastel

A half-hour drive brings you to ***Bernkastel-Kues**. Bernkastel-Kues is two villages: Bernkastel on one side, Kues lying just across the bridge on the other side of the river. In this wine valley, Bernkastel stands out as being the most picturesque larger village. You will fall in love with this quaint wine village where colorful, 400-year-old, half-timbered houses are grouped around a flower-filled marketplace and beautiful medieval houses extend for several blocks. A couple of blocks up the main street is an interesting toy and doll museum.

For a closer look at another castle overlooking the river, follow Bernkastel's main street up a narrow valley to **Berg Landshut,** a ruined castle set in vineyards that tumble to the river below. A restaurant has been incorporated into the ruined keep and the view is impressive. The narrow lane beside the castle winds you back into the village to emerge beside the **Hotel Zur Post,** one of our recommended hotels in Bernkastel. If you want to stay near the river in one of our favorite hotels, try the **Hotel Historische Schlossmühle** near Horbruch, 20 kilometers southeast of Bernkastel-Kues.

An hour's drive brings you to **Trier,** one of Germany's oldest cities founded by the Roman Emperor Augustus in 15 B.C. Follow signposts for Centrum Park and make your way on foot to **Porta Nigra,** the largest fortified gateway in the Roman Empire. Still intact, it stands guard over the city nearly 20 centuries later. This gate is like a giant wedding cake of 3½ tiers standing nearly 30 meters high. (*9 am–6 pm April to end of October, closed Mondays.*) The tourist office by the Porta Nigra will supply you with a city map (splurge for the larger one) showing you the historic sights of the city all found within a few blocks of the gate. (*Walking tours of the city in English leave at 2 pm April to October.*) With your back to the Porta Nigra, walk up the main shopping pedestrian street, the Simeonstrasse, passing the Turkish-looking **Dreilonigen-Haus,** built in 1260, to the Hauptmarkt (marketplace) where a colorfully painted fountain is surrounded by ancient timbered houses. The **Dom** (cathedral) lies just a block off the square, a surprisingly spacious, simply adorned edifice where behind the altar you can peer into an ornate shrine that is purported to contain the robe of Christ.

Retrace your steps to your car and with the aid of your detailed map, following signposts for Universitat, drive to the **Roman Amphitheater** that was built above the town to provide up to 20,000 people with gladiatorial entertainment. After the Roman Empire fell, the site was used as a quarry, and now soft, grassy mounds have taken the place of the stone seats. (*9 am–6 pm April to end of October, closed Mondays.*) If walking around Roman amphitheaters is not your cup of tea, turn just beyond the amphitheater up a narrow lane and into the vineyards onto the **Weinlehrpfad**, an educational walking route through the vineyards that offers bird's-eye views of the amphitheater.

When it is time to leave this lovely wine region of the Mosel, it is only a short drive to Germany's borders with Luxembourg, France, and Belgium. You can take an autobahn to join Würzburg (*The Romantic Road and the Neckar Valley*), Baden-Baden or Freiburg (*Highways and Byways of the Black Forest*), or Eisnach (*Exploring Eastern Germany*).

The proximity of **Luxembourg**, an hour's drive from Trier, makes the capital of Luxembourg too exciting a proposition to pass by. Leave Trier across the Römerbrüke bridge signposted for Luxembourg and the autobahn. Arriving in Luxembourg, follow signposts for Centrum and parking, and set out on foot to explore. Walk to the Place d' Armes and the tourist office where you are given maps, a walking tour brochure, and information on this cosmopolitan city atop the rocky Bock promontory. As long ago as 963 Count Siegfried built his fortress here and, in spite of it being a heavily fortified position, the Burgundians took the city in 1443. Over the next four centuries the best French, Spanish, Austrian, and German military engineers fortified the city, turning it into the "Gibraltar of the North." The most interesting part of their fortifications was a vast network of underground casemates (tunnels) that sheltered thousands of soldiers and their horses along with kitchens, bakeries, and military workshops. The Treaty of London in 1867 stipulated the dismantling of the casemates and only a small portion of them remain today, the **Casemates Pétrusse** and **Casemates Bock**. (*Bock open 10 am –5 pm March to October, Pétrusse 11 am–4 pm July to September.*)

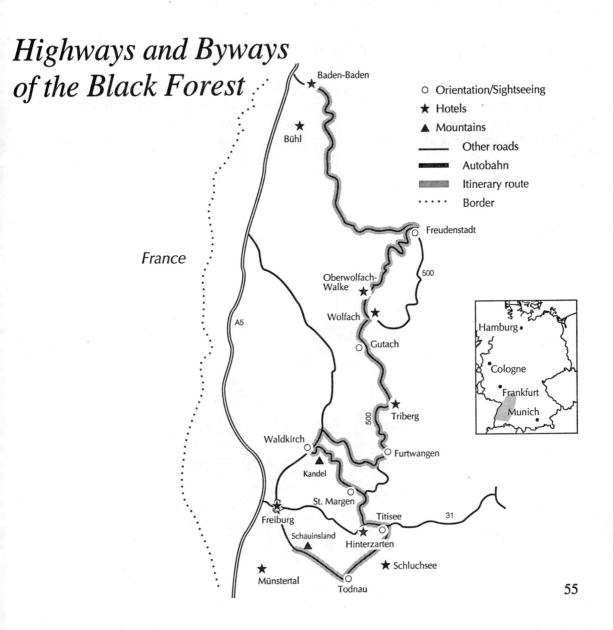

Highways and Byways of the Black Forest

Baden-Baden

Bühl

France

Freudenstadt

500

Oberwolfach-Walke

Wolfach

Gutach

A5

500

Triberg

Waldkirch

Furtwangen

Kandel

St. Margen

Freiburg

Titisee

31

Schauinsland

Hinterzarten

Münstertal

Schluchsee

Todnau

○ Orientation/Sightseeing
★ Hotels
▲ Mountains
— Other roads
▬ Autobahn
▓ Itinerary route
····· Border

Hamburg •

Cologne •

• Frankfurt

Munich •

55

Highways and Byways of the Black Forest

Without a doubt the Black Forest (named for its dense, dark forests) is one of Europe's most attractive holiday areas. Called the Schwarzwald in German, the Black Forest is a range of rolling hills 160 kilometers (100 miles) from north to south and 60 kilometers (37 miles) from east to west. Besides being famous for its vast tracts of thick pine forest, the region is popular for its cuckoo clocks, spa resorts offering clean-mountain-air cures and healing mineral waters, endless hiking possibilities, cherry cakes (Schwarzwalder torte), pretty villages, and rolling green pastures dotted with farmhouses.

Recommended Pacing: You can easily accomplish this itinerary with a night in Freiburg (skip Freiburg if you are arriving from nearby), Triberg, and Baden-Baden. However, our preference would be to base yourself in the south (Freiburg, Hinterzarten, Badenweiler, or Schulchsee) or middle (Triberg, Wolfach, or Oberwolfach) for two nights to complete the southern Black Forest sightseeing. Travel the Hochstrasse to Baden-Baden where you will need two nights if you plan on visiting the baths or one night otherwise.

With a gorgeous setting at the base of the mountains, **Freiburg** is the capital of the Schwarzwald. The dark green forests come right down within a block or two of this large city. Full of character, the pedestrian-only old center was founded in 1120 and is laden with numerous quaint buildings. On **Münsterplatz** (main square) you find the beautiful **Münster Unserer Lieben Frau** (cathedral) whose tall spires crest all vistas. Inside the cathedral 14th-century sculptures depict sin and temptation. The nave's gorgeous 14th-century stained glass was donated by the guilds and each window shows the emblem of the guild that donated it. Three very attractive buildings are found on the south side of the Münsterplatz: the **Kaufhaus** with its steep roof and pointed turrets, the baroque **Erzbischöfliches Palais** (Archbishop's Palace), and the **Haus zum Schönen Eck** which now houses the music academy. Here you also find the delightful **Oberkirchs Weinstuben**, a cozy wine tavern-hotel combination. Little streams run down each street between the cathedral and the Swabian gate: known as **Bächle**, these little waterways are the city's trademark.

A half-hour drive from Freiburg along the scenic 31 (signposted Donauschingen) will bring you to Titisee but rather than taking the direct route, detour down scenic byways by leaving Freiburg following the white signposts depicting a gondola. Following the tram tracks to their terminus in the suburbs, the road narrows and climbs steeply as it weaves back and forth beneath the cable car that soars to the summit of the **Schauinsland** (mountain). Pause at the summit, catch your breath and admire the view of Freiburg way below you and beyond it the plain stretching to the distant horizon.

Traversing the high mountain meadow, you find the hamlet of **Horsgrund** nestling in a sheltered fold of the mountain. As you re-enter the forest turn right (signposted Todnau) and begin a 12-kilometer descent to the valley floor passing through the villages of **Muggenbrun** and **Afterseg**.

Turn left in **Todnau** (signposted Donauschingen) and follow this broader valley whose sides rise steeply into the dark forest. Climb through **Brandenburg** ever higher to crest the pass at the ski resort of **Feldburg** and travel down to the cool waters of the **Titisee**. Join the 31 in the direction of Freiburg and exit after Neustadt for Titisee (the resort with the same name), following signposts for parking and Ortmitte. The resort is invariably crowded with tourists and hiring a rowboat is a pleasant way to escape the throngs of visitors.

Regain the 31 going towards Freiburg and exit on the 500 for Triburg (this is also the exit you take if you have come directly from Freiburg). Detour into the village of **Hinterzarten**, a resort noted for its clean mountain air, where pretty little houses and hotels cluster round a grassy green (see hotel descriptions). Walking paths that lead in every direction are replaced in winter by cross-country skiing trails. The 500 is an extremely scenic road passing through wide vistas of farmland with patches of dark-green forest. If the weather is clear, consider leaving the main road to take a particularly scenic loop to Furtwangen.

Leave the 500 at **Thurner**, turning left onto a country road for St. Margen (signposted Freiburg). Travel through a broad green valley with a sky-wide landscape of rolling hills speckled with farms and patchworked with dark-green woodlands. A ten-minute drive brings you to the center of the attractive village of **St. Margen** where you turn right (signposted Glotteral). Detour into **St. Peter** to visit **Klosterkirche**, the ornate baroque church attached to the large abbey. Heading towards Waldkirch, the road twists and climbs to the summit of the **Kandel**, one of the few mountains whose summit offers a view of the surrounding countryside. Traveling through thick forest, the road twists and turns down to the small non-touristy town of **Waldkirch** and on to the adjacent town of **Glotheral** where you turn right for the much prettier village of **Simonswald** strung along the road as it winds up the narrow valley to **Obersimonswald**. You climb into the trees high above the farms that nestle each in its grassy patch of pastureland to **Güttenbach**, a small industrial town at the summit. From here the road drops steeply to Furtwangen where you rejoin the 500.

Furtwangen is famous for its cuckoo clocks. Visit a full complement of them in the interesting **Deutsches Uhrenmuseum** (German Clock Museum) that presents the history of timekeeping. Besides the chirping birds, there are wristwatches and electrical and very modern timepieces. (*9 am–5 pm, April to November 1st.*)

Leaving Furtwangen, the 500 passes through some very pretty countryside and travels through **Schönwald** where the cuckoo clock was born. Schönwald was the home of Franz Anton Ketterer who at the beginning of the 18th century thought of combining a clock with bellows. He incorporated a cuckoo carved in wood with a timepiece whose tiny bellows marked the hours with the notes of a cuckoo call. Records show that clocks were manufactured in the Black Forest as early as 1630, but when cuckoo clocks were invented, they became the rage. Today clock-making remains a considerable industry for the region, and, although factories exist, the production of cuckoo clocks is sometimes still a home business with the whole family working on the intricately carved boxes and painted dials.

Triberg, located in the heart of the Black Forest just a few kilometers beyond Schönwald, is an attractive town and the **Parkhotel Wehrle** an ideal place to stay. The town has one main street comprised of clock shop after clock shop whose selection, variety, and competitive prices will amaze you. Just as you come into town you find the very interesting **Schwarzwaldmuseum** (Black Forest Museum) with the bronze of a larger-than-life lady in traditional dress outside. Inside you get a good look at the costumes, carvings, clocks, and traditions of the region. (*9 am—6 pm May to September, 10 am—noon and 2–5 pm October to April, closed Sundays.*) Above the town is the **Gutach waterfall** that cascades over 160 meters (500 feet) through the forest.

Leaving Triberg, turn left at the end of town (signposted Hornburg) and follow the 33 through tunnels beside the rushing River Gutach to **Hornburg** and on to **Gutach** where just beyond the town you find the *****Schwarzwälder Freilichtermuseum** (Black Forest Open-Air Museum), a complex of ancient farmhouses brought here from all over the Black Forest and set in a meadow beside the river to show what rural life was like in days gone by. All of the rustic rooms are furnished and you see not only little cottages but also grand mansions. Many of the homes are typical Black-Forest *Eindachof* (one-roof farms) that come with family accommodation, bakery, granary, barn, workshops, and cattle trough all under one large thatched roof. Wander from house to lovely house and admire the rustic furnishings and old farm implements. By the entrance you find several touristy restaurants and nifty-gifty shops. (*8:30 am–5 pm April to October.*)

Shortly after leaving the museum, turn right on the 294 for the short drive to **Wolfach** where, just as you leave the main road (signposted Centrum), you find the **Glasshütte** (glass museum) and **Kris Kringle Markt** (Christmas Market) before going through the town wall onto the town's main street. (We suggest **Gasthof Hecht** as an inexpensive hotel.) Cross the river and follow signposts for Oberwolfach which bring you onto a pretty country road leading through a narrow valley dotted with farmhouses through **Oberwolfach** to the tiny hamlet of **Oberwolfach-Walke** where you turn right as you cross the river and find the **Gasthof Hirschen**, one of our favorite German inns. Follow the river up the valley past sawmills with their logs and plans stacked beside the road for the half-hour drive to Freudenstadt.

Schwarzwälder Freilichtermuseum

At the main road turn right if you want to tour the town of **Freudenstadt** whose market square is the largest in Europe or turn left (signposted Strasbourg), leaving the town behind as you climb into the forest and turn right onto the **Schwarzwald Hochstrasse** (Black Forest High Road). This very aptly named road travels along the crest of the hills through dense coniferous forest, winding back and forth, up and down through the trees with only occasional clearings offering glimpses of steep valleys of dark trees. Every time you come to a clearing you find a resort hotel (often with food and trinket booths in its car park). A 68-kilometer drive brings you to Baden-Baden where you follow signposts for Centrum which bring you to Lichtentalerstrasse from where it is a short distance to the three hotels recommended in our hotel section.

*Baden-Baden was the playground of Europe's rich and famous in the middle of the 19th century. Anyone who was anyone came to soak in the curative waters and gamble at the casino. Today it is an attractive town where everywhere you want to visit is located within a 15-minute walk (park your car for the duration of your stay). Promenade yourself down the famous **Lichtentaler Allee**, strolling along a pleasant lane through the park that runs beside the river from the casino. Baden-Baden nightlife centers on the **Kurhaus** set amidst park-like gardens beside the swiftly flowing Oosbach river. Here you find restaurant, café, ballroom, and casino (take your passport to register: you must be over 21, must not be wearing tennis shoes, men must wear jackets and ties). Even if you do not gamble, it is fun to tour the casino and watch those who do. Across the river from the casino lies the pedestrian old town full of cobbled streets lined with delightful shops.

The highlight of a visit to Baden-Baden is taking the *kur*, partaking of the curative waters. Pluck up your courage and opt for the ***Friedrichsbad** (Roman-Irish Bath), a two-hour ritual that involves a complex routine that is explained in the blue English instruction sheet that you pick up as you purchase your ticket (it's well worth the extra small charge to include the soap-and-brush massage). Up the stairs (men one side, women the other), insert your ticket to gain admission, put your clothes in the basket, put your card in the locker to get a key, walk self-consciously to the showers, grab a towel, don slippers, and follow the numbers (and English explanation) on the walls. Relax in a hot room for 20 minutes, followed by an even hotter steam room (remember to lie on your towel—it's that hot); inhale steam from the curative waters; forget your modesty as you enter the pool (station 9)—it's men and women mixed (this came as an unexpected surprise); enjoy an invigorating massage; suffer a cold plunge; and finish with a relaxing rest wrapped in a warm towel beneath a blanket in a dimly lit room. (*9 am–10 pm, opens 2 pm Sunday, last entry 7 pm.*)

The adjacent **Caracalla Therme** offers a water experience with bathing suit. Pick up the English sheet as you buy your card, put the card in a locker to get a key, and set off to enjoy an indoor-outdoor water wonderland of pools, waterfalls, showers, saunas, tanning lights, cold plunges, and sunbathing. (*8 am–10 pm, last entry 8 pm.*)

Closed to traffic, Baden-Baden's Old Town, nestled below the collegiate church, is a wonderful place for shopping. The stores display their elegant wares artistically, competing with the smells from the nearby pastry shops that summon you to an afternoon tea break. Baden-Baden is also a sportsman's paradise—golf, riding, tennis, fishing, and hiking are all available in the vicinity. Race week is held each year in August when Baden-Baden becomes a sophisticated meeting place for the wealthy "horsey set." One of the town's traditional attractions is the **Merkur mountain railway**. Built in 1913, it reopened after repairs in the spring of 1979 and you can now travel up the incline and enjoy sweeping vistas from the observation tower at its summit.

Leaving Baden-Baden, you can take the autobahn to Heidelberg (to join *The Romantic Road and the Neckar Valley*, 1 hour), the Frankfurt airport (2½ hours), or join the *Castles of the Rhine and Mosel* just outside Wiesbaden (3 hours).

Highways and Byways of the Black Forest

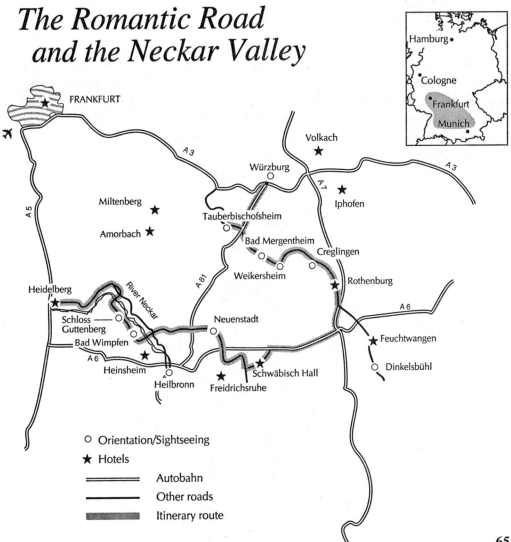

The Romantic Road and the Neckar Valley

FRANKFURT

Hamburg

Cologne

Frankfurt

Munich

A3

Volkach

Würzburg

A7

Iphofen

Miltenberg

Tauberbischofsheim

A5

Amorbach

Bad Mergentheim

Creglingen

Weikersheim

Rothenburg

A81

River Neckar

Heidelberg

A6

Schloss Guttenberg

Neuenstadt

Bad Wimpfen

Feuchtwangen

A6

Dinkelsbühl

Heinsheim

Heilbronn

Freidrichsruhe

Schwäbisch Hall

○ Orientation/Sightseeing

★ Hotels

═══════ Autobahn

─────── Other roads

▓▓▓▓▓▓ Itinerary route

65

The Romantic Road and the Neckar Valley

The Romantic Road (or Romantische Strasse) is one of Germany's most famous tourist routes—a road that travels between the towns of Würzburg in Franconia and Füssen in the Bavarian Alps. Every bend along the way between Würzburg and Rothenburg is spectacular. However, the beauty of the scenery wanes after leaving Rothenburg, so this itinerary deviates from the traditional route. Rather than traveling the entire 340-kilometer stretch of the Romantic Road, this itinerary samples the northern highlights of Germany's most traveled route and then detours west at Rothenberg to incorporate the enchanting city of Schwäbisch Hall and the picturesque university city of Heidelberg. (The southernmost portion of the Romantic Road is included in the Bavarian itinerary.)

Rothenburg

The Romantic Road and the Neckar Valley

Suggested Pacing: A full day's sightseeing takes you from Würzburg to Rothenburg—we suggest an early start after spending the night in one of our recommended hotels in the area (Miltenberg, Amorbach, Volkach, Iphofen). Stay two nights in Rothenburg (take an afternoon drive to Dinkelsbühl). Make an early-morning start from Rothenburg to arrive at Schloss Guttenberg in time for the 3 pm eagles' flight before driving on to Heidelberg (if you are not a fast-paced traveler, overnight in Schwäbisch Hall en route). One night in Heidelberg is plenty for me but you may well enjoy two.

The 12th-century diplomat, Gottfried von Viterbo, described **Würzburg** as "lovely, like a rose set in deep-green foliage—sculpted into the valley like an earthly paradise." It no longer seems like a paradise but it certainly is a lovely city with two outstanding sightseeing venues: the Episcopal princes' Residenz and the Marienberg Fortress. Try to secure a parking place in the vast forecourt of the well signposted *Residenz, one of the finest baroque palaces in Europe, constructed between 1720 and 1744. It was built as the very grandest of homes for the prince-bishop who decided that his home in the nearby Marienburg Fortress simply wasn't grand enough. Admire its architecture from the landscaped gardens and peep into the colorful **Hofkirche** (to the right near the garden) before entering the palace. If your arrival does not coincide with a tour in English, purchase the English guidebook so that you can follow along. Climb the magnificent grand staircase (it appears on the DM 50 bill) and admire the splendid oval Imperial Hall with its magnificent frescoes where several characters have slipped out of the frescoes to become statues. From here you join an escorted tour of the Imperial Apartments, following along in your English guidebook as you move from one lavishly decorated room to another. (*Tour in English 11 am and 2 pm, 9 am–5 pm April to September, 10 am –4 pm October to March, closed Mondays.*)

Vineyards climb up to the **Festung Marienberg** (Marienberg Fortress) overlooking the town from the other bank of the River Main. The fortress has evolved over the years and now contains the **Mainnfränkisches Museum** of regional art and folklore including some old wine-making implements. The most beloved exhibits are the sculptures of

Tilman Riemenschneider who lived in Würzburg from 1483 to 1531—you will see another of his masterpieces later in the day. (*10 am–5 pm April to September, 10 am–4 pm October to March, closed Mondays.*)

Festung Marienberg

Leave Würzburg on the autobahn traveling south towards Stuttgart (allow four hours for the 100-kilometer journey from Würzburg to Rothenburg). Exit at **Tauberbischofsheim** and travel 2 kilometers to this appealing, small medieval town. The local history museum in the castle (Schloss) is well signposted. (*2:30–4:30 pm Easter to October, closed Mondays.*)

Follow the Tauber river valley and the Romantic Road for the short drive to **Bad Mergentheim**. The old order of the Teutonic Knights left Prussia to reside here in the castle in 1525 and remained until they were disbanded in 1809. Their **Deutschordensschloss** now houses a museum that traces the knights' history from the battles of the Crusades to becoming a charitable institution (entrance under the archway). (*2:30–5:30 pm weekdays, 10 am–12 noon and 2:30–4:30 pm weekends, March to October.*)

Detour into the village of **Weikersheim**. From the ample parking lot it's just a few steps to the attractive Marktplatz and the castle. The ***Dorfmuseum** (on the market place) is well worth the entrance fee. On the first floor are several rooms set up to show how the locals lived in years gone by with displays of country-simple antiques, amongst them some lovely examples of painted beds, chests, and cupboards. The second floor is full of farm implements and the floor under the eaves covers winemaking in the area. (*8 am–6 pm April to October, 10 am–12 noon and 2–4 pm November to March.*) The adjacent 18th-century **Schloss Weikersheim** is filled with its original furniture, tapestries, porcelain, and gloomy family portraits. Once you are on the hour-long tour (German only) it's hard to escape as you are locked into each floor of the castle as you enter it. Skip the tour, and go instead to admire the statues in the formal garden and the view of the Tauber valley. (*9 am–6 pm April to October, 10 am–noon and 2–4 pm November to March.*)

Your road follows the Tauber as it weaves south, passing under the clock-tower building in **Schaffersheim** and narrowing as it goes down the main street of **Rottingen**. Leave the Romantic Road to travel through the narrow streets of **Creglingen**, a mixture of old and new houses, and follow signposts in the village for ***Herrgottskirche**, a squat little church on the edge of town. Your entrance ticket includes a pompous English brochure that requires detailed study to glean useful information. Of the five altars in the church, the masterpiece, the Assumption of Mary (1505–1510) by Tilman Riemenschneider, is **the** reason for visiting. Study the different expressions on the faces of the disciples surrounding Mary. On the altar base Riemenschneider carved himself as the second of the three scribes. (*8 am–6 pm April to October.*) Across the road you find a little **Fingerhut**, thimble museum. (*8 am–6 pm April to October.*)

Leaving the church, the country road leads you up a narrow valley, across peaceful farmland, and through quiet rural villages to enter through the old city gates into ***Rothenburg**, truly one of Europe's most enchanting towns (you can only drive and park your car within the walls if you are staying at a hotel—they provide you with a parking permit). Walking down the cobblestoned streets of Rothenburg is rather like taking a stroll through an open-air museum: there is history in every stone.

Rothenburg's old houses, towers, and gateways that have withstood the ravages of the centuries are there for you to explore. Tourists throng the streets but somehow the town has the ability to absorb them and not let their numbers spoil its special magic. Being such a popular tourist destination, Rothenburg has a rich choice of places to stay: our selections are covered in the *Hotels* section.

Rothenburg has narrowly escaped destruction on several occasions. In 1945 the Allies ordered Rothenburg destroyed as part of the war reprisals but an American general, remembering the picture of Rothenburg that hung on his mother's wall, tried to spare the town. His efforts were successful and although Rothenburg was somewhat damaged, the town remained intact. During the Thirty Years' War, General Tilly's army laid siege to the town and, despite spirited resistance, breached the walls. Tilly demanded that the town be destroyed and its councilors put to death. He assembled the town councilors to pass sentence on the town and was offered a drink from the town's ceremonial tankard filled with 3½ liters of the best Franconian wine. After having drunk and passed the cup among his subordinates, Tilly then, with a touch of humor, offered to spare the town and the lives of the councilors if one of its representatives could empty the tankard in one go. Nusch, a former mayor, who seems to have been good at drinking, agreed to try. He succeeded and saved the town. Apparently he slept for three days after the feat. Several times a day (*11 am, noon, 1 pm, 2 pm, 3 pm, 6 pm, 7 pm, 8 pm, 9 pm*) in the marketplace the doors on either side of the clock open and the figures of Tilly and Nusch reenact the historic drinking feat.

For an entertaining, informative insight into the history of the town join the *nightwatchman on his nightly rounds (*April to end of December, meet under the clocktower in the market square*). The English tour begins after the 8 pm drinking feat and arrives back at the square just in time for the 9 pm event. (The German tour leaves at 9:30 pm.)

Rothenburg

The brochure *Rothenburg Worth Seeing, Worth Knowing* is carried by all hotels and the tourist office—with this and map in hand set off to explore. Be sure to include a section of the *city walls*: climb the stairs to the walkway and follow the covered ramparts which almost encircle the town (the stones with names are placed in honor of those who donated money for the walls' restoration). Particularly if you have in tow adolescents whose delights gravitate toward the gruesome, make a stop at the **Mittelalterliches Kriminalmuseum** (Museum of Medieval Justice). Here you will find displayed various instruments of torture such as the headpiece for women who gossiped and the dunking chair for bakers who did not make their loaves the correct size. (*9 am–6 pm April to October, 2–4 pm November to March.*) The **Reichsstadt Musuem** in the Dominican Convent offers an English explanation sheet that guides you through rooms full of furniture (including the convent kitchen and a chemist's shop), past lots of paintings of Rothenburg, and encourages you to find the Meistertrunk (Kürfurstenhumpen), the cup that pretends to be the one used at the drinking feat. (*10 am–5 pm April to October.*) Wander down ***Herrengasse** where the merchants and patricians lived in their elegant mansions, through the old gate with its little after-curfew entrance, and glance back to see the scary mask mouth where defenders of the town poured hot tar down on their attackers. The pretty castle garden offers lovely countryside views. Rothenburg has many lovely shops and boutiques, one of the most enchanting being **Kathe Wohlfahrt's Christkindlmarkt**. Claiming to offer the world's largest selection of Christmas items, a tiny storefront near the market square opens up to a vast fairyland of decorated Christmas trees and animated Stieff animals. The town's culinary specialty is *Schneeballen*, a dessert looking like snowballs, made up of layers of thin strips of pastry rolled up, deep fried, and then dusted with confectioner's sugar, but I have never seen anyone actually eating them.

Consider escaping the daytime crowds that flock to Rothenburg by taking a half-day outing just a little farther down the Romantic Road to Dinkelsbühl. En route is **Feuchtwangen,** a small town whose market square is referred to as "Franconia's festival hall." Of interest are the **Romanesque cloisters,** and the **Heimatmuseum** (Franconian Folklore Museum) that traces furnishing styles through the ages from country farms to baroque and Biedermeier. The town also has one of the region's most delightful inns— the **Romantik Hotel Greifen Post**.

South of Feuchtwangen is the historic old town of **Dinkelsbühl,** a town that prospered in the 15th and 16th centuries at the junction of trade routes. Its narrow streets filled with historic houses lie behind the walls with their towers and four gateways. The most handsome houses are found on the main street, Dr Martin Luther Strasse, particularly the **Deutsches Haus** with its overhanging balconies. The **Heimatmuseum** (Folklore Museum) in the Spitalhof traces the town's history with furniture, kitchen utensils, torture instruments, and a portrait of King Adolphus of Sweden. The town's siege by Adolphus's army is re-enacted every year in mid-July to commemorate the town's salvation by the village's brave children in the Thirty Years' War.

With sightseeing it will take you a full day to follow our route from Rothenburg to Heidelberg. Get a fast start on the day by taking the autobahn (about an hour's drive) to **Schwäbisch Hall**, a town that profits from the fact that it is not very heavily visited by tourists. Built on a steep hillside sloping down to the River Kocher, the town contains many well preserved medieval houses. The Marktplatz is one of the prettiest in Germany and always teeming with activity—a real town center with women carefully selecting their produce for the evening meal from small stalls in the square (*market days Saturday and Wednesday*) and children neatly dressed in uniforms chatting gaily on their way to school. The monumental **Fischbrunen** fountain with its statues of Samson, St. Michael, and St. George sits at the base of the 53 steps that lead up to **St. Michael's Church**. A statue of the archangel is found in the church's porch. Inside the church admire the high altar with its painted and sculpted scenes by unknown Dutch artists. Opposite the church sits the **Rathaus,** an elegant, baroque-style building. Also on the market square you find the **Romantik Hotel Goldener Adler.** Follow the cobbles down to **Obere** and **Untere Herrengasse** with their fine, half-timbered houses.

Leaving the 14 in the direction of Stuttgart, then after 6 kilometers turn right for **Waldenburg**. A 12-kilometer drive through pretty countryside brings you to the town which you enter along the defense wall with a sheer drop on either side. Meander beneath the castle ramparts down to the plain. Another 12-kilometer drive brings you to **Neuenstein** where, amidst the town's narrow streets, you find **Schloss Neuenstein** which we were unable to tour because the owner's daughter was getting married that day. (*Mid-March to mid-October, closed Mondays.*)

On to **Öhringen** (6 kilometers), an industrial, workaday town, **Neuenstadt** (follow signposts for the autobahn then Neuenstadt, 13 kilometers away), and **Bad Friedrichsal** (8 kilometers). Cross the Kocher river and turn left to **Bad Wimpfen**. Leave the broad river valley and climb up to park near the town walls. Walk to the Marktplatz (it's a little town so you will not get lost) and obtain a town map from the tourist office in the **Rathaus.** Walk beside the town hall to the **Blamer Turm** (blue tower) whose turreted top was the home to the nightwatchman in years gone by. It is not worth the entrance fee to climb the tower (more dramatic towers await). Continuing along the wall, you have a panoramic view of the valley from the viewpoint adjacent to the **Kaiserpfalz** which now houses the town's museum with its displays of Roman remains. (*10 am–noon and 2–4 pm April to mid-October, Wednesdays to Mondays.*) On to the **Roter Turm** (red tower) where you can climb a small section of wall before continuing through the little cobbled streets and looping back to the market place. Leaving the town, the road zigzags down to the broad river valley, weaving through the village of **Hensheim** towards **Gudshem**. Do not turn over the river to Gudshem, but left to Schloss Guttenberg which you see perched atop the hillside in front of you.

Schloss Guttenberg is particularly fun to visit because not only does it have an interesting museum (displays on three floors of the tower and the opportunity to walk along the ramparts and climb the tower), but it also has the ***Deutsche Greifenwarte Claus Fentzloff** (German Raptor Research Center). The aviary has some magnificent eagles, vultures, and owls from around the world. Try to time your arrival to coincide with the 3 pm flight demonstration. Claus Fentzloff, his wife Bettina, and their assistants demonstrate eagles and vultures skimming just over your head across the ramparts then swooping beyond the castle walls to ride the updrafts. The explanation is in German but if you indicate to Claus that you do not understand German, he also offers a short explanation in English. (*9 am–6 pm March to November, raptor flight demonstration 11 am and 3 pm.*)

Continuing along the quiet river road, pass **Schloss Hornburg** on the opposite bank. Cross the river onto the 37 (signposted Heildelberg) and **Schloss Zwinger** comes into view. For another castle experience deviate into **Hirschhorn** and visit **Schloss Hirschhorn** where all of the intact building now comprises a castle hotel. There are lovely views of the Neckar river valley from the hotel's terrace. Three little castles decorate the skyline of **Neckar Steinach** and from here a few more river bends bring you to Heidelberg.

Heidelberg receives an overrated review in most guidebooks—there are just too many tourists. Nevertheless, it cannot be denied that the crowds make this a particularly dynamic city (there are lots of young people). Surprisingly, it was the romantic operetta *The Student Prince* that put Heidelberg on the tourist map. Unlike so many less fortunate German cities, Heidelberg has been spared the ravages of recent wars. The streets of its old town are a maze of cozy restaurants and lively student taverns—we enjoyed our visits to **Schnookeloch** (Haspelgasse 8) and **Roter Ochsen** (Hauptstrasse 215). Above the town looms the ruin of its picture-postcard, pink-sandstone castle: you can walk up to the castle, but it is easier and more fun to take the **Bergbahn** (mountain railway) from the Kornmarkt. The **Heidelberg Schloss** (castle) is now mostly a ruin, but still great fun to explore, and offers spectacular views of the town and the river from the terrace. The **Ottheinrichsbau** (1559) with its decorative façade is a particularly lovely building. Beneath the Ottheinrichsbau lies the **Deutsches Apotheken Museum** (Apothecary Museum), tracing the history of pharmacy and displaying balances and herbal boxes. (*10 am–5 pm daily.*) The best views of the castle and the town are from the **Philosophenweg** (Philosophers' Walk) on the northern bank of the Neckar river. Cross the Alte Brucke or Old Bridge spanning the Neckar—the Philosophers' Walk is clearly indicated by signs (lit at night).

City life centers on the pedestrian **Hauptstrasse** where you find the town's most impressive building, the 16th-century **Romantik Hotel Zum Ritter St. Georg.** Just a few steps from the Hauptstrasse you find the most attractive **Zur Backmulde** hotel.

Enjoy your sightseeing in the old-world city of Heidelberg, then when it is time to continue your journey, you have many convenient options: you can easily take the autobahn south to the Black Forest or north to the Rhine and Mosel, or, if your holidays must end, it is only an hour and a half's drive to the Frankfurt airport.

Heidelberg

The Romantic Road and the Neckar Valley

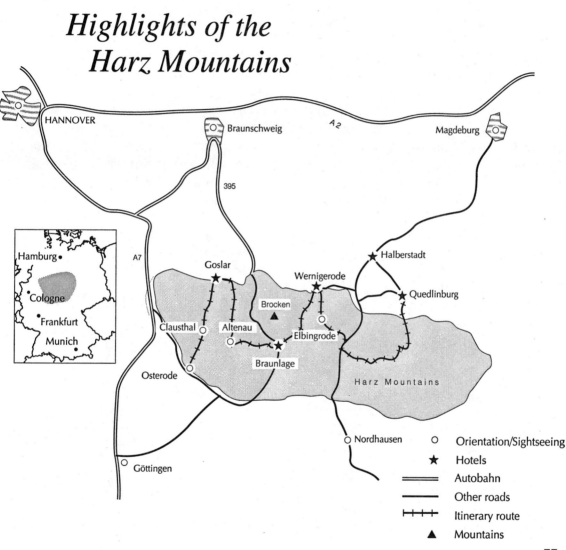

Highlights of the
Harz Mountains

HANNOVER

Braunschweig

A 2

Magdeburg

395

A7

Hamburg

Cologne

Frankfurt

Munich

Goslar

Wernigerode

Halberstadt

Brocken

Quedlinburg

Clausthal   Altenau

Elbingrode

Braunlage

Osterode

Harz Mountains

Nordhausen

Göttingen

○   Orientation/Sightseeing

★   Hotels

Autobahn

Other roads

Itinerary route

▲   Mountains

Highlights of the Harz Mountains

Rising from the plains, the Harz mountains are the tallest in northern and central Germany. The mountains' summits are not towering (they are more like rolling hills than mountains) but their sheltered valleys, cool blue lakes, green, forested slopes, and tumbling streams provide some most attractive scenery and plenty of opportunities for summer walks and winter cross-country skiing. Little resort villages nestle amidst the mountains while sitting at their feet three outstanding medieval towns (Goslar, Wernigerode, and Quedlinburg) vie for your attention with a parade of outstanding half-timbered homes, decorative town halls, towering castles, and interesting museums.

Wernigerode, Schloss Wernigerode

Recommended Pacing: Concentrate your first day's sightseeing in Goslar and spend your first night in the Harz here (our recommended hotel only just made it into the guide) or in the resort of Braunlage. Follow this with one night in Wernigerode (two if you take the steam train into the Harz) or a night in Quedlinburg if you, like us, enjoy exquisite, not-overly-restored medieval homes (some may interpret this as shabby).

Nestling at the foot of the Harz mountains, **Osterode's** brightly painted half-timbered houses make exploring the historic city center an attractive proposition. (Follow signposts for Innerstadt Ring, park your car, and walk into the pedestrian precinct.) The historic **Rathaus** (town hall) was built in 1522 and beneath its ornate bay window hangs a whale rib that is supposed to protect the town from flooding and inclement weather. Continuing along the street from the town hall, you come to the **Marktkirche** (market church) on the Kornmarkt. The church dates back to the Middle Ages and until 1936 the town's nightwatchman lived in the little flat just below the spire—it was his job to sound the alarm in case of fire. Festivals and flea markets are held at the Kornmarkt along with the weekly market on Saturdays.

Leaving Osterode, follow signposts for Goslar (241): a dual carriageway takes you to the base of the mountains where a narrower, forest-lined road continues up into the mountains to the twin towns of **Clausthal** and **Zellerfeld**. At the top of the hill in Zellerfeld you find the **Bergwerkmuseum** dedicated to mining in the Harz. Apart from displays of old-fashioned mining paraphernalia, rooms have been set up to give you a glimpse of eras long past showing how the miners lived and worked. Leaving the first museum, you cross a rustic courtyard to explore buildings full of old-fashioned wooden mine machinery and walk through a short length of underground mining tunnel. (*9 am–5 pm daily.*) The blue-painted **Marktkirche Zum Heiligen Geist** (Holy Ghost Parish Church) with its stubby onion domes was built between 1636 and 1642 and is the largest wooden church in Germany.

Goslar

From Clausthal-Zellerfeld the 241 winds down through vast forests to ***Goslar** where a full day's sightseeing awaits you in this lovely city full of historic buildings. Try to park at the Kaiserplatz (signposted). Here you find the majestic 11th-century **Kaiserpfalz** (Imperial Palace), one of the largest non-church buildings in the empire now displaying military paintings in its vast hall. (*10 am–3pm daily.*) Amble down the pedestrian-only cobbled streets, past timbered houses to the Marktplatz. Occupying a corner of the square, the old town merchants' guildhall is now the **Hotel Kaiserworth** (see hotel section) where statues of German emperors guard the portals. Here you are only steps away from the **Rathaus** (town hall) with its Hudigungssaal (chamber of allegiance) displaying German emperors on the wall and the life of Christ on the ceiling. (*10 am–4 pm daily.*) The different scenes on the clock on the market square represent the 1,000-year-old mining history of the region (the clock performs at 9 am, noon, 3 pm, and 6 pm). The tourist office is also located on the square.

Follow the cobbled street beside the Kaiserworth to the **Goslar Museum** with its displays of life in old Goslar, a geological overview of the Harz, and displays of minerals. One room contains art treasures from the cathedral and the Goslar gospel. (*10 am–4 pm, closed Mondays*.) Follow the tumbling River Gose past the **Lohmühle** (tanning-mill) with its ancient waterwheel to the **Puppen Museum** (Puppet Museum) in the basement of an antique shop on Hoher Weg. The **Barock Café** next door serves scrumptious cakes.

At Münzstrasse 11, the **Tin Figure Museum** is situated in the coach house of an inn which was built in 1644 and used as a stopping place for the mail coach. Here you see displays of over 1,000 little tin figures depicting historic scenes. (*10 am–4 pm, closed Mondays*.) Just round the corner on Jakobistrasse you find the **Mönchehaus Museum of Modern Art** in an imposing farmer's townhouse that dates back to 1528. It has exhibitions of modern art and works by the prize-winners of the Kaiserring, an art award given by the town of Goslar. Its garden is full of sculptures. (*Open 10 am–5 pm, closed 1pm–3pm, closed Mondays*.)

Leaving the town center, retrace your steps towards Clausthal-Zellerfeld for a very short distance and turn left for the brief drive to the ***Rammelsberger Bergbaumuseum**. The Rammelsberg Mine on the edge of Goslar closed in 1988, the only mine in the world to have been in continuous operation for over 1,000 years (968 to 1989). Everything is the way it was on the mine's last day of operation. Don your hard hat and miner's garb and follow your tour guide (tours are given in German but several of the guides speak English and give bilingual tours) past the 10th-century waste heaps, down long, low (well lit) tunnels to the 12th-century Rathstiefster gallery, visiting ingenious wooden water wheels used for removing water from deep underground. You emerge in a more modern tunnel to see the little yellow train that carried the miners deep underground. The tour concludes with a film (in German) showing activities at the mine. Plans are afoot to offer a tour where you don not only mining garb but take your hammer and lamp underground to the face to mine your own rock sample. (*9:30 am–4:30 pm daily*.)

Leave Goslar on the 82 signposted Bad Harzburg which brings you onto the 6 (also signposted Bad Harzburg). As you go onto the dual carriageway, stay to the right as yours is the first exit (immediate): the 498 to Oker. Oker is an industrial town and after passing through it you quickly regain the forests and the mountains as the 498 follows a tumbling stream up a steep grade to the **Oker Dam**. This wild valley is understandably a favorite walking spot for summer visitors and there are several parking places where you can hike beside the tumbling stream. The road traces the dam for several kilometers to arrive in **Altenau** (an attractive resort town) where you turn left for the 17-kilometer drive to Braunlage.

Before reunification the resort town of **Braunlage** was on the border (the edge of the Harz mountains as far as tourists from the West were concerned). Now it is a central touring location and you can do no better than to make the **Romantik Hotel Zur Tanne** your base for explorations of the area.

The tragicomically named village of **Eland** ("misery") lies 7 kilometers from Braunlage where the well paved road turns to cobbles. Turn left for Wernigerode, a 17-kilometer drive down **Mount Brocken**. It is said that on Walpurgisnacht, April 30, cackling witches astride their broomsticks gather on the summit of the mountain to cavort and cast their wicked spells. Arriving at the northern foot of the mountains in ***Wernigerode**, secure a parking place on one of the little side streets near the pedestrian Altstadt and make your way to the Marktplatz where you find the magnificent ***Rathaus** (town hall) whose slender spires and intricate woodwork occupy one side of the square. Directly facing the town hall is the **Hotel Weisser Hirsch**, a lovely, modern hotel behind an ancient, timbered façade. The **Oberfarrkirchof** is a picturesque little nook behind the town hall. House number 13, the House Gadenstedt, dating from the 15th century, is one of the loveliest houses in the town. The nearby Kochstrasse contains the smallest house in town—its little door is only 1.7 meters high and the house is only 4.2 meters up to the eaves. Number 72 Breite Strasse was built in 1674 and you can hardly see the original half-timberwork for the amount of intricate carving that decorates it. A horse's head and horseshoes over the door of 95 Breite Strasse indicate that this was for over 300 years a blacksmith's shop, **Krell'sche Schmeide**. The museum contains a display of all things pertaining to blacksmithing and outlines the lifestyles of two families who lived here. (*1–5 pm Wednesdays to Sundays, 10 am–3 pm Fridays.*) The tourist office is on Nicolaiplatz. High above the town the ***Schloss Wernigerode** dominates the skyline. While it is possible to walk up to the castle (a half-hour walk through the suburbs), a less strenuous approach is to take the little tractor-train from just behind the market place. There has been a castle here since the 13th century but beyond the ancient portcullis what you see today is an ornate,

Rathaus (*town hall*), *Wernigerode*

19th-century baroque castle-style home. Guided tours are available in German or you can tour the castle with the aid of an English brochure and walk from one beautifully furnished room to another. (*10 am–5 pm, closed Mondays except in summer.*)

Wernigerode is the headquarters of the Harzer Schmalspurbahnen (HSB) which operates the great little trains of the Harz that give you magnificent views of the mountains. Their brochure *Great Adventures with Narrow-Gauge Steam* outlines three railway adventures, two of which leave from Wernigerode. The ***Harzquerbahn** leaves from the

Hauptbahnhof and, steaming between houses and gardens, the little train chugs into the forest, winding its way up through the trees as it climbs into the mountains. Following a long tunnel, the track becomes steeper and steeper as the train approaches Drei-Annen-Hohne where the track divides: the Harzquerbahn continues across the Harz to Nordhausen (three hours from Wernigerode) while the **Brockenbahn** begins the climb of the Brocken mountain. From Drei-Annen-Hohne the Brockenbahn train climbs ever steeper to the summit of the Brocken, offering magnificent views of the **Hochharz National Park**. (*8 trains a day May 28 to November 5, tel: [03943] 558126, fax: [03943] 32107.*)

While this itinerary's next major destination, Quedlinburg, lies just 40 kilometers distant across the plains, take a more circuitous back road through the mountains. Leave Wernigerode (with the castle on your left) on the 244 for the 7-kilometer climb into the mountains to the pleasant little resort of **Elbingrode** where the **Büchenberg Mine Museum** is found just outside the town. A tour of this former tin mine gives you an insight into the working life of a miner in the Harz. (*Tour 10 am, noon, 2 pm, 3 pm— additional tours on weekends, open all year.*)

A 5-kilometer drive brings you to **Rübeland**, a mountain village set amongst limestone cliffs and noted for its caves. Park near **Baumans Höhle** and choose between a tour of this cave system or **Hernmanns Höhle**, a series of caves found just across the River Bode. We chose Baumans because of the availability of a tour and were led on a 45-minute walk through passages to caves with magnificent displays of stalagmites and stalactites (the tour was in German and information in English was not available). We understood that the tour of Hernmanns was very similar but included a pool that contained "cave fish," blind, white, eel-like creatures that live out their lives in darkness. (*9:45 am–4:15 pm daily.*)

Cross the River Bode and leave Rübeland past the entrance to Hernmanns Höhle towards Hasselfelde. The road travels up through the trees, into a tunnel, and emerges on a dam with a vast tract of water stretching to the right and the valley falling away steeply to the left. Turn left on the 81 (signposted Blankenburg) and after 1 kilometer pass through **Wendefugh** (a speck of a village), go up through the trees, and turn right for Altenbrak, following the River Bode as it tumbles down the most picturesque of valleys for 4 kilometers to the village of **Altenbrak** whose houses are straddled along the road. Carry on to the few houses that comprise **Tresburg** where you turn right up the **Bodetal Valley**, following walking paths whose rustic little bridges span the tumbling little river, to **Aldrode**, a quiet farming community set high in the mountains. Turn right and a 5-kilometer drive across heathland takes you down to the tree-lined main street of **Friedrichsbrun** and on to **Bad Suderode** (8 kilometers) where nearly every old house (most in need of a coat of paint) has an ornate balcony.

Seven kilometers across the plain brings you to *Quedlinburg. Cross the river (following signposts for Centrum) then secure a parking place and walk to the Marktplatz where you find the tourist office and the sturdy stone **Rathaus** (town hall). Within the old town there are 1,500 half-timbered houses, many of them crumbling and in need of restoration, looking much as they must have in the Middle Ages. The entire town center is an architectural gem. Map in hand, explore the little streets behind the Rathaus, venturing down little alleyways where you can touch the leaning houses on either side of the cobbled walkways to emerge on streets with elaborate, picture-perfect façades. On a low promontory just a short walk from the Marktplatz you find the **Schloss Quedlinburg** and the **Stifskirche** (collegiate church) **of St. Servatius** which is considered the most beautiful Romanesque church in north and central Germany. It is a surprisingly spacious, simply adorned edifice built between 1070 and 1129. The treasury chamber contains valuable religious relics and the room next to it contains fragments of a knotted wall hanging discovered in the 19th century. The adjacent **Schlossmuseum** houses 16th- and 17th-century Flemish and Italian paintings and gives you an impression of life at the time of the founding of the Damenstift, a religious institution run for ladies by nuns. The terrace gives you a spectacular view of the town's rooftops. (*9 am–5 pm,* *closed Mondays*.) The **Klopstockhaus**, a magnificent patrician home at the foot of the castle, has been used as a museum for over 90 years. (*9 am–5 pm, closed Mondays and Tuesdays*.) The **Ständerbau** (half-timbered house, Wordgasse 3), built in the 13th century, is the oldest half-timbered building in the town and was a home until 1965. The tiny rooms with all their nooks and crannies house an exhibition on the half-timbered architecture of Quedlinburg. (*10 am–5 pm May to September, closed Thursdays*.) At 11 Steinweg you find the simply decorated **Hotel Zur Goldenen Sonne**, a pleasant place to stay in the heart of the town. From Quedlinburg a two-hour drive finds you in Berlin, Potsdam, or Dresden where you can join the *Exploring Eastern Germany* itinerary, or travel north to Hamburg and *Schleswig Holstein—the land between the seas.*

Quedlinburg

　　　　　Highlights of the Harz Mountains

Exploring Eastern Germany

Hamburg

Cologne

Frankfurt

Munich

POLAND

Gohren-Lebbin

A14

A24

BERLIN

Potsdam

E30

A2

E30

E55

E36

Lübbenau

SPREEWALD

E36

Cottbus

A9

Leipzig

A14

Meissen

A24

E55

Dresden

A7

Eisenach

Erfurt

Weimar

Bad Hersfeld

A5

E40

E40

Giessen

E40

A5

FRANKFURT

E40

CZECH REPUBLIC

○   Orientation/Sightseeing

★   Hotels

─────   Other roads

═════   Autobahn

▓▓▓▓▓   Itinerary route

· · · · ·   Borders

Exploring Eastern Germany

For 40 years East Germany slept under a mantle of secrecy. Then, in November, 1989, the stunning word spread throughout the world: "The Wall" had been torn down. In October, 1990, the reunification became official, and the doors to East Germany opened. While miracles have happened, all is not yet complete: cranes dot the skyline of every town and village, and traffic snarls are a problem near larger towns. Eastern Germany cannot yet compete with the excellent hotels and perfectly groomed towns in the rest of the country, but don't wait too long to visit—it is fun to be a part of history and witness the transformation taking place. In this itinerary we have hand-picked eastern Germany's most historical towns and cities (Eisenach, Erfurt, Weimar, Meissen, Dresden, Potsdam, and Berlin) and added intriguing palaces and mighty castles for good measure, along with the opportunity to take a punting trip through the quiet canals of the Spreewald, enjoying "pickle stops" and a historic Sorb village.

Parade of Princes, Dresden

Recommended Pacing: If you want to get a leisurely start, overnight in Wartburg Castle, otherwise make Weimar your first overnight. A night here with two nights in Dresden and two nights in Potsdam or Berlin (three if you do extensive sightseeing in Berlin) gives you a good overview of the cities of eastern Germany. If you are not a cities person, head for the Spreewald: being punted down a countryside canal is an experience unique in all of Europe.

Situated on the edge of the vast stretches of the Thuringia forest, **Eisenach** is a bustling city with miles of urban sprawl on its outskirts and traffic snarls downtown, so, until the road infrastructure improves, be prepared to move around town at a snail's pace. Follow the well signposted route to your destination, *****Wartburg**, one of Europe's finest Romanesque castles, perched atop a wooded hill southwest of town. Leaving the main road, follow the small lane that weaves up through the forest to the castle to the parking lot, a ten-minute walk from the fortification at the summit. Buy your entrance ticket and cross the moat then go under the portcullis and into the courtyard to stand in line to purchase a second ticket for the guided tour of the castle (buy a guidebook in English to help you understand this German-only tour). It was this castle that inspired Ludwig II to build his fanciful Bavarian castles and Richard Wagner to write his opera *Tannhäuser*. The restored castle is largely Romanesque but furnishings, artwork, and tapestries are original pieces from the medieval to the baroque eras of this castle.

One of the most interesting rooms is the Elisabeth Gallery where six large frescoed murals depict the tale of Elisabeth, a Hungarian princess who came to live at the castle in 1211. She died when only 24, but became a legend due to her work with the peasants— nursing those who were ill and helping the destitute. Another room in the castle, the Elisabeth Room, has a gorgeous mosaic, consisting of more than a million pieces of glass, mother-of-pearl, and gold leaf, which also tells her story.

After leaving the tour, return to the courtyard and take a few minutes to visit the few simple rooms where Martin Luther hid after being excommunicated in 1521. The walls are decorated with Lucas Cranach's portraits of Luther and his wife. Luther spent his time translating the New Testament into German—it was Luther's preaching and writing in German that established German as an important language. (*8:30 am–4:30 pm April to October, 9 am–3:30 pm November to March.*) Many tourists visit Wartburg Castle without realizing that one wing of the castle complex houses the **Hotel auf der Wartburg**.

Wartburg Castle
Eisenach

Fortunately Eisenach's other interesting sightseeing spot, Johann Sebastian Bach's birthplace, ***Bachhaus**, lies outside the crowded city. Watch carefully—just a few minutes before entering the town center turn left (signposted Bachhaus) and follow the road to a tree-shaded square with a statue of Bach set in a tiny park. Facing the statue is a cheerful, mustard-yellow house where Johann Sebastian Bach lived as a boy. The tour of Bach's home is not structured: follow the well marked signs throughout the house which is furnished in much the same way as it was when Bach was a child. The tour ends at the chamber music room where every 20 minutes a program of Bach's music, both live and taped, is cleverly woven together with a presentation about his life and work. To sit in this lovely, small music chamber dappled with sunlight filtering in from the garden while listening to Bach's music is indeed magical. After the demonstration, you may choose to traverse the flower-filled garden to another section of the house in which Bach memorabilia and sheet music are displayed. (*1:30–4:30 pm Mondays, 9 am–4 pm Tuesdays to Fridays, 9 am–noon and 1:30–4:30 pm Saturdays and Sundays.*)

Leaving Eisenach, return to the autobahn and continue east. It is only about 45 kilometers to the turnoff heading north to the old university town of **Erfurt**. Do not be discouraged by the size of the city because beyond the sprawling, ugly suburbs lies an attractive city center. Park in any of the designated parking areas near the pedestrian old town and set off on foot for the **Krämerbrücke** (Kramer bridge), a narrow street of little shops and galleries in colorfully painted, half-timbered houses that spans the river. Walk its length and you come to the vast Domplatz with its monumental staircase leading up to the triple-spired **Dom** (cathedral). In the interior notice the beautifully carved choir-stalls and the exquisitely detailed stained-glass windows (1370–1420) round the altar. The adjacent triple-spired **Severikirche** was built between 1280 and 1400.

The **Domplatz,** crowded with market stalls on Wednesdays, has a couple of very attractive houses: **Grüne Apotheke** (Green Apothecary) and the restaurant **Zur Hohn Lilie.** Further appealing homes are also located on **Fischmarkt Platz** where you find the attractive **Gildehaus** restaurant and where you may perhaps be tempted to snack on one of the tantalizing freshly grilled bratwurst sandwiches from the street vendors.

Leaving Erfurt, follow signs for Weimar, 25 kilometers away. It is possible to return to the autobahn, but the quickest route is a smaller back road that heads directly east from Erfurt to Weimar. The traffic crawls through the sprawling suburbs but take heart, since after you park your car you are treated to an attractive town center. Follow signposts for the Hotel Elephant as you near the town center for this brings you to the pedestrian Markt Platz where you find the tourist information office and the **Hotel Elephant** (you can drive into the square to drop your luggage if you are staying at the hotel). Two other recommended places to stay are the **Hotel Schwartze**, 6 kilometers south near the autobahn, and the **Weimar Hilton** overlooking **Ilm Park**.

Weimar's status as a cultural capital led to Germany's democrats putting the town's name on the new republic in 1919. Over the years the town's princes nurtured those with artistic and musical talents, including Lucas Cranach, Franz Liszt, and Johann Sebastian Bach. Similarly, the court nurtured Germany's leading writers: Goethe, Schiller, Wieland, and Herder. Goethe spent over 50 years here. He moved into *Goethehaus in 1782 and lived here until his death in 1832 (from the market square take Frauentorstrasse to Frauenplan). His home is by and large the way it was when he lived here: you see the study where he worked, manuscripts and all, and his bedroom with the armchair in which he died. (*9 am–4 pm, closed Mondays.*) Goethe frequently dined in the adjacent **Zum Weissen Schwan** and housed his overflow of visitors here. The Swan has two delightful, cozy dining rooms, an excellent choice for an up-market place to eat.

A few streets away lies the **Schillerhaus**, Schillerstrasse 12, where Schiller came to live for three years prior to Goethe's death. It was here that he wrote *Wilhelm Tell*. Behind the house an interesting museum depicts the writer's life and work. (*9 am–4 pm, closed Mondays.*) Goethe and Schiller were great friends and a large statue of them together stands outside the **Deutches Nationaltheater** on Theaterplatz.

The exterior of the **Stadtshloss** (castle) has been restored and the wing facing the park is now open as an art gallery that houses, amongst other things, an important collection of paintings by Lucas Cranach. (*9 am–5 pm, closed Mondays.*) Cross the river Ilm (on the bridge behind the museum) and stroll though the woodlands and lawns, following the river to **Goethe's Gartenhaus** (garden house) which he received as a present from August the Strong in 1776. He liked it so much he lived there till 1782 and it always remained his favorite retreat. The country-simple furnishings in the garden house are very different from the ornate decor in his later home. (*Closed Mondays.*)

On a sadder note, just 11 kilometers northwest of town lies **Buchenwald.** Drive through the woodlands to the buildings at the end of the road where you find a bookshop and an auditorium which shows a movie. Narrated in German, this jerky, very dated film is somehow more poignant than some slick, commercial production (and it is impossible to miss the story line). The images generated by this concentration camp are horrific, but a part of history not to be forgotten. The camp installations are gone and a monument pays tribute to the 65,000 victims who died here. (*8:45 am–4:45 pm, closed Mondays.*)

Depending upon road conditions, it is about a two- to three-hour drive from Weimar to Dresden, a distance of 200 kilometers. The drive takes you through pretty, rolling farmland, pasture, forest, and low-lying hills. ***Dresden**, a large, sprawling city, is not as well signposted as you would wish, so it is handy to have a city map in hand to navigate yourself to the Altstadt.

Dresden, the city with a great past, is well on its way to a great future. The famous skyline of palace domes and majestic church steeples on a bend of the River Elbe was razed by Allied bombers on February 13, 1945 and it is only since reunification that the city has experienced a rebirth with cranes and building sites restoring ruins to their former glory. An example of painstaking renovation is Taschenbergpalais (the Taschenberg palace), a magnificent home commissioned in 1706 by August the Strong for his mistress, the Countess Cosel. Today, behind a painstakingly restored façade, you find the elegant **Kempinski Hotel Taschenbergpalais**, the finest address in Dresden. We also recommend the **Hotel Bülow Residenz** just across the river in the Neustadt.

Begin your sightseeing at the Catholic cathedral, **Hofkirche**, whose lacy spire faces Augustusbrücke. Just beside the cathedral is the **Brühlsche Terrace**, praised as the "balcony of Europe"—only members of the nobility were allowed to enjoy this riverside view until 1814 when the broad flight of stairs was built to allow everyone to enjoy it. If you wish to know why the city's hero, August the Strong, was given his name, study the cast-iron railing of the terrace and find his thumb mark—what a pity the rail was

Zwinger Palace, Dresden

installed ten years after his death! Follow the ***Parade of Princes**, a tile mural made up of 24,000 Meissner porcelain tiles stretching down Auguststrasse that depicts the princes and kings of the region. The reconstruction of the **Frauenkirche** (Church of Our Lady) is under way and the building that was once considered the most beautiful Protestant church in Europe is rising slowly from the ashes. Turning behind the **Residenzschloss** (castle), walk behind the Catholic cathedral to the **Semperoper** (Semper Opera House) where statues on the façade portray Shakespeare and Sophocles, and Goethe and Schiller flank the entrance.

Saving the very best for last, enter Dresden's greatest treasure, the ***Zwinger Palace**, where you will concentrate much of your sightseeing. Just to walk into the enormous courtyard, which seems the size of multiple football fields, is awesome. Surrounding this lovely garden courtyard is the palace, which contains a mind-boggling assortment of museums. The ***Gemäldegalerie Alte Meister** (Old Masters Gallery), full of magnificent paintings by Canaletto, Raphael, Rubens, Rembrandt, Van Dyck, and many other famous artists, is world-famous. (*10 am–6 pm, closed Mondays.*) Your gallery ticket gives you entrance to the adjacent **Rüstkammer Museum** with its displays of ancient military hardware. (*10 am–6 pm, closed Mondays.*) The **Porzellansammlung** (Porcelain Museum—entrance on Sophienstrasse) houses an important collection of Meissen, Japanese, and Chinese porcelain. (*10 am–6 pm, closed Thursdays.*) The **Wallpavillion** houses the **Mathematisch-Physikalischer Salon** (Salon of Mathematics and Physics) with its collection of mathematical and measuring instruments (it has lots of barometers, thermometers, and clocks). (*9:30 am–5 pm, closed Thursdays.*)

Steamer trips depart from the Terrassenufer, underneath the Brühlsche Terrasse. A 90-minute boat trip takes you upstream to Loschwitz and Blasewitz where the boat tacks around and returns you to the city center. (*Operates April to mid-November.*) A longer trip takes you upstream past the Elbe palaces of Albrechtsburg, Lingner, and Eckberg to Pillnitz Palace, where you can leave the steamer and visit the park and palace before returning to the city center two hours later. (*Operates all year, reduced program October to April. Sächsische Dampfschiffahrts, Lingneralle 3, 01096 Dresden, tel: [0351] 4969203, fax: [0351] 4969350.*)

The 1,000-year-old town of **Meissen** is only a 25-kilometer drive from Dresden following the River Elbe north. The heart of Meissen is on a knoll overlooking the Elbe where the beautiful cathedral and the castle decorate the plaza. Follow the sign of the crossed blue swords (the hallmark of Dresden china) through the old town at the base of the castle which leads you directly to the ***Staatliche Porzellanmanufaktur** (porcelain factory) at 9 Leninstrasse. Parking is limited and there are a great many buses. Upon entering the building, buy two tickets, one for the museum and one for the work demonstration. While the tour through the work area is in several languages, it is helpful to have the English booklet describing the making of this world-famous china which dates back to 1708 when Johann Friedrich Böttger, working for August the Strong, discovered the secret of making "white gold" (porcelain china). August founded an isolated factory at Albrechtsburg castle, keeping the workers almost prisoners to protect the secret. In 1865 the factory was transferred to its present site. After the tour visit the museum in the same building. Here you see incredible examples of Meissen china dramatically displayed in the regal setting of these lovely old rooms. Most of the pieces you see date from the 1700s and are extremely ornate: clocks, figurines, dinnerware, candelabra, statuettes—almost anything you can name has been duplicated in this fine white china. The style might not be your taste—much is a bit flamboyant, to be sure— but you cannot help appreciating the incredible craftsmanship involved in the making of each piece of art. A shop sells china and there is a pleasant little café just by the front door. (*8:30 am–3:30 pm, closed Mondays.*) The understandable popularity of the china factory means that Meissen's other tourist attractions are, sadly, often overlooked: the **Dom** (cathedral) and **Albrechtsburg Castle**, high above the town and visible from afar, are masterpieces of Gothic architecture. (*1–6 pm Mondays to Saturdays, 10 am–3 pm Sundays.*)

Leaving Dresden, follow the signs to autobahn 55 heading north to Berlin. The road is well maintained and the countryside quite flat so, unless there is a lot of traffic, it is an easy 95-kilometer drive north. You pass large farms of cultivated fields and drive through some pretty pastoral countryside. Watch your map carefully: when highway E55 joins the E36 to Berlin, you turn south toward **Cottbus** and then almost immediately take the turnoff marked to **Lübbenau**, which is where you will take your boat excursion to explore the water alleys of the *Spreewald. Follow the road into town (signposted Häfen with a little boat and waves) and continue to the boat landing (you cannot miss it—there is a small plaza where many boats are tied up along docks lining the River Spree). As you walk along the docks you see a large selection of boats, each with a sign posted with the price and the length of the trip offered. Tours last from two to six hours and boats leave when they are full of passengers.

Spreewald

The Spreewald is an enormous maze where the Spree divides into tiny fingers, creating a lacy pattern of canal-like waterways which wind lazily in every direction under a canopy of trees. For many centuries the Spreewald has been home to the Sorbs who have their own language and folk customs. (I saw pictures of quaint costumes, but did not see any.) Along the banks of the river the Sorbs have built small houses which vary in style but which are all simple wooden structures with high-pitched roofs crowned on each corner with a carved snake wearing a crown.

You can experience the magic of this area only by taking one of the boat excursions. First choose your boat: the two-hour tour is excellent, giving you a good sample of the area and also time to stop at **Lehde**, a Sorb village where you can have a cup of tea and visit the museum made up of a cluster of typical wooden homes furnished with old, country-style furniture. Each canoe is almost identical: a blackened wooden shell—sort of a cross between an Indian dug-out canoe and a Venetian gondola. Benches are set in rows down the length of the canoe and your "gondolier" stands at the back and poles you through the shallow waters. As the boat left the dock, I was reminded of the jungle cruise at Disneyland. The boats pass under many humped bridges from which paths disappear mysteriously into the forest. Your gondolier makes a "pickle stop," for the Spreewald is famous for its pickles and merchants sell these spicy wares along the riverbanks. As the canoe glides through the water you are surrounded by constant activity: boats pass piled high with hay or carrying laughing children on their way to school or the postman delivering his mail—all attesting to the fact that there are few roads into this world of yesteryear. The **Schloss Lübbenau** and the **Turm Hotel** are our recommended places to stay in the delightful little town of Lübbenau.

When it is time to leave the Spreewald, it is an easy drive of about 125 kilometers along the well marked autobahn 55 to Berlin. But, instead of continuing on to the center of the city, we suggest you make your base southwest of Berlin in **Potsdam**. To reach Potsdam, turn west on highway 30 (about 22 kilometers before Berlin) and follow signposts to **Schlosshotel Cecilienhof**. Looking for all the world like an English country manor, the Schlosshotel Cecilienhof was built by Kaiser Wilhelm in 1916 and became the royal residence of the Crown Prince Hohenzollern. The mansion is surrounded by a large park graced with lakes, trees, green lawns, and forest. The manor house is especially important because it was here that Churchill, Truman, and Stalin met in 1945 to work out the details for the Potsdam Treaty that proposed the economic and political destiny for the defeated Germany. Although a fire destroyed some of the rooms of historical interest, you can still see where the various delegates lived and worked while they planned the treaty and there are many interesting photographs depicting the historical event. The park-like grounds surrounding Cecilienhof are also open to the public, but it is only a lucky few who stay on to spend the night in the lovely hotel rooms that occupy several of the wings. (*9 am–5 pm, closed 2nd and 4th Mondays.*)

Potsdam also offers a sensational attraction: the palaces and gardens of ***Sanssouci**. Frederick II chose Potsdam instead of Berlin as his permanent residence because he wanted a place where he could escape the pressures of being a ruler and pursue his interests in philosophy and the arts without care—*sans souci*. He had the Sanssouci palace built to his own design between 1745 and 1747, but this was just the beginning of an entire series of palaces set in vast, landscaped grounds. Be sure to wear sturdy shoes because it is almost a half-hour's walk between some of the buildings. Map in hand, explore the tantalizing paths (strategically highlighted with sculptures) which weave through forests and glens as they connect one palace to another. If you have the stamina, you can easily spend a full day exploring the gardens and palaces. Important stops are: ***Sanssouci Palace** with its elaborate rooms in the rococo style which you can tour with a German-speaking guide; the even larger **Neues Palais** (New Palace) where you don felt overshoes—do not miss the grotto made from shells and semi-precious stones; the **Orangerie**, an enormous building used to grow plants and house guests in sumptuous apartments; the **Grosse Bildergalerie** (Art Gallery), an ornate gallery displaying paintings by Caravaggio, Reni, Rubens, Van Dyck, and others; and the **Chinesisches Teehaus** (Chinese Tea House), a fanciful pavilion with gilded palms for columns and an ornate green-and-gold pagoda-style roof—Chinese porcelain is displayed inside. Other attractions include **Neptune's Grotto**, the **Obelisk Portal**, the **Trellis Pavilion**, the **Dragon House**, the **Sicilian Gardens**, **Charlottenhof Palace**, the **Temple of Friendship**—and on and on. There is a staggering amount to see and do. Obtain a map and guidebook (in English) from the information booth beside the car park and set off to explore. Even if you do not tour the interiors, just walking through the vast, park-like grounds makes this a very worthwhile visit. The Sanssouci Palace is a real highlight: tickets go on sale at 9 am and tours are often sold out by early afternoon, so buy your ticket as soon you arrive and visit the other sights before returning at your allotted time. (*Sanssouci: 9 am–5 pm mid-May to mid-October, to 4 pm in February, March, and late October; to 3 pm November to January, closed 1st and*

3rd Mondays. Neues Palais: same hours as palace but closed Fridays. Grosse Bildergalerie: 9 am–noon, 12:45–5 pm mid-May to mid-October.)

In sharp contrast to Potsdam, **Berlin** is dynamic and vigorous. Europe's largest city can be somewhat overwhelming in size for those who have been touring the countryside, but while the major sights are quite spread out, the public transportation system enables you to get around easily. If you are staying in Potsdam, you can take a train into the city or if you are staying in Berlin, we recommend the **Hotel Mondial** or the deluxe **Maritim Grand Hotel.** Your first stop in Berlin should be the tourist office at the Europa where you can obtain information on sightseeing tours that range from 90 minutes to half a day. The tours leave from the adjacent Kaiser Wilhelm Memorial Church.

Equipped with maps and a transportation pass, you can cover the main sights of Berlin in a day (just). Set amidst the traffic outside the **Bahnhof Zoo** (Zoo station) is the **BVG transportation kiosk** where you purchase your 24-hour transportation pass and pick up maps before boarding the number 100 bus in front of the Zoo station (*runs every 10 minutes*). Proceeding down the Kurfürstenstrasse (before the tunnel), you pass, on the right, the **Europa Center,** a modern building with a large Mercedes sign on top, **Gedächtniskirche** (Kaiser Wilhelm Memorial Church) whose burnt, blackened, bombed-out shell stands as a memorial to the dead of two world wars, and, on the left, the two majestic stone elephants that guard the entrance to the **Berlin Zoo.** Turning left into **Tiergarten,** a grassy park, the 67-meter-high **Siegressaül** comes into view (a huge column surmounted by a statue of Victory). Immediately on the left comes **Schloss Bellevue,** the German White House, official residence of the President of the Republic (if the flag's flying he's at home). The arch-shaped building on your left is the **Kongresshalle** (House of Culture) with sculpture by Henry Moore floating on its lake. Approaching the **Reichstag,** notice its bullet-riddled, patched-up façade. The German parliament met here for the first time in 1990, marking the end of almost four decades of political separation. (*10 am–5 pm, closed Mondays.*) Just round the corner you go under the 200-year-old ***Brandenburg Gate** whose majestic columns support the goddess of peace upon her horse-drawn chariot. During the years when Berlin was divided, the Brandenburg Gate became a symbol of oppression instead of the symbol of peace it was originally conceived to be. Driving up **Unter der Linden,** the famous avenue "under the lime trees," you pass the much-photographed statue of Frederick the Great high atop his horse. Behind the statue is **Humboldt University** which was attended by Marx and Lenin and next to it sits a Greek temple-like façade, a memorial for the Germans who died in the world wars. Cross the river onto "Museum Island" and alight to tour the Pergamon Museum, a highlight of any visit to Berlin. (If you do not want to visit the Pergamon at this time, stay on the bus for another five minutes to its terminus as it retraces its route to the Bahnhof Zoo.)

Walk along the river to the second neoclassical building which contains the ***Pergamon Museum,** named for its most prized possession, the enormous Pergamon Altar. This beautifully preserved altar dating from the 2nd century B.C. was brought from the west coast of Turkey and erected in an enormous hall. Pay the small extra cost for the half-hour tape-recorded tour that gives you a real perspective on this masterpiece of Hellenistic art. Almost as impressive is the adjacent Babylonian Processional Street where lions stride along the street's walls to the soaring blue-and-ochre tiles of the Ishtar Gate (604–562 B.C.). (*10 am–5 pm daily.*)

Leaving the Pergamon to the right, turn left before the railway lines on Georgestrasse for the short walk to the Friedrichstrasse U-bahn station where you take the U6 in the direction of Alt Mariendorf beyond Stadtmitte to Kochstrasse. A vast office complex now occupies the site of Checkpoint Charlie but the adjacent ***Haus Am Checkpoint Charlie** tells the fascinating history of the wall and the many ingenious escape attempts. Displays and video take you through 15 little rooms to conclude in the Checkpoint Charlie café. (*9 am–10 pm daily.*)

Back in the underground take the U6 towards Alt Mariendorf for one stop to Hallesches where you change to the U1 (in the direction of Ruhleben) across town to Sophie

Charlotte Platz. A ten-minute walk up Schlossstrasse brings you to Charlottenburg Palace. At number 70 Schlossstrasse (opposite the palace) visit *Ägyptisches Museum (Egyptian Museum), worth a visit if for no other reason than to gaze into the eyes of Nefertiti, an incredible bust over 3,000 years old yet depicting a woman as beautiful as any modern movie star. (*10 am–5 pm, closed Mondays.*)

Schloss Charlottenburg (Charlottenburg Palace) is one of those palaces that is more impressive outside than in. Rather than taking the guided tour (in German), go around the building and stroll along the inviting paths that lead you through elaborate, sculptured gardens to woodlands and lakes. If you want to take a peek inside, visit the Galerie der Romantik in the Knöbelsdorf wing, a gallery containing works by 19th-century Romantic painters. (*10 am–5 pm, closed Mondays.*) Leaving the palace, take the number 109 bus which runs from just beside the palace down Kaiser Frederich Strasse and along the Kurfürstendamm (the Ku'Damm), a boulevard lined with chic boutiques, outdoor cafés, and grand hotels, and returns you to the Bahnhof Zoo. It would be a shame to leave Berlin with experiencing Europe's biggest department store, Kaufhaus des Westens (KaDeWe) (U-bahn 1 Wittenburgplatz). With over 2,400 employees, KaDeWe offers a vast array of goods for sale from souvenirs to sweaters. Choose from 1,800 kinds of cheese in the food hall or just take the glass elevator to the self-service café with its impressive views. (*9:30 am–6:30 pm, Saturdays till 2 pm, Thursdays till 8 pm, closed Sundays.*)

From Berlin you can go northwest to Hamburg to follow *Schleswig Holstein—the land between the seas* or southwest to Quedlinburg to join *Highlights of the Harz Mountains*.

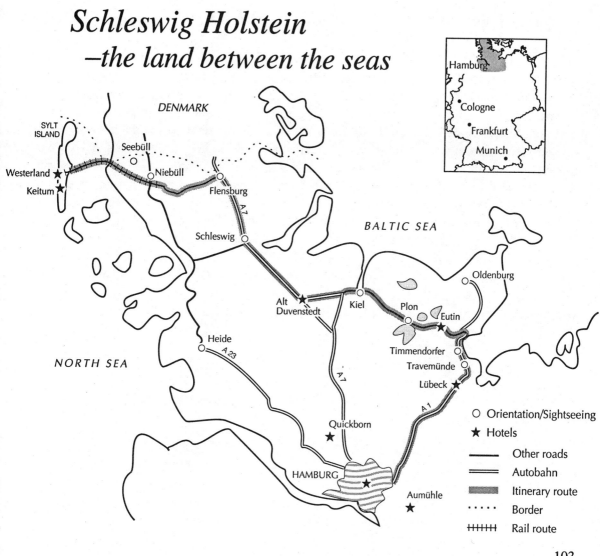

Schleswig Holstein
–the land between the seas

DENMARK

Hamburg

Cologne

Frankfurt

Munich

SYLT
ISLAND

Seebüll

Westerland

Niebüll

Keitum

Flensburg

A 7

BALTIC SEA

Schleswig

Oldenburg

Alt
Duvenstedt

Kiel

Plon

Eutin

Heide

A 23

Timmendorfer

NORTH SEA

A 7

Travemünde

Lübeck

A 1

Quickborn

○ Orientation/Sightseeing

★ Hotels

HAMBURG

—————— Other roads

══════ Autobahn

Aumühle

▓▓▓▓▓▓ Itinerary route

· · · · · Border

++++++ Rail route

103

Schleswig Holstein–the land between the seas

Schleswig Holstein is Germany's most northerly province. With Denmark at its tip, this broad finger of land divides the placid Baltic from the wild North Sea. Along the North Sea shore, dikes protect the sky-wide landscape from being claimed by the sea's crashing waves. Safe behind dikes, sheep and cattle graze while crops grow in serene pastures. Offshore, dune-fringed islands brave the sea. Any visit to Schleswig Holstein would not be complete without a trip to one of the islands, so this itinerary takes you and your car on top of a train for a rocking ride across the Hindenburgdamm to Sylt. This island boasts an impressive landscape of sand dunes and exposed, steep cliffs sheltering quaint little thatched villages from bracing sea breezes. In sharp contrast, the Baltic coast is hilly, with long, graceful fjords extending far inland from the gently lapping ocean. Here kilometer after kilometer of white sand beaches provide a holiday haven for northern Europeans who brave the chilly waters and relax in gaily colored, canopied beach chairs while their children decorate sand castles with sea shells. Between these two seas lies *Holsteinische Schweiz* (Swiss District), a confusing name as there are no mountain peaks, just a lovely area of wooded, rolling hills sprinkled with sparkling lakes.

Schleswig Holstein–the land between the seas

Recommended Pacing: Spend two nights in Hamburg to appreciate the flavor of this large city then an early-morning start will enable you to be on Sylt by nightfall. The expense of the train to Sylt discourages you from spending only one night here. Try to include a visit to the Nolde Museum in Seebüll on your way to or from the island.

Northern weather tends to be cool and rainy, so pack your warm sweaters and rain gear. But be prepared to be surprised—the weather is unpredictable, so with a bit of luck you will have balmy, cloudless days as you explore this lovely region far from the beaten tourist paths.

Hamburg is a mighty trading and industrial center on the banks of the River Elbe. Understandably, Hamburg was a target for World War II bombings—by the end of the war the town was little more than a heap of rubble. But with great determination, much of the city has been rebuilt in the old style so that today it has the mellow feel of an older age. Hamburg's sights are spread around a large area, so the most efficient way to get from place to place is on the U-bahn, or subway system, whose stations are marked on the city's tourist map. Hamburg has many excellent hotels listed in the *Hotels* section.

The *Aussenalster* is a beautiful body of water stretching from the city into the suburbs. Promenade the **Jungferstieg**—the most popular spot is the terrace of the **Alsterpavilion**—along its tributary, the **Binnenalster**. Take a ferry from the **Alterrundfahrt** around the Aussenalster. (*10 am–6 pm, every half hour, April to end of October.*)

In the city center include the following on your sightseeing agenda: **St. Mickaelis-Kirche** (Hamburg's symbol) which offers a great view of the port and city from atop its 449 stairs and the palatial **Rathaus** (city hall), built at the end of the 19th century, at the center of the popular shopping district. Its square, **Rathhausmarkt**, is the site of summer beer and wine festivals.

A boat trip around the port gives you an idea of the enormous size of the port complex. Boat trips leave from landing stage number 2, St. Pauli-Landungsbrücken. (*8 am–6 pm,*

April to September.) If you are in Hamburg on a Sunday morning, plan on visiting the **Altona Fischmarkt**, an open-air market at the water's edge offering everything—fruit, flowers, rabbits, socks, antiques, and, of course, fish. The show starts at six, but plan on arriving before nine. No need to eat before you arrive: there are plenty of food stands selling everything from delicious hot grilled sausages to crunchy rolls filled with smoked eel or pickled herring. Just a short walk for sailors from their ships, Hamburg's notorious red-light district has grown up along the **Reeperbahn** and surrounding streets, where erotic entertainment knows no bounds. This raunchy area, just west of the city center, is an anomaly in what is otherwise a very straight-laced city. (Reeperbahn 136 is where the Beatles started their career.)

After a few days of city adventures, you will be ready for a change—something quiet and relaxed, a complete change of pace from the bustling city. Drive into the downtown area and follow signs for the autobahn 1 to Lübeck. ***Lübeck** was the leading city of the Hanseatic League, a group of towns who banded together for trade advantages during the 13th to 16th centuries. About an hour's drive finds you beside the canal skirting the town's medieval fortifications. Follow the walls to the north and enter the town through the **Burgtor,** a gate built in 1444, into Grosse Burgstrasse whose tall, red-brick buildings have impressive façades. On the left the **Heiligen-Geist-Hospital**, three red-brick gables each separated by slim, pointed turrets, now serves as a home for the elderly. Turn right opposite the hospital and on Breite Strasse you find the seamen's tavern, now a restaurant, **Haus der Scheffergesellcraft** with its long wooden tables set beneath brass lanterns hanging from ancient beams. Farther down Breite Strasse you see the tall, slender, twin steeples of the **Marienkirche**, St. Mary's church, rise above the town. In the nearby Marktplatz you find tourist information and the **Rathaus**, Lübeck's impressive town hall, covering two sides of the square. Holenstrasse leads from the market square to the impressive **Holstentor Gate**, a squat fortress crowned by twin towers shaped like enormous witches' hats. The gate houses the town history museum

Holstentor Gate, Lübeck

which displays a model of the city in the 17th century, weapons, model ships, and instruments of torture. (*10 am–4 pm, closed Mondays.*)

Leaving the old town of Lübeck, drive to the north for 15 minutes to the popular Baltic resort of **Travemünde**. It is fun to drive along its riverfront road seeing the boats and ferries on one side and the crowded little seaside shops on the other and then to drive along its wide, sandy beach fringed by modern hotels.

As you leave Travemünde, follow road 76 which parallels the coastline going north. If the weather is sunny and warm, you may want to get into the German holiday spirit and join the crowds on the beaches at the coastal resorts of **Timmendorfer Strand** or **Scharbeutz-Haffkrug**. In pleasant weather sun worshipers soak up the sun from the shelter of their canopied beach chairs while offshore the Baltic waters come alive with the sails of gaily colored sailing boats and wind surfers.

Follow the 76 as it turns inland at Scharbeutz-Haffkrug. Leaving the flat coastal landscape behind you, enter a region of gently undulating farmland sprinkled with lakes both large and small. Narrow threads of land often separate one lake from another. The region is known as **Holsteinische Schweiz** (Swiss District) not because of its Alpine peaks, of which there are none, but because it shares a similar rock formation with Switzerland. About a half-hour's drive brings you to the lakeside town of **Eutin**. This is a colorful medieval town with a quaint central pedestrian square. Park by the old moated castle and meander down to the lakefront through a gorgeous forested park, following the promenade that leads you along the shores of the lake, the **Eutiner See**.

Farther on, lovely lake vistas are provided by the drive around the **Keller See** to Malente-Gremsmühlen. Take the road along the northern shore through **Sielbeck** for the prettiest views. **Malente-Gremsmühlen** is the departure point for motor-boat tours of the beautiful five lakes to the west of town. The frustration of catching only glimpses of the lakes through the trees is removed when you glide along them on a boat.

Just a short distance to the west is **Plon**, positioned atop a small hill overlooking the region's largest lake, the **Grosser Plonnersee**. Drive through the town to the quaint, cobbled marketplace near the church. Park your car and walk up the narrow, cobblestoned alley to the castle terrace where you have a lovely view of the lake below.

Leaving Plon, you follow road 76 for the half-hour's drive to the outskirts of **Kiel**. Unless you are interested in busy freight and yacht harbors, do not go into the city but take the road 404 to the 4 and on to the suburban town of **Molfsee**. Here you will find the **Freilichtmuseum**, Schleswig-Holstein's Open-Air Museum, a collection of rustic farms and country homes dating from the 16th through the 19th centuries that have been brought here and reassembled. It is great fun to watch the local craftsmen operating the old smithy, potter's shop, mill, and bakehouse. You can explore the old houses and barns and retire to the timbered inn for welcome refreshments. (*10 am–6 pm, 9 am–5 pm Sundays, closed between November and April and on Mondays except in July and August.*)

Make your way to the autobahn 7 going north (Schleswig and Flensburg) and exit at the ancient Viking stronghold of Schleswig. Soon after you leave the autobahn (before you reach the main town), watch for signs to the road going to the left to the baroque **Schloss Gottorf**. The **Archäologisches Landes-Museum** (archaeological museum) displays Viking artifacts such as dishes and fishing nets. Their prize exhibit is the 4th-century Viking ship, the **Nydam-Schiff**. Long and slender, the 36-oarsman boat was preserved in the marshes. (*9 am–5 pm daily March to October, 9:30 am–4 pm November to February, closed Mondays.*)

Schleswig's old town (Altstadt) hugs the northern bank of the Schlei inlet. Its Gothic brick **Dom** (cathedral) dates from the 12th century and is noted for its handsome carved altar (1521) in the chancel. Admire the 14th-century cloisters with the floral motif on their vaults. Also in Schleswig (around Friedhofplatz) is the picturesque fishermen's quarter called **Holm**. Don't miss this tiny, but ever-so-special hamlet—it is truly picture-perfect. Explore its quaint lanes, follow the circular road that wraps around the park and toy-like church, and stroll down to see the fishing boats at the water's edge.

Continue north on the 7 taking to the exit for Niebüll. Do not go into the town, but follow the well posted signs of a car atop a railway car for the train to Sylt. On your way to or from the island make a little side trip from the car station to the north to visit the **Nolde Museum**, the home of Emiler Nolde the painter, in **Seebüll**. His house is a 12-kilometer drive north via Neukirchen. Over 200 paintings, watercolors, and drawings are displayed and his studio shows his religious paintings. The Nazis condemned him as a painter (ironically he was a die-hard racist and a member of the Nazi party) and it's touching to see the vast collection of miniature watercolors (*Ungemalte Bilder*) that he

Train to Sylt

painted between 1941 and 1945 when the Nazis forbade him to paint. (*10 am–5 pm April to October, 10 am–noon and 2–4 pm November to March, Monday to Friday.*)

You cannot drive your car to the island of ***Sylt**, but take it on top of a railway carriage along the causeway that connects the island to the mainland. There is no need to make advance reservations—purchase your round-trip ticket as you drive into the railway yard. Do not worry about catching a particular train for there are between 11 and 16 departures each day. The car-train trip seems excessively expensive for such a short journey, so plan to stay awhile on the island.

Leaving the ticket office, you drive your car onto the train and sit in it for the 50-minute bumping ride past fields of sheep and Holstein cows towards the shoals that lead to the Hindenburg Levee which connects the island to the mainland. From your lofty perch atop the train you can appreciate the centuries-long battle to keep the sea from flooding this flat, low-lying land. A series of dikes protects the land from the water and the farms are built on earthen banks which become islands if the dikes fail. Crossing the sea dike, the train arrives in the island capital, **Westerland**, a town of elegant boutiques, sophisticated nightspots, and a casino.

The island is lovely, a long narrow strip, much of it sand dunes facing the North Sea. Dikes, sand dunes, and cliffs protect the island from North Sea storms. Forty kilometers of white sand attract summer sun-worshipers—bathing suits are as welcome as none—and canopied beach chairs provide snug shelter from the wind. Hardy Germans enjoy swimming in the chill North Sea waves, but you will probably find the wave pool in Westerland (or your hotel pool) more to your liking.

There are many small hotels on Sylt but, if you want to splurge, choose the island's loveliest, the **Benen Diken Hof** in Keitum. If you like lots of action, the beautifully decorated **Hotel Stadt Hamburg** in Westerland is another recommendation.

*****Keitum** is the island's prettiest village, an old Friesian settlement of squat, thatched cottages, lilac bushes, and tree-lined streets. Keitum's low-slung houses are topped by thick roofs of reeds gathered from the tidal marshes, just the kind of house from which you would expect Hansel and Gretel to emerge. High garden walls protect against storm flood tides and winds. On Museumweg you can visit the **Old Friesian House**. Built in 1739 by a sailing captain, the red-brick old Friesian farmhouse passed into the hands of a 19th-century historian who assembled a history of the island. The house and the furnishings are such that a Friesian of two centuries ago would feel immediately at home. Next door the **Sylter Heimatmuseum** (folklore museum) contains collections of island seafaring memorabilia and coins, porcelain, and costumes dating back hundreds of years.

Inspired perhaps by their forefathers, modern artisans have set up their shops in nearby houses. (*10 am–noon and 2–5 pm April to October, closed Tuesdays.*)

As you explore farther afield, you pass Keitum's **St. Severin church**, a landmark for seafarers since it was built seven centuries ago. The island's days as an important maritime center are long past, yet once a year, on the eve of February 22, the islanders pile straw, reeds, and wood into a huge bonfire as a symbolic send-off for the island's sailors.

Devote a day to exploring the island and its villages huddled behind the sand dunes, then use the remainder of your stay for relaxation—hike to the **Rotes Kliff** and see the water turning red as it erodes the cliff. Behind the cliffs climb the 53-meter **Uwe Dune**, a vantage point for seeing the North Sea to the west and the mud flats to the east. Bird watchers head for **Vogelkoje** bird sanctuary.

When your island holiday is over, if your destination is Denmark, you can take a ferry to Havenby or retrace your steps to **Niebüll** for the short drive to the Danish border. For those who are returning to Hamburg, follow the road south across the flat polder lands that have been reclaimed from the sea. The waters offshore are shallow: sea dikes keep them at bay, protecting the lush green pasture and farmlands behind.

Hotels

If you are looking for an isolated hideaway far from the oft-trod tourist paths, the Hotel Töpferhaus fits the bill. Hugging the shores of the tranquil Bistensee and surrounded by manicured gardens, the Hotel Töpferhaus commands a serene setting. On our first visit, the Töpferhaus was a small hotel with guestrooms in a simple, whitewashed farmhouse. This original part of the inn remains but a new section has been built, adding 21 deluxe guestrooms and a restaurant with a view of the Bistensee gently lapping at the lawn in front of the hotel. As a result of the expansion, the hotel has gained a sophisticated elegance, but happily there is no jarring, commercial feeling to spoil the mood. The setting remains superbly pastoral, the warmth of welcome sincere, and the furnishings throughout extremely tasteful. All the guestrooms are appealing, but I especially love numbers 30 to 32—on the ground floor with French doors opening out to the garden. The Töpferhaus is not the kind of hotel for an overnight stop, but rather an enchanting place to stay for at least several days to enjoy the unspoiled solitude of the countryside. The Töpferhaus is quite difficult to find: Take the autobahn 7 north from Hamburg and get off at the Rendsburg exit. Turn east on 203 (towards Eckernforde) and after about 2 kilometers you see a sign for the Hotel Töpferhaus: turn left and the narrow road brings you to the hotel. Do **not** go to Alt Duvenstedt—it is on the other side of the autobahn.

HOTEL TÖPFERHAUS
Owner: Ulrich Harms
24791 Alt Duvenstedt am Bistensee, Germany
Tel: (04338) 402 Fax: (04338) 551
46 rooms
Double: DM 190–320 Suite: DM 250–350
Open all year
Credit cards: all major
Restaurant open daily
100 km N of Hamburg, 35 km W of Kiel

Der Schafhof, one of Germany's loveliest hotels, sits on a hillside dotted with grazing sheep near the town of Amorbach. Built in 1721, the main building originally belonged to the estate of the Amorbach Benedictine Abbey and is now owned by the Winkler family who in years gone by were titled millers hereabouts. Der Schafhof is still an operating farm with all the farming paraphernalia of barns, tractors, ducks, and geese next to the hotel. Just inside the front door is a snug lounge warmed on cool evenings by a blazing log fire. Here you find a gourmet restaurant serving sumptuous cuisine and fine wines, while more casual dining is offered in the Benedictine Room in the adjacent barn which dates back to 1524. While there are some lovely bedrooms in the main house, those in the barn are especially delightful. In fact, the decor is consistently beautiful in all of the bedrooms, whether you choose the spaciousness of a suite or the coziness of a beamed bedroom tucked under the eaves. For relaxation enjoy walks across farmland, a game of tennis, the sauna, solarium, or simply soaking up the countryside view from the terrace. From Amorbach take the 47 towards Michelstadt for about a kilometer and you find signposts directing you for the 3-kilometer drive to Der Schafhof.

DER SCHAFHOF
Owners: Charlotte & Lothar Winkler
Otterbachtal
63916 Amorbach, Germany
Tel: (09373) 97330 Fax: (09373) 4120
18 rooms, 5 suites
Double: DM 180–250 Suite: DM 350–490
Open all year
Credit cards: all major
Restaurant open daily
80 km SE of Frankfurt, 67 km NE of Heidelberg
Relais & Chateaux

The Residenz Heinz Winkler, conveniently located in the quaint village of Aschau just a five-minute drive south of the expressway that links Munich and Salzburg, is a real charmer. The hotel is easy to find: as you drive into Aschau you will see a small hill rising from the town. Perched on this hill is a picturesque church with twin onion domes, and right next to the church is the Residenz Heinz Winkler. This stately home, at one time an annex of Hohenaschau Castle whose history dates back to the early 15th century, is now a sumptuous Relais and Chateaux hotel. From the moment you enter, the mood of sophisticated elegance is set: light streams through large plate-glass windows into a spacious lobby with a marble floor enhanced by a handsome Oriental carpet. The hotel has several dining rooms, each with its own personality, from elaborately formal to cozy-Bavarian. On warm summer days, you have the option to dine outside on a protected terrace that affords a sweeping view of the mountains. If you appreciate truly fine cuisine, you will be pleased to note the hotel has the remarkable accomplishment of being awarded three Michelin stars! The mood of subdued grandeur continues in the bedrooms that are all elegantly appointed with fine furniture and lovely fabrics.

RESIDENZ HEINZ WINKLER
Owner: Heinz Winkler
Kirchplatz 1
83229 Aschau, Germany
Tel: (08052) 17990 Fax: (08052) 179966
32 rooms
Double: DM 220–350 Suite: DM 450–580
Open all year
Credit cards: all major
Restaurant open daily
82 km SE of Munich, 64 km W of Salzburg
Relais & Chateaux

The tiny wine village of Assmannshausen sits at a slight widening of the narrow Rhine river gorge and, limited by its location and unspoilt by modern development, remains a cramped cluster of old houses overlooking the river. Fronting the Rhine, the Hotel Krone has been providing hospitality to weary travelers since 1541. The hotel's wisteria-covered terrace and raised restaurant provide lovely places for dining while watching the busy river life glide by. Much of the building dates from the turn of the century and has an interior perfectly in keeping with the exterior, with large, rather heavy pieces of lovingly polished furniture set against dark paneled walls. Some of the bedrooms are in the main building while others are located in the adjacent annex—all have been beautifully refurbished and are absolutely decorator-perfect, each accompanied by a luxurious marble bathroom. All the rooms are attractive but the spacious junior suites are especially appealing. The rooms in the front are choice since these offer the added advantage of a view of the Rhine: I particularly liked rooms 83 and 90 (double rooms), each with a seating area tucked into the tower. River steamers dock just a two-minute walk away: if you arrive by boat, the hotel will send someone to meet you and tend to your luggage. Assmannshausen is on the Rhine, 5 kilometers northwest of Rüdesheim.

HOTEL KRONE
Owners: Family Hufnagel-Ullrich
65385 Rüdesheim-Assmannshausen, Germany
Tel: (06722) 4030 Fax: (06722) 3049
55 rooms
Double: DM 294–339 Suite: DM 434–820
Open all year
Credit cards: all major
Restaurant closed January 10 to February 20
70 km W of Frankfurt, 31 km W of Mainz

Come dream a romantic dream or two in this imposing hillside fortress. Surrounded by dense forest, the Burg Schnellenberg has been in existence since 1225 and over the years has been altered, added to, and finally restored into an elegant castle hotel. The halls display enormous old oil paintings. The bedrooms vary in their size and aspect: you may find yourself in a cozy paneled room with a window seat overlooking the trout ponds or high atop a winding turret staircase in a room with 20-foot-high ceilings and a lofty view over the surrounding countryside. The furniture is large and old—not as old as the castle but very old nonetheless. The main dining room is splendid: several rooms with lofty ceilings, an enormous old tapestry decorating the main wall, and groupings of elegant tables and chairs. A further dining room is decorated in a hunting-lodge motif and beneath it lies a cozy wine-cellar bar. Other cellars comprise a museum where rows of cases are filled with weapons and suits of armor. Tucked away in the upper castle is a 17th-century family chapel whose vaulted ceiling is covered with decorative biblical frescoes.

BURGHOTEL SCHNELLENBERG
Owners: Family Bilsing
57439 Attendorn, Germany
Tel: (02722) 6940 Fax: (02722) 694169
42 rooms, 7 suites
Double: DM 275 Suite: DM 285–330
Closed Christmas to mid-January
Credit cards: all major
Restaurant open daily
3.5 km E of Attendorn, near the Biggesee
Gast im Schloss

If your heart always longs to be in the countryside, stay at the Fürst Bismarck Mühle on your next visit to Hamburg. It is just a five-minute walk to the station where you can hop on a train for the half-hour ride to the heart of the Hamburg. The Fürst Bismarck Mühle, a charming cottage-like white mill with a gabled roof, is set in a forest overlooking a peaceful pond. On the side of the inn, a stream rushes by—a reminder that this was formerly a mill for grinding corn. The entrance is accented by cheerful, bright-red double doors. Excellent meals are served in the beamed-ceilinged dining room which has an heirloom armoire, carved chests, portraits, and oil paintings (all authentic antiques from the Bismarck family). Tall windows on three sides capture the sunlight and views of the pond and forests. A flight of stairs leads up to the seven comfortable, home-like guestrooms. All are furnished with antiques and have traditional, color-coordinated fabrics used for the draperies, upholstery, and bed coverings. I loved room 5, overlooking the pond, but all are very appealing. In 1871 King Wilhelm I gave the Sachsenwald Forest (which included the old corn mill) to Chancellor Otto von Bismarck and the property still belongs to the family. Although the inn is filled with memorabilia from the Bismarck family, the old mill has been leased and superbly managed by Jochen Dölger and Monika Diehl for nearly 20 years.

FÜRST BISMARCK MÜHLE
Owners: Monika Diehl & Jochen Dölger
Mühlenweg 3
21521 Aumühle, Germany
Tel: (04104) 2028 Fax: (04104) 1200
7 rooms
Double: DM 190
Open all year
Credit cards: MC, VS
Restaurant closed Wednesdays
25 km E of Hamburg

The Brauerei-Gasthof-Hotel Aying is a famous brewery, restaurant, and hotel, all rolled into one typically Bavarian package. The hotel's wisteria-covered façade is easily spotted thanks to a giant, blue-striped flagpole marking the entrance. The front doors and entry area are painted a bright blue, complemented by many decorative flower designs and German proverbs inscribed on the ceiling beams. Fresh bouquets and large dried flower arrangements abound in all the public areas, and traditional hearts-and-flowers painting adorns almost every nook and cranny—on armoires, beams, staircases, and old chests. The restaurant offers candlelit dinners in front of a large open fireplace. The romantic scene is completed with Dutch-blue tablecloths set with pretty china and glassware. Traditional Bavarian specialties of ham and pork (and, of course, all varieties of the famous Ayinger beer) are offered with pride. The guestrooms are all extremely inviting. Some are decorated with Bavarian-style painted furniture while others have a more traditional, elegant look. One of my favorites is room 1, with pretty fabrics in tones of peaches and greens. As a special little touch, beer is left as a gift in each room. Aying is an attractive Bavarian brewery town, with the advantage of being in the country, yet very convenient to Munich.

BRAUEREI-GASTHOF-HOTEL AYING
Owners: Family Franz Inselkammer
Zornedinger Strasse 2
85653 Aying bei Munchen, Germany
Tel: (08095) 705 Fax: (08095) 2053
28 rooms
Double: DM 220–300
Closed last 2 weeks in January
Credit cards: all major
Restaurant & beer garden open daily
25 km SE of Munich

The Romantik Kurhotel was built by Herzog Friedrich Franz von Mecklenburg in 1793 as a holiday retreat where he would come to the Baltic Sea for his health. Thus started the concept in Germany of a spa holiday, a trend that continues to be extremely popular today. During the Communist regime, the Kurhotel was confiscated but, with the reunification, the Metz family returned to Bad Doberan to reclaim their family home. They found it a disaster: dark, dingy, and very depressing. Happily, Dr. Metz's wife (who oversaw the renovation) has impeccable taste. After studying both Scandinavian and English decorating journals, she came up with her own style, combining the fresh, clean, uncluttered look of Scandinavian design with lovely, traditional English fabrics. The mood of understated elegance is set as you enter the reception hall where classical music is playing. Soft-white predominates throughout, with bouquets of freshly cut flowers and pretty slip-covered chairs in handsome English stripes adding just the right dash of color. There are two main dining rooms: each is traditional in feel, with Biedermeier-style chairs, handsome draperies, pastel colors, and fresh flowers. The guest bedrooms continue the country-manor look with English fabrics in color schemes of soft yellows or pretty greens. Note: The hotel is located in the center of town facing the small park.

ROMANTIK KURHOTEL
Owner: Dr. Horst Metz
Am Kamp
18209 Bad Doberan, Germany
Tel: (038203) 3036 Fax: (038203) 2126
60 rooms
Double: DM 175–195 Suite: DM 245
Open all year
Credit cards: all major
Restaurant open daily
17 km W of Rostock, 210 km NW of Berlin

Bad Hersfeld is a handsome North German town with, at its heart, a large market square lined with old burghers' houses, part of which has been turned into a pedestrian mall. It is in this pedestrian zone, with its tables and chairs spilling over onto the square, that you find the Romantik Hotel Zum Stern. Bustling and welcoming, the inn has been offering hospitality to weary travelers for over 500 years. In recent years, as the volume of trade has grown, the hotel has expanded back from the square so that accommodations are provided both in the old section and a modern extension. Try to secure one of the darling rooms in the original hostelry. With their blackened beams, creaking floorboards, and antique furniture, they are a real prize. I especially liked room 101 with its view of the market square. A new wing of rooms has been opened in a little house across the courtyard and these are furnished with most attractive country-pine reproduction furniture. A small indoor swimming pool is found at the rear of the building overlooking a little garden. Regional specialties highlight the menu in the country-style dining room. Walter and Waltraud are the fourth generation of the Kniese family to operate this hotel.

ROMANTIK HOTEL ZUM STERN
Owners: Waltraud & Walter Kniese
Linggplatz 11
36251 Bad Hersfeld, Germany
Tel: (06621) 1890 Fax: (06621) 189260
45 rooms
Double: DM 190–240
Open all year
Credit cards: all major
Restaurant open daily
170 km NE of Frankfurt, 26 km W of Erfurt

The simple Hotel Am Markt sits on the corner of a quiet cobbled square where Baden-Baden's old town meets the famous Friedrichsbad (Roman-Irish Bath) and is an excellent, less expensive choice for a place to stay in this lively town. Andrea and her sister Doris take great pride in their little hotel. There is a lot of old-world charm in the dining room with its Windsor chairs arranged round little tables beneath the paneled ceiling and the day's newspapers hung on reading poles for guests to browse. The restaurant is for residents only and closed for dinner on Sundays and Wednesdays. Beyond the traditional dining room Andrea and Doris have chosen to decorate their hotel in a pleasing, uncluttered, modern style. Rooms on the first two floors are larger high-ceilinged rooms whose floor-to-ceiling draperies stretch beyond the windows to cover the wall. Bedrooms under the eaves are smaller with lower ceilings. Because less than half of the rooms have en-suite showers or bathrooms it is important that you request one when making a reservation. Follow the blue hotel signposts in Baden-Baden to the Hotel Am Markt located directly behind the Friedrichsbad. The hotel has parking on the square and in a nearby garage.

HOTEL AM MARKT **NEW**
Owners: Family Bogner
Marktplatz 17/18
76530 Baden-Baden, Germany
Tel: (07221) 22747 Fax: (07221) 391887
27 rooms (12 with en-suite bathroom)
Double with bath: DM 141
Open all year
Credit cards: all major
Restaurant closed Sundays & Wednesdays
110 N of Freiburg, 35 km S of Karlsruhe

Romantik Hotel "Der Kleine Prinz" (The Little Prince) is a most appealing luxury hotel, conveniently located close to shopping, parks, and spa facilities in the popular resort town of Baden-Baden. The owners, Edeltraud and Norbert Rademacher, are often at reception to greet guests personally. Norbert worked in hotels in the United States for many years, so he is very attuned to American tastes. Edeltraud is responsible for the decor of the lovely rooms. She loves English and French antiques and has taken great care in choosing fabrics, carpet, and bathroom decor to complement the lovely furniture, so you find the Louis XVI room very different from the English Victorian room. (A few bedrooms that do not have antiques have Portuguese pine furniture.) A great many of the bedrooms are suites with separate sitting areas—all have every luxurious appointment and a great many have whirlpool tubs. The dining room (where breakfast and exquisite dinners are served) has murals from St. Exupéry's heartwarming fable *The Little Prince*. As a whimsical touch, a large mural of this irresistible red-haired hero is painted on the exterior wall of the hotel and a small memento appears in every guestroom. The hotel has parking in a nearby garage.

ROMANTIK HOTEL "DER KLEINE PRINZ"
Owners: Edeltraud & Norbert Rademacher
Lichtentaler Strasse 36
76530 Baden-Baden, Germany
Tel: (07221) 3464 Fax: (07221) 38264
22 rooms, 11 suites
Double: DM 350–395 Suite: DM 450–795
Open all year
Credit cards: all major
Restaurant open daily
110 N of Freiburg, 35 km S of Karlsruhe

You cannot help being captivated by the wisteria-laden, yellow-painted façade of the Badhotel Zum Hirsch located at the heart of the historic old town of Baden-Baden in a pedestrian zone of smart shops. The Hirsch has been a hotel for almost 300 years and was a family concern until 1982 when it was bought by Steigenberger Hotels. Steigenberger have renovated and modernized the hotel, taking great care to preserve its traditional atmosphere. Upstairs you find the formal restaurant that opens up to a broad terrace whose tables and chairs are an ideal spot for people-watching. While 206 and 306 are the largest rooms, 219 and 319 are the nicest. All the bedrooms have lovely old furniture and sparkling modern bathrooms where you can choose mains or spa water for your bath. The first proprietor of the Hirsch obtained permission for the thermal spring to be connected to the bathing cabinets of his hotel and the tradition has been continued—the curative waters flow directly from the thermal spring to the hotel's bathrooms. The hotel also has a health spa where you can receive various curative treatments and massages—foot massage is a specialty. The hotel is 5 kilometers from the railway station. Motorist can drive through the pedestrian streets to unload their luggage and are then given a pass to a nearby car park. Parking places are limited so it is best to make a parking reservation when requesting your room.

BADHOTEL ZUM HIRSCH **NEW**
Manager: Gerhard Eckarth
Hirschstrasse 1
76530 Baden-Baden, Germany
Tel: (07221) 9390 Fax: (07221) 38148
58 rooms
Double: DM 248–288
Open all year
Credit cards: all major
Restaurant open daily
110 N of Freiburg, 35 km S of Karlsruhe

Badenweiler is an old spa town where the architecture is predominantly heavy Victorian and the clientele come for the curative powers of the water. Such is the town's desire to promote a quiet, restful atmosphere that the main streets are closed to cars between 1:30 and 2:30 pm. Set in a quaint older section of town, the Sonne is the oldest gasthaus in Badenweiler and is ably run by the Esposito family. Vittorio hails from Italy and, although he speaks no English, his warm Italian welcome crosses all language barriers, more than making up for his lack of English. Son Michael is happy to help with translating. The focus of the antique-filled living room is an old blue-and-white-tile stove with an inviting bench on which you can snuggle up and enjoy its warmth. Many guests stay for a week or longer so there is a large dining room for pension guests and two cozy restaurants for shorter-stay guests. Bedrooms come in all shapes and sizes and are found in the main building, a modern annex in the garden, and an old house across the street. If you are traveling with family, there are several apartments available with bedrooms and separate living rooms. The southern reaches of the Black Forest are around you—spectacular walks and drives abound. Note: Turn up Luisenstrasse, opposite the Cassiopeia Therme (a large, modern complex by the park), and you arrive in the hotel's cobbled courtyard.

ROMANTIK HOTEL ZUR SONNE
Owners: Renate, Vittorio & Michael Esposito
Moltkestrasse 4
79405 Badenweiler, Germany
Tel: (07632) 75080 Fax: (07632) 750865
37 rooms, 6 suites
Double: DM 140–200 Suite: DM 200
Closed mid-November to mid-February
Credit cards: all major
Restaurant closed Wednesdays
35 km S of Freiburg, 40 km N of Basel

Bamberg is an absolute delight, a medieval city exuding the appeal of yesteryear. It is almost too picturesque to be real with the Rathaus (city hall) perched on a tiny island in the middle of the river that flows through the center of town. In fact, to cross the river one follows a tunnel through the arcaded Rathaus, which also forms one of the walled entrances to the city. Just a few minutes' walk from the Rathaus, marvelously positioned fronting the Regnitz river, is the Hotel Brudermühle. It is an attractive, three-story, light-yellow building with green shutters and dormer windows peeking out from under the steeply pitched red roof. Originally a mill dating from the early 14th century, the structure now houses a small, modern hotel. The owners, Erna and Georg Vogler, have increased the hotel's charm with a few well chosen antiques. Just off the lobby is an attractive restaurant where good home cooking of regional specialties is served. The guestrooms are small and the decor is simple, but you'll be quite happy if you're lucky enough to snare one the choice rooms: number 5 (overlooking the river) or number 1 (a sunny corner room with a view of both the river and the famous Rathaus).

HOTEL BRUDERMÜHLE
Owners: Erna & Georg Vogler
Schranne 1
96049 Bamberg, Germany
Tel: (0951) 955220 Fax: (0951) 9552255
16 rooms
Double: DM 170
Open all year
Credit cards: MC, VS
Restaurant closed Mondays
61 km NW of Nürnberg, 230 N of Munich

Bamberg is a beautiful town and a destination which deserves more attention than given in travel literature. From a distance, the six spires of its church pierce the skyline. At its center, Bamberg is a complex of quaint cobbled, pedestrian streets, outdoor cafés, bridges, and enchanting houses gracing and lining the waterfront. Not more than a few blocks from the old section of town is a simple hotel with a wonderful restaurant—the Romantik Hotel Weinhaus Messerschmitt. The charming, well-known, Franconian-style restaurant (in the Pschorn family since 1832) always includes local specialties on the menu. The hotel has only 15 rooms for overnight guests. The bedrooms are found up a marvelous wooden, handcarved stairway and are identified from other offices and private rooms by numbered wine bottles which hang over each door. The bedrooms are simple but sweet in decor. Down comforters deck the beds and the bathroom facilities are modern but enhanced by lovely old fixtures. At night it is difficult to shut out the street noise but a welcome cognac left by the considerate management might be all you need to sleep.

ROMANTIK WEINHAUS MESSERSCHMITT
Owners: Lydia & Otto Pschorn
Langestrasse 41
96047 Bamberg, Germany
Tel: (0951) 27866 Fax: (0951) 26141
13 rooms, 2 suites
Double: DM 189 Suite: DM 225
Open all year
Credit cards: all major
Restaurant open daily
61 km NW of Nürnberg, 230 N of Munich

The Jagdschloss Thiergarten is a small, ever-so-pretty hunting lodge (well-known for its excellent cuisine) with eight rooms to accommodate overnight guests. The spacious bedrooms are individually furnished, not with a sleek elegance, but more like guestrooms in a country home. There are several intimate, pastel-toned dining rooms, just brimming with charm. The Kamin (translates as "fireplace") has just a few elegantly set tables warmed by a dramatic fireplace. The Venezianischer Salon highlights a dramatic, very intricate, two-tiered, hand-made, 300-year-old Venetian glass chandelier. The Barocksaal, used for brunch on Sundays and also banquets or weddings, is found in the imposing rotunda, open to a meticulously restored, detailed ceiling. Formerly, when the hotel was primarily a hunting lodge, guests actually shot from the vantage point of a balcony that wrapped around the rotunda. In warm weather tables are set out on a stretch of grass behind the castle, under the shade of cherry and apple trees. Open as a hotel for more than 40 years, the Schloss Hotel Thiergarten provides a delightful retreat from the neighboring city of Bayreuth. To reach the hotel, drive south from Bayreuth on expressway 9 and take the Bayreuth-Sud exit, following signs to Thiergarten.

SCHLOSS HOTEL THIERGARTEN
Owners: Renate & Harald Kaiser
Obertheirgärtner Strasse 36
95406 Thiergarten-Bayreuth, Germany
Tel: (09209) 9840 Fax: (09209) 98429
8 rooms
Double: DM 220–260
Open all year
Credit cards: all major
Restaurant closed Mondays
75 km NE of Nürnberg, 6 km S of Bayreuth
Gast im Schloss

The Hotel Haus Lipmann has been in the same family since 1795 and Marion Thölen Lipmann, your gracious hostess, is always on hand to see that her guests are well looked after. This quaint little hotel is especially appealing because it is located at the heart of one of the prettiest villages along the Mosel—with its picturesque medieval buildings, church, and ruined castle, Beilstein is a gem. The dining rooms are just as attractive as the exterior: you may find yourself in a small farmhouse-style room before an old fireplace, in the warm, paneled main dining room, or feasting in the knights' hall surrounded by collections of old weapons. When weather permits, you can move out-of-doors to the wisteria-covered terrace and watch the life on the gentle Mosel river glide by as you sip a glass of excellent Mosel wine produced from the Lipmanns' own grapes. Upstairs are five nicely decorated guestrooms. Ask for one of the bedrooms in the front of the house with an antique bed and a splendid river view. Brother Joachim offers tasting in his cellar across the square as well as running the town's little wine museum. Beilstein's wine festival takes place during the first weekend in September. The Haus Lipmann makes an excellent base for exploring the Mosel.

HOTEL HAUS LIPMANN
Owner: Marion Thölen Lipmann
Marktplatz 3
56814 Beilstein, Germany
Tel: (02673) 1573
5 rooms
Double: DM 120–150
Open mid-March to mid-November
Credit cards: none accepted
Restaurant open daily
111 km NW of Mainz, 11 km SE of Cochem

Stefan and Claudia are the fifth generation of the Geiger family to operate this lovely hotel that dates back to 1865. It is very much a family hotel with guests returning year after year. (As a child Claudia came here every year with her family then when she was grown she made a return visit and fell in love with Stefan.) Set in meadows on the southern slopes of the Kälberstein mountain, this weathered chalet is attractively decked with green shutters, wooden balconies, and overflowing flowerboxes, while its interior displays traditional Bavarian decor. The heart of the hotel is its lovely, old, paneled dining room with its handsome ceilings, planked floors scattered with Oriental carpets, and heart-carved chairs with red-print cushions set around beautifully laid tables. A comfortable, old-fashioned sitting room adjoins this room. Bedrooms are in three buildings—all have Tyrolean charm (except one which has Biedermeier furniture) and views of the mountains. I particularly enjoyed those in the Garden wing with their room-wide views. Relax in the indoor or outdoor swimming pools or simply just sit and soak up the scenery. From Munich follow signposts to Bad Reichenall and from there take the road to Stanggass which brings you to the hotel on the outskirts of Berchtesgaden.

HOTEL GEIGER
Owners: Claudia & Stefan Geiger
Stanggass
83462 Berchtesgaden, Germany
Tel: (08652) 965555 Fax: (08652) 965400
46 rooms, 6 suites
Double: DM 160–300 Suite: DM 300–500
Closed mid-November to mid-December
Credit cards: VS
Restaurant open daily
150 km SE of Munich, 25 km S of Salzburg
Relais & Chateaux

The delightful Hotel Watzmann is centrally located in Berchtesgaden across from the Franziskaner Kirche on the main road through town. It was originally built as a brewery in the 1600s and is now a family-run hotel filled with antiques, memorabilia, and charm. The yellow façade with its green shutters and bright-red geraniums is set back from the road behind a large terrace filled with tables, umbrellas, and, on a warm day, many patrons. The public areas and two dining rooms contain plenty of old prints, painted antique furniture, and hunting trophies, as well as beamed ceilings and old ceramic stoves. Menu selections are traditionally Bavarian, featuring delicious pork and game dishes. The hotel has 38 bedrooms, only 17 of which have private baths, and none of which are equipped with phones or televisions. Bedrooms are comfortable, clean, and well appointed with reproduction Bavarian-style furniture and large family suites are also available. The upstairs hallways are decorated with door panels painted in Bavarian floral designs and a collection of colorful old archery targets. Antique chests, armoires, and paintings are also displayed in abundance. This is a very warm Bavarian inn, owned and managed with personal care by the English-speaking Piscantor family.

HOTEL WATZMANN
Owner: Family Hinrich Piscantor
Franziskanerplatz 2
83471 Berchtesgaden, Germany
Tel: (08652) 2055 Fax: (08652) 5174
38 rooms
Double: DM 148 with shower & toilet
Closed November to December 23
Credit cards: all major
Restaurant open daily
150 km SE of Munich, 25 km S of Salzburg

Many hotels with super-expensive rates claim to be deluxe, but few deliver. Not so with the Maritim Grand Hotel: this truly outstanding hotel gives you everything you could possibly expect in an elegant hotel—and more. Although large, the Maritim Grand Hotel has the warmth and friendliness usually encountered only in small, family-run establishments. From the front desk receptionist to the maid who brings fresh towels, everyone exudes a caring yet professional manner. You enter into one of the grandest lobbies imaginable with a broad staircase sweeping majestically up to the second level which forms a galleried balcony. As you gaze far above to the domed skylight, the floors rise ever higher like a tiered wedding cake, each level with a balcony overlooking the lobby below. The architectural effect is reminiscent of the "Hyatt" style, but the mood is sophisticated and traditional instead of contemporary. Although large, the lobby is cleverly designed with intimate nooks and crannies which encourage friends to gather and talk quietly. The beautifully decorated guestrooms offer more amenities than I have ever seen in a deluxe hotel: large bath towels, towel warmers, toothbrushes, combs, hair dryers, fancy soaps and shampoos, and even such a thoughtful extra as an umbrella to use on rainy days.

MARITIM GRAND HOTEL
Manager: Thomas Wachs
Friedrichstrasse 158–164
10117 Berlin, Germany
Tel: (030) 23270 Fax: (030) 23273362
358 rooms, 35 suites
Double: from DM 480 Suite: from DM 700
Open all year
Credit cards: all major
Restaurant open daily
3 blocks E of the Brandenburg Gate

Because so many buildings in Berlin were demolished in World War II, most of the hotels are of comparatively new construction. Such is the case with the Hotel Mondial but, happily, it is very inviting and, instead of being starkly modern, has an appealing warmth. The location is ideal, on the nicest stretch of Berlin's fascinating shopping street, the Kurfürstendamm. The hotel sits far enough back from the street to allow space for a sidewalk café where tables are set under shady trees, a favorite place for guests to sip a glass of wine or glass of beer while watching the world of Berlin pass by. The exterior is mostly glass, but it is not gaudy. Bronzed green trim, marble, and dark glass create a sedate, somewhat traditional feel. The attractive reception area and intimate bar are modern, but not cold, with a predominantly rose color scheme. To the left of the lobby, excellent meals are served in the Krautergarten restaurant, decorated in shades of green. There is a parking garage, not free, but still a blessing as it is a convenient, safe place to park your car. All the double rooms have private baths and are offered at a range of prices. None of the rates is a bargain (everything in the heart of Berlin is expensive), but the lowest priced rooms continue to offer one of the best values for a quality hotel in the city.

HOTEL MONDIAL
Manager: Herr U. Hayer
Kurfürstendamm 47
10707 Berlin, Germany
Tel: (030) 884110 Fax: (030) 88411150
75 rooms
Double: DM 230–480 Suite: from DM 690
Open all year
Credit cards: all major
Restaurant open daily
In the heart of Berlin

Berlin is a large, bustling city, yet incredibly close by is an oasis of forests and lakes called the Grunewald. If you don't mind a short drive into the city, you can stay in the Grunewald (Green Forest) at the Forsthaus Paulsborn and not only spend much less than you would for a comparable hotel in Berlin, but also have the fun of staying in a 19th-century hunting lodge, surrounded by woodlands and just steps from the Grunewaldsee (Grunewald Lake). In addition to being a hotel, the Forsthaus Paulsborn is well-known as a restaurant where the talented Bernd-Peter Heide, the hotel's manager, has been chef for many years. On weekends the dining room is bustling with guests who come to enjoy a meal in the countryside. When the weather is warm, meals are also served outside. The Forsthaus Paulsborn is an appealing, small, lodge-like building, painted white with two small turrets and a steeply pitched red-tile roof. The approach to the restaurant (which also serves as the reception desk for the hotel) is through a beautifully tended garden. On the ground floor of the hotel is the main restaurant, plus a series of small dining rooms for private parties. A staircase leads to the bedrooms. Although the bedrooms are simple and the decor rather dated, they all have private bathroom, television, and direct-dial phone. One of my favorites, room 14, has a view of the lake from the pretty sitting area in the round bay window.

FORSTHAUS PAULSBORN
Manager: Bernd-Peter Heide
Am Grunewaldsee
14193 Berlin, Germany
Tel: (030) 8138010 Fax: (030) 8141156
10 rooms
Double: DM 195–235 Suite: DM 235
Open all year
Credit cards: all major
Restaurant closed Mondays
10-minute drive downtown, exit 2 off the 115

Bernkastel is one of the most charming of the larger towns along the Mosel river. Fronting the river are large turn-of-the-century hotels: venture behind them and you find winding, cobblestoned streets lined by 400-year-old half-timbered houses. Among these side streets you find the Doctor Weinstuben. Named after the local tax collector, Doctor Wein, who lived here in the 17th century, the house went on to become a wine room then a hotel when a modern block of rooms was built across the courtyard in 1974. While an effort was made to put an old-world exterior on the annex, the accommodations are modern, functional hotel rooms. Their decor is clean and bright but far from memorable. Each room has a private bathroom. By sharp contrast, the hotel has put a great deal of effort into making the restaurant in the old wine room reflect the atmosphere of this pretty little wine town. A large hay wagon stands as a decorative centerpiece and around it the lofty room has been divided into intimate dining nooks with beams and dark wood.

HOTEL DOCTOR WEINSTUBEN
Owner: Manfred Schantz
Hebegasse 5
54470 Bernkastel-Kues, Germany
Tel: (06531) 6081 Fax: (06531) 6296
19 rooms
Double: DM 150–160
Open March to December
Credit cards: all major
Restaurant closed Thursdays
75 km SW of Koblenz

Bernkastel is actually one of twin towns (the other is Kues) on either side of the River Mosel. This picture-book wine village is famous for its oh-so-pretty half-timbered houses and cute wine cellars on the streets that surround the town hall. The Hotel Zur Post is very professionally run by owners Hella and Bernhard Rössling. True hoteliers, the Rösslings do a superb job and are always striving to improve their hotel. Located slightly away from the center of town just steps away from the banks of the Mosel, the Zur Post has a mustard-colored façade complemented by dark green shutters and windowboxes of red geraniums. The oldest part of the Zur Post dates from 1827 and wings of rooms have been added in a similar, old-world style. The bedrooms are all very similar in decor, having modern fitted furniture complete with TV, phone, and mini-bar. All are large enough to have sitting areas and everything is meticulously maintained. One of the restaurants is quite delightful with walls and ceilings entirely of carved pine complemented by dried flower arrangements and bright tablecloths. The other two snug restaurants have less charming decor.

HOTEL ZUR POST
Owners: Hella & Bernhard Rössling
54470 Bernkastel-Kues, Germany
Tel: (06531) 2022 Fax: (06531) 2927
42 rooms
Double: DM 150–180
Closed January
Credit cards: all major
Restaurant open daily
75 km SW of Koblenz

The Störzer family have lovingly converted a building which dates from 1500 and added an annex to offer guests 43 delightful rooms in a village whose inhabitants probably number even fewer than the guests in the hotel. In this rural setting, mornings might be disturbed by the sound of milkcarts or a tractor. The Romantik Hotel "Die Bierhütte" incorporates the Bavarian theme throughout in its decor. Stenciling, found bordering doorways, is used to identify rooms and furnishings are in light wood enhanced by lovely, handpainted designs—so typical of the region. All the rooms in the new annex have either a balcony or terrace, depending on whether they are found on the first or second floor and the entire basement of the annex is devoted to a playroom equipped with toys, sauna, solarium, ping-pong table, and fitness room. In the main building, the restaurant, Wappenstupen, is named for the coats of armor displayed on the walls, the Gaststube is a cozy room available for either a meal or refreshments, and the cheery breakfast room benefits from the morning sun. A lovely terrace overlooking the lake is used for dining on warmer days.

ROMANTIK HOTEL "DIE BIERHÜTTE"
Owners: Family Ludwig Störzer
94545 Bierhütte
Hohenau, Germany
Tel: (08558) 315 Fax: (08558) 2387
43 rooms
Double: DM 150–230 Suite: DM 280–300
Open all year
Credit cards: all major
Restaurant open daily
205 km NE of Munich, 135 km E of Regensburg

A wonderfully rustic, country-home atmosphere prevails at the Landhotel Schindlerhof. A recently renovated and enlarged farm complex, it is built around a large open courtyard where tables are set in summer for cocktails and evening barbecues. Inside, the two dining rooms are country-cozy, yet also retain a certain elegance. The walls and ceilings are warm knotty pine, matched by light-pine furniture throughout. Hanging baskets, sheaves of harvest wheat, and dried and fresh flowers brighten all corners of the rooms, while charming rose-and-white-checked tablecloths are complemented by lace curtains and pink candles. The menu is imaginative and varied, offering cosmopolitan gourmet selections as well as fresh, health-food entrees. In all areas of the Schindlerhof, host Klaus Kobjoll's attention to the smallest detail is infallible. From thoughtful touches such as welcoming fruit baskets in each guest bedroom, packets of German gummy bears underneath the pillows, to a complimentary glass of sherry or champagne upon arrival, every comfort is attended to. Guest bedrooms are all fresh and new, but never sterile. Light-pine, antique reproductions furnish the spacious rooms, all of which have a writing table, good lighting, discreet color television, mini-bar, and telephone.

LANDHOTEL SCHINDLERHOF
Owner: Klaus Kobjoll
Steinacher Strasse 6–8
90427 Nürnberg-Boxdorf, Germany
Tel: (0911) 93020 Fax: (0911) 9302620
71 rooms
Double: DM 225–260
Open all year
Credit cards: all major
Restaurant
10 km NW of Nürnberg, near airport

The little town of Braubach lies on the Rhine almost opposite Koblenz. In amongst a mixture of modern and old houses you find the Zum Weissen Schwanen leaning against the old city wall where the large tower extends into the street. Step behind the half-timbered façade and you enter a gem of an unpretentious, rustic tavern with warm pine paneling, bottle-glass dimpled windows hung with hand-crocheted curtains, and simple pine tables and carved chairs. Your genial hosts, Erich and Gerhilde Kunz, will probably be there to welcome you. Although their English is limited, warm smiles and exuberant gestures overcome any language barrier. Several lovely bedrooms are found in the inn itself, all with spotless modern shower rooms and country antique furniture. Additional rooms with fitted furniture are found in the stable block behind the inn, while more delightful rooms with rustic handicrafts surrounding old pine beds topped with plump pillows and comforters lie in a nearby watermill. Room 141 Mägdestube is an especially appealing bedroom with lovely craftsman-style furniture. Many of the bedrooms contain two single beds with footboards that make them cramped for tall people. The Kunz family has a restaurant in the mill where a huge wooden waterwheel turns slowly at the building's center. The hotel gives you a wonderful feel of days gone by.

HOTEL ZUM WEISSEN SCHWANEN
Owners: Gerhild & Erich Kunz
Brunnenstrasse 4
56338 Braubach, Germany
Tel: (02627) 559 Fax: (02627) 8802
16 rooms, 1 suite
Double: DM 120–140 Suite: DM 200
Open all year
Credit cards: all major
Restaurant closed Wednesdays
100 km NW of Frankfurt, 13 km SE of Koblenz

You will have no problem finding the Romantik Hotel Zur Tanne: its pretty little façade graces the town's main street. Probably one of your genial hosts, Helmut or Bärbel Herbst, will be there to greet you. Their warm welcome, excellent English, and concern for their guests' comfort add to an enjoyable stay. From a tiny entrance the hotel opens up to reveal a large dignified dining room. This is the center of activity, for the hotel has gained a well-deserved reputation for excellent meals and impeccable service. Up the winding front staircase you find a few country-cozy bedrooms—I suggest you request one of these when making a reservation. A wing of modern rooms, decorated in shades of green, stretches out from the rear of the old inn. The hotel's most rustic room is its cheery bar where guests gather for after-dinner drinks and discussions of the day's events. Budget travelers can find more simple accommodations at the Guesthouse Zur Tanne on the edge of town. Braunlage is in the heart of the Harz mountains. In summer, besides sightseeing, delightful trails in the forests beckon, while winter offers the opportunity for cross-country skiing. Since the opening of the German border, the Harz region presents for exploration an appealing ring of quaint medieval towns such as Goslar, Wernigerode, and Quedlinburg. Last, but not least, don't miss the nostalgic steam-engine train ride through the lovely Harz mountains.

ROMANTIK HOTEL ZUR TANNE
Owners: Bärbel & Helmut Herbst
Herzog-Wilhelm Strasse 8
38693 Braunlage, Germany
Tel: (05520) 93120 Fax: (05520) 3992
21 rooms
Double: DM 165–225
Open all year
Credit cards: all major
Restaurant open daily
69 km S of Braunschweig

The name of this delightful 17th-century inn, "Die Grüne Bettlad" ("Green Bed"), refers back to its early history, when, so the story goes, the beautiful wife of the dipsomaniac innkeeper blatantly entertained her suitors in a green bed conveniently set next to a large ceramic oven. For the past two generations the hotel has been owned by the gracious Günthner family and is now ably run by Peter, the talented chef, and Sabine, his lovely wife and hostess. This is a restaurant with rooms and guests are expected to dine at the restaurant. The small front lobby sets the mood of the inn with a gaily painted reception desk and a large antique cradle. Through adjoining doors, guests find the intimate and charming restaurant where, in the evening, candlelight casts a romantic glow over tables set with crisp, pretty linens and fresh flowers. Whitewashed walls set off the cheerful red-and-green color scheme and a clutter of artistically placed prints, religious statues, copper molds, and wall sconces. From the lobby an old wooden spiral staircase leads to an upper lounge and bedrooms. Each of the guestrooms is spotlessly clean and features hand-painted furniture. Although the food is superb and the accommodations delightful, the nicest aspect of this tiny inn is the warmth and caring of the owners.

HOTEL "DIE GRÜNE BETTLAD"
Owners: Sabine & Peter Günthner
Blumenstrasse 4
77815 Bühl-Baden, Germany
Tel: (07223) 24238 Fax (07223) 24247
6 rooms
Double: DM 180–210 Suite: DM 250
Closed Christmas to mid-January & 2 weeks in July
Credit cards: AX
Restaurant closed Sundays & Mondays
14 km S of Baden-Baden

If your taste is for fancy, sophisticated decor, the hotel for you in the lovely town of Celle should be the Fürstenhof Celle. Whereas most of the buildings in Celle are quaint timbered houses, the Fürstenhof is a stately, 17th-century, peach-colored palace reflecting the influence of its famous Italian architect, Stechinelli. For many years the estate belonged to one of Europe's well-known aristocratic families, the Hardenbergs, and in 1970 Count Christian-Ludwig von Hardenberg took over the property and converted it into a luxury hotel. Two timbered buildings (once the stables and carriage house) stretch out in front of the two-story palace forming a courtyard where tables are set in the shade of 300-year-old chestnut trees. Inside, the hotel is ornately glamorous— especially the grand salon where Grecian columns support a mirror-paneled ceiling and comfortable leather chairs form intimate groups for afternoon tea. From the salon, a dramatic staircase leads up to the only four bedrooms located in the original building. Be sure to ask for one of these spacious, antique-filled rooms (all of the others are located in a modern, hotel-like wing without much personality). There are two places to dine: an elegant, gourmet restaurant (with a well deserved Michelin star) and a charming, rustic restaurant (in the former stables) serving regional specialties.

FÜRSTENHOF CELLE
Owner: Count von Hardenberg
Hannoversche Strasse 55–56
29221 Celle, Germany
Tel: (05141) 2010 Fax: (05141) 201120
71 rooms, 5 suites
Double: DM 225–430 Suite: DM 340–560
Open all year
Credit cards: all major
Restaurant open daily
45 km NE of Hannover, 118 km S of Hamburg
Relais & Chateaux

The two-tone green façade of the Hotel Utspann (a narrow, colorfully painted, timbered house dating from 1644) reflects the marvelous character of old Celle. At first glance, the hotel looks small, but as you walk through the entrance and into the back courtyard, it is evident that the hotel actually incorporates six 17th-century houses, cleverly renovated into one building by the architect, Andreas Mehls. The cluster of houses forms a central patio with tables and chairs set for a relaxing moment under the trees. The bedrooms are all different in decor, yet each has a similar folksy-cute look. Ursula Mehls is an avid collector, and all of the rooms are brimming with antique toys, old plates, copper pots, baskets of silk flowers, country-style fabrics, painted tables, hanging plants, and Oriental throw rugs. My favorite is the prettily decorated Rostock room, tucked under the eaves with windows overlooking the street. An added bonus is the Hotel Utspann's intimate little restaurant where there are only five small antique tables set for dining. An upright piano along one wall, framed musical manuscripts, fresh green plants set in the deep window niches, fresh flowers, pretty linens, and soft candlelight create a romantic ambiance for excellent, home-cooked meals. Note: You can drive to Hotel Utspann, which is located on the edge of the pedestrian-only section of town.

HOTEL UTSPANN
Owner: Ursula Mehls
Im Kreise 13
29221 Celle, Germany
Tel: (05141) 92720 Fax: (05141) 927252
17 rooms
Double: DM 212–295 Suite: DM 295–420
Closed Christmas & New Year
Credit cards: all major
Restaurant closed Sundays
45 km NE of Hannover, 118 km S of Hamburg

Cochem hugs the banks of the winding River Mosel. It is a delightful village that thrives on the production of wine and the influx of tourists who come to wander through its streets lined by old houses and to climb to the castle guarding the heights. Leaning against the remnants of the old town wall, the Alte Thorschenke is a lovely, old-fashioned German inn. From the tiny lobby, a beautifully carved, creaking wooden staircase spirals up to the old-fashioned bedchambers. Several have romantic antique four-poster beds and French armoires. Request one of these older rooms as the majority of the hotel's accommodations are modern, rather dated rooms built at the rear of the hotel. A special treat is the hunting-lodge-style dining room with its handsome oil paintings, great old portraits, hunting trophies, and Oriental carpets accenting beautiful planked wooden floors. Surrounding the village, steep vineyards produce excellent white wines, for Cochem is at the heart of the Mosel wine region. Consequently, wine sampling from the hotel's long wine list or in one of the taverns along the river is a popular pastime. The Alte Thorschenke has its own 500-year-old winery where the best Mosel wines can be tasted and bought at low prices.

ALTE THORSCHENKE
Managers: Annegret & Walther Kretz
Bruckenstrasse 3
56812 Cochem, Germany
Tel: (02671) 7059 Fax: (02671) 4202
45 rooms
Double: DM 165–225
Closed January 5 to mid-March
Credit cards: all major
Restaurant open daily
51 km SW of Koblenz, on Mosel river
Gast im Schloss

Miraculously, Cologne's cathedral was not flattened by the Allied bombers that devastated the rest of the city during the Second World War. Its tall, delicate spires still rise above the skyline and the pedestrian square surrounding the cathedral is still the meeting point for visitors from all over the world. Jutting out into the square is the Dom Hotel, one of the grand old stylish hotels of Europe. The public rooms are gracious and formal. Relaxed and informal dining can be enjoyed in the Wintergarden restaurant with its natural plants and palm trees, comfortable rattan chairs, and a breathtaking view of the cathedral. In summer the terrace café provides a less formal dining spot: from here you can almost touch the cathedral—a perfect location for watching busy Cologne whirl by. Heavy marble stairways lead to wide, recently renovated hallways and grand, high-ceilinged bedchambers. Large windows hung with beautiful, full-length drapes and elegant antique furniture add to the luxurious ambiance. One warning: the rooms are not soundproofed and while the noise of the square recedes late at night, the cathedral bells continue to ring.

DOM HOTEL
Domkloster 2a
Manager: Herr Horst Berl
50667 Cologne, Germany
Tel: (0221) 20240 Fax: (0221) 2024444
125 rooms, 2 suites
Double: DM 430–730 Suite: DM 1,300
Open all year
Credit cards: all major
Restaurant open daily
Near cathedral in heart of Cologne

The Haus Lyskirchen is an excellent choice for a moderately priced hotel in Cologne. The hotel occupies a side street just off the River Rhine. From the pier, only a short distance from the hotel, steamers depart for the popular Rhine day trip from Cologne to Mainz. A ten-minute stroll through the old town brings you to the cathedral, just far enough away that you can hear the distant echo of its bells. The Haus Lyskirchen is a blend of styles. To the left of the modern lobby is a small country-style dining room where, if you are too tired to venture out after a busy day's sightseeing, you can enjoy an intimate dinner. An appealing little paneled bar provides a cozy spot for after-dinner drinks. In sharp contrast, a display of modern art leads you to the stark, modern breakfast room where you partake of a sumptuous, buffet-style breakfast. Some bedrooms are just like a mountain chalet (all cozy in pine); the others, which are brighter, have been completely renovated and are furnished in white-ash wood. A large indoor swimming pool and underground parking are added bonuses. Cologne hosts conventions during January, February, March, April, September, and October: if you plan to visit during these times, book well in advance.

HAUS LYSKIRCHEN
Owner: Family Marzorati
Filzengraben 26–32
50676 Cologne, Germany
Tel: (0221) 20970 Fax: (0221) 2097718
94 rooms
Double: DM 215–340
Closed Christmas
Credit cards: all major
Restaurant closed Sundays and holidays
10-minute walk to city center

Deidesheim is a particularly nice village on Die Deutsche Weinstrasse, The German Wine Road. Occupying a corner of the village square, the Hotel Deidesheimer Hof has a formal appearance, for this was once a Bishop's residence and is now a sophisticated Relais and Chateaux hotel. Sampling wines is an obligatory pastime and there is no more pleasant a spot for the task than the flower-filled terrace that spills onto the village square. Beyond the lobby you find a number of delightful, country-style restaurants offering German cuisine. The kitchen is supervised by Manfred Schwarz who has received a Michelin star for the gourmet food he serves in his cavernous, more formal, cellar restaurant. Upstairs you find the sunny breakfast room with its bright, royal-blue chairs set against white walls accented with yellow-and-blue draperies. The bedrooms are furnished in a very sophisticated modern decor as befits a Relais and Chateaux Hotel. Deidesheim's wine festival takes place during the second week of August.

HOTEL DEIDESHEIMER HOF
Owner: Anita Hahn
Am Marktplatz 1
67146 Deidesheim, Germany
Tel: (06326) 1811 Fax: (06326) 7685
18 rooms, 2 suites
Double: DM 180–310 Suite: DM 340–420
Closed first week of January
Credit cards: all major
Restaurant open daily
88 km S of Mainz, 23 km SW of Mannheim
Relais & Chateaux

With the opening of the Hotel Bülow Residenz Dresden has a small, luxury hotel which is full of character. Found on a quiet side street of old houses, the hotel is in the Neustadt just across the from the heart of Dresden. This baroque building with its façade dating back to 1730 has been restored, keeping the elegant exterior and adding a traditional-modern interior. At the heart of the hotel is a vine-covered courtyard set with tables and chairs for enjoying breakfast or afternoon coffee and cake outdoors. While we enjoyed casual fare in the Austrian/Italian restaurant across the street, the hotel has a formal restaurant serving more elegant food in hushed surroundings. The barrel-vaulted wine-cellars are now a cozy piano bar. Found on four floors, the spacious bedrooms are each accompanied by a luxurious bath- or shower-room. A two-minute walk brings you to the golden statue of August the Strong sitting atop his horse gazing across the Augustusbrücke which spans the Elbe to the historic heart of Dresden. Here you find the Zwinger (museums), a monumental palace that August the Strong used as a background for sumptuous festivals and housing his vast art collection. To find the hotel locate the Albertplatz in the Neustadt (a circular traffic island with roads radiating from it like spokes of a wheel) and take Konigstrasse, then turn left on Obergraben to Rähnitzgasse.

HOTEL BÜLOW RESIDENZ   **NEW**
Manager: Ralf Kutzner
Rähnitzgasse 19
01097 Dresden, Germany
Tel: (0351) 80030 Fax: (0351) 8003100
24 rooms, 7 suites
Double: DM 440–490 Suite: DM 490–600
Open all year
Credit cards: all major
Restaurant open daily
Across the river from city center

The Kempinski Hotel Taschenbergpalais has the ultimate location in Dresden: flanked on one side by the magnificent Zwinger museum and the Semper Opera House and on the other by the castle and the cathedral. The exterior of the hotel is an exact reconstruction of the baroque-style Taschenbergpalais that King August the Strong built for his mistress, the Countess Cosel, in 1706. Now you too can live like a king at the jewel in the crown of the luxurious Kempinski hotel chain. The vast lobby is flanked by an arcade of luxurious boutiques which leads you to the intimate lounges and restaurants that range from Paulaner (a casual restaurant) to Intermezzo, the hotel's gourmet dining room. In summer the vast inner courtyard is set with tables and chairs for *al fresco* dining. The elegant, contemporary decor extends to the bedrooms with their stylish burled furniture, comfortable gray armchairs, and jaunty decor of navy-blue bedspreads banded with red and gold topped with large red and smaller white pillows. After a day's sightseeing, relax at the health club with its Turkish baths, sauna, solarium, and indoor swimming pool. Park you car in the car park under the hotel (DM 25 per day in 1995) and explore the heart of this famous city of art on the banks of the River Elbe.

KEMPINSKI HOTEL TASCHENBERGPALAIS   **NEW**
Manager: Günther Haug
Taschenberg 3
01067 Dresden, Germany
Tel: (0351) 49120 Fax: (0351) 4912812
188 rooms, 25 suites
Double: DM 430–570 Suite: DM 600–950*
*Breakfast not included
Open all year
Credit cards: all major
Restaurant open daily
In city center

We first stayed at the Hotel auf der Wartburg, located in what was formerly East Germany, in 1990 (only a few days after the reunification of Germany). On our second visit a few years later, we were astounded at the miraculous changes. Bathless guestrooms with outdated, dreary decor had emerged like butterflies from their cocoons into some of the best-looking rooms in all of Germany. Each of the bedrooms is individual in decor, yet all have the same refined, English-country-manor look with beautiful fabrics used in the color-coordinated draperies and upholstered chairs. One of my favorites, number 104 (a deluxe corner room decorated in rich greens and yellows) looks out to the forest. Less expensive room 102 (overlooking the front courtyard) is also a charmer in tones of reds and golds. Some of the most romantic rooms are tucked up under the eaves with tiny garret windows capturing miniature views of the wooded hills. Just steps from the hotel is the museum section of Wartburg Castle, one of Germany's real gems. The hotel is easy to find. Leave the autobahn at Eisenach following signposts to Wartburg. As you near the castle, take the small signposted lane that winds uphill through the forest to the castle. There is a parking area at the top with a barricade. Continue about 500 meters past the parking to the courtyard in front of the hotel.

HOTEL AUF DER WARTBURG
Manager: Hans Joachim Hook
Wirtschaftsbetriebe
99817 Eisenach, Germany
Tel & fax: (03691) 5111
35 rooms, 3 suites
Double: DM 260–310 Suite: DM 380
Open all year
Credit cards: all major
Restaurant open daily
On hilltop, 3 km S of Eisenach
Gast im Schloss

We searched in vain for a small hotel with charm in Nürnberg and finally settled on a delightful alternative only 22 kilometers to the north. The Schwarzer Adler exudes country charm even though it is located near the large cities of Nürnberg and Erlangen. The hotel's façade is prettily laced with intricate timbering and has green-shuttered windows above windowboxes full of bright-red geraniums in summer. A small stream flows behind the inn and a pretty church sits nearby. Once inside, you will not be disappointed, for the inn is beautifully decorated in a cozy style perfectly suited to its picturesque façade. An antique wooden spiral staircase winds up from the lobby to the Müller family's quarters on the second floor, and continues to the third floor where the guest accommodations are tucked into cozy dormers. Although these rooms are not large, they are spotlessly clean and very appealing; decorated with tasteful, light-pine furniture, fluffy down comforters with crisp, white duvet coverings, and white crocheted curtains at the windows. Since our last visit additional rooms have been added and guests have a garden between the two houses. Christiane Müller-Kinzel has renovated this historical Franconian framework house (dating back to at least 1702) with such care and attention to detail that it has won several awards.

HOTEL SCHWARZER ADLER
Owner: Christiane Müller-Kinzel
Herdegenplatz 1
91056 Erlangen-Frauenaurach, Germany
Tel: (09131) 992051 Fax: (09131) 993195
14 rooms
Double: DM 180–200
Closed Christmas & mid-August to mid-September
Credit cards: VS
Restaurant serving snacks
22 km N of Nürnberg

The Romantik Hotel Voss Haus is located on the main road through Eutin, an ever-so-quaint medieval town with pedestrian-only lanes and a picturesque square lined by 17th-century houses. The hotel fronts onto the street, but backs onto a garden with a path leading down to an exceptionally beautiful lake. The 300-year-old building is chock-full of character. The lower part of the building is brick while the upper floors are vertical panels of wood painted a deep blue, enhanced by white-framed windows and a steeply pitched red-tile roof. You enter into a large reception room (with dark-red walls) that also serves as a lounge for guests of the hotel's restaurant. There are five dining rooms. Each is individual in decor, but all are brimming with a stunning, romantic charm: dark woods, soft lighting, beamed ceilings, many oil paintings, antiques galore, pretty white dotted-Swiss curtains, and fresh flowers throughout. It is no wonder that the Voss Haus restaurant is so popular: the food, the service, and the ambiance are all faultless. In the summer, meals are also served in the back garden overlooking the lake. A curving staircase (which could use a coat of paint and new carpeting) winds up to the guestrooms which, although a bit dated in decor, are spacious and quite pleasant. The choice rooms are those in the rear overlooking the garden.

ROMANTIK HOTEL VOSS HAUS
Manager: Lars Ruelander
Vossplatz 6
23701 Eutin, Germany
Tel: (04521) 70770 Fax: (04521) 707777
16 rooms
Double: DM 160–180
Open all year
Credit cards: all major
Restaurant open daily
40 km N of Lübeck, 106 km NE of Hamburg

Four generations of the Lorentz family have perfected a tradition of welcome and quality that is ever-present in their hotel. Referenced in local records as early as 1369, the Greifen Post now offers extremely modern comforts and facilities. The inn has a number of cozy rooms that serve as restaurants. The main restaurant is very elegant, with heavy beams and hand-painted scenes staging an attractive atmosphere. Downstairs is a more casual bar and restaurant that overlooks the indoor swimming pool through stone arched windows. Here tapestry-covered, high-back chairs are set around a large open fireplace used to grill steaks and cutlets. Upstairs you find a sunny breakfast room decorated in shades of yellow where a generous buffet breakfast is artfully displayed. The Greifen Post's bedrooms can be grouped by decor: Romantik (in the flamboyant French style of Louis XIV), Biedermeier (with Biedermeier antiques), Himmelbett (with charming four-poster beds), and Laura Ashley (with English-style fabrics). I could not decide what style of room I liked best—every one is beautiful. The entire hotel shows the touch of owners who strive to have every detail of their inn perfect. Bicycles are available for exploring the nearby countryside.

ROMANTIK HOTEL GREIFEN POST
Owner: Edward Lorentz
Marktplatz 8
91555 Feuchtwangen, Germany
Tel: (09852) 6800 Fax: (09852) 68068
35 rooms, 3 suites
Double: DM 199–259 Suite: DM 289–359
Open all year
Credit cards: all major
Restaurant closed Sundays & Mondays*
*Smaller restaurant closed Wednesdays
170 km NW of Munich, 70 km SW of Nürnberg

FRANKFURT-Neu-Isenburg   KEMPINSKI HOTEL GRAVENBRUCH   MAP: 3b

A grand international hotel in the casually elegant style of a country estate, the Kempinski Hotel Gravenbruch is nestled in its own 37-acre park yet is only 15 minutes from either the heart of town or the Frankfurt airport (there is a free shuttle service every 30 minutes to or from terminal one). The hotel's refreshing rural tranquility is further enhanced by extensive health and leisure amenities: inviting indoor pool, fitness and massage rooms, heated outdoor pool, tennis courts, and beauty farm. The hotel has a resort atmosphere with various dining rooms, conference rooms, and enormous lobbies. Obviously most of the hotel is of new construction, but the nucleus of the hotel is old. The architects have constructed the additions cleverly, not only mindful of the hotel's origins, but taking advantage of the park-like setting. Most of the nicely decorated guestrooms look out to either the woods or the lake. Although much larger than most hotels featured in this guide, this star of the Kempinski hotel affiliation has much to offer—especially for your first or last night in Germany. After a long airline journey, it is refreshing to walk in the woods before taking a bite to eat and going to bed. You will find yourself reinvigorated the next day and ready to "hit the road."

KEMPINSKI HOTEL GRAVENBRUCH
Manager: Elmar Greif
Neu-Isenburg 2
63263 Frankfurt/ Neu-Isenburg, Germany
Tel: (06102) 5050 Fax: (06102) 505900
286 rooms
Double: DM 348–578 Suite: DM 708–2,258
Open all year
Credit cards: all major
Restaurant open daily
Near Frankfurt airport
On Rte 459, 11 km SE of Frankfurt

We thought that our kind of little hotel could not exist in the heart of Frankfurt where most of the buildings are new and without charm but, happily, we were proved wrong. Not only does a gem of a small hotel exist, but it is splendidly located in a very nice neighborhood, only three blocks from the train station and within easy walking distance to shopping and sightseeing. Your heart will be won at first glance at the Hotel Westend—a pretty, pastel-pink house, reminiscent of a small villa. There is a small front lawn and steps leading up the side of the house to a long, marble-floored entry accented by Persian carpets. Three intimate little parlors are at guests' disposal, each prettily decorated with antique furniture, bouquets of fresh flowers, Oriental carpets, crystal chandeliers, handsome mirrors, and oil paintings. The overall effect is one of quiet elegance, somewhat formal, yet welcoming and homelike. Guestrooms are located upstairs and all have an old-world ambiance created by pretty, pastel color schemes, white curtains at the windows, and liberal use of authentic antiques. Be sure to request a room with an ensuite bathroom as these are at a premium. An added bonus is a secluded back garden where breakfast is served during the warm summer months. Hotel Westend is truly an oasis in the busy city of Frankfurt, but with so few rooms available, you need to book far in advance for this very special hotel.

HOTEL WESTEND
Owner: Carl-Ludwig Mayer
Westendstrasse 15
60325 Frankfurt 1, Germany
Tel: (069) 746702 Fax: (069) 745396
20 rooms
Double: DM 180–350 Suite: DM 330–560
Closed for Christmas
Credit cards: all major
No restaurant: breakfast only
3 blocks from train station, central location

How fortunate that driving rain drove us into Oberkirchs Weinstuben for a fortifying drink, for we discovered that it is also a darling inn. Oberkirchs Weinstuben is actually located in two buildings: the principal building sits on Munsterplatz in the shadow of Freiburg's impressive cathedral, the other just a short cobblestoned block away. The Weinstuben serves a very satisfying lunch or dinner in a congenial, cozy atmosphere. Beamed ceilings, wooden tables, white linen, and contented chatter set the mood for the charming restaurant. It is a popular place to dine in the marvelous medieval town of Freiburg and understandably so. In addition to the restaurant, there 26 guestrooms, found either directly above the weinstube or in the neighboring building. All have been recently refurbished and are very attractive. The nine rooms above the weinstube are slightly more expensive. My special favorite is number 55, a gem of a room with a romantic view out over the square to the cathedral. Freiburg is one of the most attractive walled cities in the Black Forest region of Germany, and the Oberkirchs Weinstuben makes an excellent choice for overnight accommodation. It is somewhat difficult to maneuver by auto through the pedestrian district, but the hotel provides a map and directions for parking.

OBERKIRCHS WEINSTUBEN
Owner: Helmut Johner
Munsterplatz 22
79098 Freiburg im Breisgau, Germany
Tel: (0761) 31011 Fax: (0761) 31031
26 rooms
Double: DM 220–250 Suite: DM 280–290
Closed January
Credit cards: all major
Restaurant closed Sundays
208 km SW of Stuttgart, 71 km N of Basel

Schlosshotel Friedrichsruhe sits in manicured, park-like grounds at the edge of the village. A complex of very different buildings comprise the hotel: the 1712 hunting castle, the adjacent timbered Torhaus, a modern complex, and the beauty complex where guests can enjoy massages and skin treatments. The modern core of the hotel houses the reception area (where service is somewhat impersonal and aloof), a wing of modern bedrooms renovated in 1996, indoor and outdoor swimming pools, and the restaurants. One of the main reasons guests come here is to dine for manager and chef Lothar Eiermann holds two Michelin stars for the gourmet cuisine served in the elegant restaurant. Gourmet cuisine or more ordinary fare can be enjoyed in the informal Jagerstube where country tables and chairs are set around an old stove beneath hunting trophies. Bedrooms in the hunting castle are elegantly traditional as are those in the Torhaus and garden house. The owner Fürst Kraft lives nearby in Neuenstein castle and you can obtain details on when the castle and gardens are open to visitors from the reception desk. Friedrichsruhe is so small it does not appear on most maps. The village is signposted from Öhringen.

SCHLOSSHOTEL FRIEDRICHSRUHE
Manager: Lothar Eiermann
74639 Friedrichsruhe, Germany
Tel: (07941) 60870 Fax: (07941) 61468
37 rooms, 12 suites
Double: DM 295–390 Suite: DM 490–560
Open all year
Credit cards: all major
Restaurant open daily
6 km from Öhringen, 65 km NE of Stuttgart
Relais & Chateaux

There is something very endearing about the simplicity of the Schloss Fürsteneck. One would never just happen upon this hotel: it is set in the Bavarian hills in a village that is mostly comprised of a castle and a church. By no means luxurious, this hotel has appeal for those on a budget. The exterior is accented by colorful windowboxes while inside there are ten spotless guestrooms. The restaurant with its arched ceilings and tables appealingly decked with either blue- or red-checked cloths is very cozy. There are actually three adjoining dining rooms to choose from: the Gaststube, the Jagerzimmer (a round room with a hunting motif that overlooks a steep drop to the River Ohr), and the Kaminzimmer (named for the fireplace that warms it). The menu highlights the regional specialties and garden-fresh vegetables. This hotel has only two rooms with full bath and private toilet—the rest share facilities. Again, I stress the rooms are simple but sweet, with matching prints used for the comforter covers and the curtains. In this region one can hike between hotels: you set out with only a luncheon pack and have your bags delivered to your next hotel. Contact the hotel for specific details and arrangements.

SCHLOSS FÜRSTENECK
Owner: Adrian Forster
94142 Fürsteneck, Germany
Tel & fax: (08505) 1473
10 rooms
Double: from DM 80
Closed January to mid-February
Credit cards: AX, MC
Restaurant closed midweek
195 km NE of Munich
Near Czech Republic border

Located in the historic section of Partenkirchen, the Gasthof Fraundorfer has been in the Fraundorfer family since 1820 and is still a homey, family-run inn. Its façade is decorated with murals and windowboxes of red geraniums, while inside a restaurant with a marvelous atmosphere awaits. Walls and ceilings covered entirely in mellow, knotty pine foster a warm, rustic feeling here, where tradition is taken seriously. One of the wooden tables in the room is a *Stammtisch,* the exclusive territory of a specific group of regulars, where each person always sits in the same place—in fact, some of the chairs have brass plaques engraved with the occupant's name. Photos of Stammtisch regulars, some dating back 50 years, adorn the wall above the table. Home-cooked meals with German beers and wine are served in this charming dining room accompanied by accordion music and slap-dancing. Some of the guestrooms are located in Gästehaus Barbara, a remodeled house located just behind the hotel, while others are in the original Gasthof. The rooms vary in size and furnishings, although all are in traditional Bavarian style. Do not expect elegance, but homey comfort. All rooms have private bath, phone, and television, and some have balconies or additional rooms for children. This inn is truly a friendly place and a very good value in the center of such a popular tourist town.

GASTHOF FRAUNDORFER
Owners: Barbara & Josef Fraundorfer
Ludwigstrasse 24
82467 Garmisch-Partenkirchen, Germany
Tel: (08821) 2176 Fax: (08821) 71073
32 rooms
Double: DM 126–156 Suite: DM 186–342
Open all year
Credit cards: all major
Restaurant closed Tuesdays
89 km S of Munich

In the charming village of Partenkirchen, just across from the picturesque church whose bells toll the hour, the Posthotel Partenkirchen reflects its colorful history as a postal station. Four generations of the gracious Stahl family have maintained the old-world tradition and excellent standard of service. Delightful antiques are displayed beautifully in all the public rooms and maids are forever busy polishing and scrubbing each and every corner. A cozy bar sits just off the grand entry and is warmed by a lovely stove. Trunks and painted armoires line the hallways that lead to traditional accommodations. Rather than a particular one or two, it seemed that the majority of the hotel's 60 rooms were decorated with antiques and attractive fabrics, though the carpets seemed a little worn on a 1995 visit. The bathrooms have all been remodeled in a luxurious style. On the first floor, the largest room is number 2: wood-paneled, it looks out over the back streets through thick walls. Although much smaller, my favorite is number 53, a corner room on the top floor. It is paneled cozily both on the walls and ceiling with antique wood set off by handsome tapestry-like bedspread and draperies. Sliding doors lead out to a wrap-around balcony which enjoys an unobstructed view of the Zugspitze. However, no matter what room you have, you will certainly be enchanted by this delightful hotel.

POSTHOTEL PARTENKIRCHEN
Owners: Lisa & Otto Stahl
Ludwigstrasse 49
82467 Garmisch-Partenkirchen, Germany
Tel: (08821) 51067 Fax: (08821) 78568
58 rooms, 2 suites
Double: DM 200–250 Suite: DM 270–320
Open all year
Credit cards: all major
Restaurant open daily
89 km S of Munich

Like so many of the hotels in what used to be East Germany, the handsome Schloss Blücher has undergone a tremendous face-lift since reunification. For many years Schloss Blücher, which is serenely located amidst forests and lakes, was used by the government as a holiday retreat. The castle was not well tended and looked quite dreadful when first taken over by the present owner but today, with a complete face-lift, the castle has returned to its former glory. You enter a very large, quite formal, reception hall with an intricately paneled ceiling that soars two stories high. The reception area has ornate, upholstered furniture in a deep-red fabric which sets off the rich-blue carpet. A majestic, wide staircase with beautiful wooden banisters leads to the second level where a balcony wraps around the room, open to the floor below. Beyond the reception area is a lounge with large windows looking out to a peaceful wooded landscape. The hotel is well-known for its kitchen, and to the right of the foyer there is a series of dining rooms, formal but extremely attractive. My favorite is one fashioned from the original chapel with an intricately sculpted ceiling and stained-glass windows. The guestrooms were designed by an Italian decorator: the custom-made, ultra-modern furniture is obviously very expensive and, although not to my taste, is undoubtedly popular with many guests.

HOTEL SCHLOSS BLÜCHER
Manager: Uwe Sabrowsky
Schlossplatz
17213 Göhren-Lebbin, Germany
Tel: (039932) 175 Fax: (039932) 17999
40 rooms, 2 suites
Double: DM 220–265 Suite: DM 375–450
Open all year
Credit cards: AX, VS
Restaurant open daily
150 km N of Berlin, 86 km S of Rostock
Gast im Schloss

I have often included a town because of a wonderful hotel but in this case I am including a hotel because of a wonderful town. Made rich by mining in the nearby Harz mountains, Goslar was a flourishing regional capital long before Columbus set sail for America. Time has been kind, and wandering along the narrow cobbled streets is like taking a walk into a history book. Occupying a corner of the large pedestrian market square, the Kaiserworth was built in 1494 as the guild house of the cloth workers. The stunning façade, with carvings of emperors beneath the eaves, was completed in the 17th century. The Oberhuber family purchased the hotel several years ago and have meticulously restored and repainted the exterior to perfection. Regrettably, rather than restoring the public rooms they have updated them, using modern bleached oak. However, because the older bedrooms are somewhat bedraggled in their decor we advise that you request one of the refurbished (bleached oak) bedrooms. These are the most expensive rooms: I particularly liked room 110, a large corner bedroom, and room 114, a smaller refurbished room. Step outside your hotel at six in the evening and watch the concert of the city clock whose four different scenes represent the thousand-year-old mining history of the region.

HOTEL KAISERWORTH
Owner: Karin Oberhuber
Markt 3
38640 Goslar, Germany
Tel: (05321) 21111 Fax: (05321) 21114
51 rooms
Double: DM 170–240
Open all year
Credit cards: all major
Restaurant open daily
90 SE of Hannover, 70 km S of Braunschweig

It is always a real delight to discover a newly built hotel that offers all the up-to-date comforts without sacrificing an old-world ambiance. A fine example is the Hotel Alpenhof, which does not pretend to be old, yet maintains a romantic mood of Bavarian country charm. Soaring mountain peaks form the backdrop for this modern, chalet-style hotel with balconies both in front and back, accented by windowboxes filled with red geraniums. You enter into a cheerful reception area that opens onto a cozy yet sophisticated bar where a fireplace warms the room in winter. From the bar, steps lead down to the paneled dining room divided into several eating areas. My favorite is an intimate, wood-paneled (both walls and ceiling) room adorned with pewter trays, antique mugs, brass lamps, an antique tiled oven, and tables set colorfully with blue tablecloths and napkins. When the weather is warm, meals are also served outside in a pretty rear garden. This is a deluxe hotel with many amenities including a solarium, sauna, and magnificent indoor pool with arched windows looking out to the trees. The bedrooms continue the standard of excellence: the furnishings are new, but traditional in style and of superb quality. Splurge and request one of the more expensive back bedrooms with a balcony capturing the view of the majestic, soaring, granite peaks of the Zugspitze.

HOTEL ALPENHOF
Owners: Margaret and Albert Falkenstein
Manager: Karl Buchwieser
Alpspitzstrasse 34
82491 Grainau, Germany
Tel: (08821) 8071 Fax: (08821) 81680
36 rooms
Double: DM 240–340
Closed mid-November to mid-December
Credit cards: MC, VS
Restaurant open daily
94 km S of Munich, 6 km SW of Garmisch

It is rare to discover a hotel with guestrooms offering an unobstructed view of the mountains, but the Hotel Post, located in the small village of Grainau, close to the famous resort of Garmisch-Partenkirchen, is a happy exception. If you love collecting memories of dramatic mountain peaks, ask for rooms 18, 19, 20, or 21. From your balcony you have a perfect view of green meadows stretching up the hillside to the enormous, soaring, granite peaks of the Zugspitze. The Hotel Post is a very simple hotel—not for those expecting luxury or quaint accommodation. The guestrooms are fresh and clean, but basic and with very dated decor. However, the breakfast room is much more appealing, with beamed ceiling, provincial-print tie-back curtains, attractive wooden chairs, tables set with linen cloths, and oil paintings and copper pots adorning fresh, whitewashed walls. The Hotel Post is around 300 years old. For the first two centuries it was a sturdy farmhouse then in 1890 it was bought by the Seufferth family who decided to take in paying guests. The family still owns the hotel and you will usually find Hannes Seufferth at the front desk. She speaks perfect English and is an exceptionally gracious hostess who has the knack of making guests feel very welcome. Hannes also has ten simply furnished apartments that she rents on a weekly basis.

HOTEL POST
Owner: Hannes Seufferth
Near Garmisch-Partenkirchen
82491 Grainau/Zugspitzdorf, Germany
Tel: (08821) 8853 Fax: (08821) 8873
20 rooms
Double: DM 120–165
Closed mid-January to mid-February
* & mid-November to mid-December*
Credit cards: AX, VS
No restaurant: breakfast only
94 km S of Munich, 6 km SW of Garmisch

The Stadtschänke is truly a gem, a superb, tiny hotel brimming with charm inside and out. Your heart will be won the moment you reach the colorful little marketplace in the center of Grossbottwar and discover the picture-perfect, 15th-century Stadtschänke. The façade is a whimsical delight—a narrow, timbered building that rises five stories high, ending in a steeply pitched roof. A huge bucket of flowers hanging from a wrought-iron brace completes the story-book look. The first two floors house the restaurant, and you must plan to dine here. Hans Könneke is the master chef, and not only is the food outstanding, but the dining rooms exude an oh-so-appealing rustic elegance. The candlelit tables, dressed with fine linens and fresh flowers, set off to perfection the rough-hewn, exposed timber walls. The inn's own local red wine completes a delicious dinner. The guestrooms, located on the third level, are small and simple, but each is decorated in perfect harmony with the mood of the house. Beamed ceilings, simple white walls, embroidered, tie-back curtains, comfortable beds, and soft pink linens create a most inviting look. My favorite room is number 3, a darling corner room overlooking the square. As a final bonus, the Stadtschänke is run by the very gracious Könneke family who add their warmth of hospitality to make your visit even more special.

STADTSCHÄNKE GASTHOF
Owners: Sybille & Hans Könneke
Hauptstrasse 36, am Marktplatz
71723 Grossbottwar, Germany
Tel: (07148) 8024 Fax: (07148) 4977
4 rooms
Double: DM 120
Open all year
Credit cards: all major
Restaurant closed Wednesdays
30 km S of Heilbronn, 35 km N of Stuttgart

Halberstadt was almost flattened by Allied bombers in January, 1945 but the medieval area around the cathedral of St. Stephanus has been carefully restored. This elegant cathedral, built from the 13th to the 15th centuries, is one of the greatest Gothic monuments in eastern Germany. Sadly, the ambiance of this area does not extend to the rest of the city which contains a great many decidedly ugly apartment buildings. The Romantik Parkhotel Unter den Linden, a totally modern hotel set behind a restored exterior, stands out as a rose amongst thorns. We were shown to the fireplace room for pre-dinner drinks and while we admired the richness of the dark paneled walls inlaid with interesting landscape paintings of the once historic Halberstadt, we felt ill at ease as we balanced in our uncomfortable red chairs placed regimentally every 3 feet round the edge of the sculptured carpet. Things improved greatly in the much more comfortable restaurant which overlooks an attractive grassy courtyard at the center of the hotel. Many of the bedrooms enjoy this same delightful garden vista. Bedrooms in the main building are spacious, decorated in a modern vein with art-deco-style headboards and furniture, each accompanied by a red-and-white-tile shower room. More glamorous gray marble shower rooms are found in the modern extension where the bedrooms are smaller and uniform in size. The hotel is well signposted from the outskirts of Halberstadt.

ROMANTIK PARKHOTEL UNTER DEN LINDEN **NEW**
Manager: Frank Butzke
Klamrothstrasse 2
38820 Halberstadt, Germany
Tel: (03941) 600077 Fax: (03941) 25188
45 rooms, 1 suite
Double: DM 210–240 Suite: DM 280
Open all year
Credit cards: all major
Restaurant open daily
57 km SW of Magdeburg

The Hotel Abtei is one of the finest small city hotels in Germany. Situated on a quiet, tree-lined street north of the center of Hamburg, the hotel seems far removed from the confusion of the city, yet is quickly accessible either by car, subway, or boat. Every detail of the Abtei, originally a gracious private home, is of the highest quality and taste: gorgeous fabrics, exquisite antiques, fine linens, comfortable mattresses (replaced every two years), fresh flower arrangements throughout, and exceptional service. Herr Lay's goal is to provide the old-fashioned quality of excellence rarely found today—his goal is to have the "smallest GRAND hotel" in Europe. The Abtei is not inexpensive, yet when compared with all the other hotels in the costly city of Hamburg, it offers real value for the price. It was voted the best hotel with under 50 rooms in Germany—and was among the top 25 of all German hotels. The guestrooms are beautifully decorated suites with well equipped, attractive bathrooms en suite. Guests may enjoy breakfast in their room, in one of the guest dining rooms, or, if the weather is warm, in the pretty garden behind the hotel. Homemade baked goods are offered in silver bread baskets, and delicious coffee or tea is served in antique pots. In the evening, dinner is served in the intimate dining room. If you like refinement and exceptional service, you will love this tiny hotel.

HOTEL ABTEI
Owner: Fritz Lay
Abteistrasse 14
20149 Hamburg, Germany
Tel: (040) 442905 Fax: (040) 449820
12 rooms
Double: DM 350–450 Suite: DM 450–490
Open all year
Credit cards: MC, VS
Restaurant closed Sundays & Mondays
In the Harvestehude section, NW of Alster Lake

Hamburg is the hub of northern Germany. Far more than an important seaport and business center, it is a city of great beauty offering a rich and varied social and cultural menu. Just north of the city center you find Alster Lake: with this expanse of water at its front and a tranquil garden at its rear, the Hotel Prem occupies a handsome downtown Hamburg location. What were originally two large townhouses were converted into a small hotel by Herr and Frau Prem more than 75 years ago. The downstairs is small: a lounge area leads to a bar and, beyond, an airy restaurant overlooks the garden. The restaurant, decorated in shades of beige and white and with arrangements of fresh flowers, brightens even the gloomiest Hamburg day. In summer the pretty garden is set with tables and chairs for outside dining. Accented with fine antiques, the bedrooms retain their high ceilings which give a spacious feeling—a few lovely rooms even have their original ornate plasterwork ceilings. The staff speak excellent English and really care that you enjoy your holiday. You can easily walk to the heart of Hamburg, and, if you like to travel by boat, one of the ferry stops is very close by. Also, only steps from your front door are the walking paths that encircle the lake. As an added bonus, the hotel provides discounted rates for guests staying on weekends.

HOTEL PREM
Manager: Ulrich Voit
An der Alster 9
20099 Hamburg, Germany
Tel:(040) 241726 Fax: (040) 2803851
59 rooms, 3 suites
Double: DM 250–370 Suite: DM 425–610
Open all year
Credit cards: all major
Restaurant open daily
N of city center, on SE shore of Alster Lake

This guide usually features small, intimate inns rather than grand hotels, but sometimes a hotel is so lovely that we feel compelled to make an exception. Such is definitely the case with the Vier Jahreszeiten. Although a large hotel, it maintains the quality and ambiance of a small inn. If you don't mind spending the money for a very deluxe hotel and want to be in the heart of Hamburg, the Vier Jahreszeiten is a wonderful choice: it is positioned proudly on the banks of the Alster Lake near the picturesque boats that ply the rivers and canals, and minutes from Hamburg's elegant shops. From the moment you enter into the exquisite lobby you are surrounded by the warmth and charm of a lovely country home. A dramatic hallway stretches beyond the reception counter with an exquisite Persian carpet in shades of gold and cream reflecting the color scheme of a gorgeous tapestry dominating the end of the room. To the left of the reception area is a cozy, club-like lounge with mellow paneling, a grandfather clock, lovely fresh flowers, and comfortable chairs and couches. Several restaurants offer a delicious variety of dining options, from casual to more elaborate meals. As you might expect, the Vier Jahreszeiten's guestrooms are beautiful and the service refined.

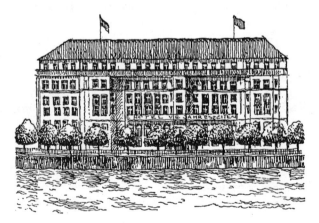

VIER JAHRESZEITEN
Manager: Stefan Simkovics
Neuer Jungfernstieg 9–14
20354 Hamburg, Germany
Tel: (040) 34940 Fax: (040) 3494602
158 rooms, 12 suites
Double DM 380–595 Suite: DM 990–1,600
Open all year
Credit cards: all major
Restaurant open daily
On the SW shore of Alster Lake

The Hufnagel-Ullrich family, who own one of our favorite hotels, the Krone in nearby Assmanshausen, offer deluxe accommodation at the Kronen Schlösschen. This attractive mansion, painted white with brown trim, is set in gardens across the highway from the Rhine. The Kronen Schlösschen has a whimsical look, with jaunty towers topped by peaked onion domes and a stepped roofline. From the courtyard, you enter into a pretty foyer with ornate stucco design and marble floors. A staircase leads up to the guestrooms, each one absolutely stunning in decor. Your choice of rooms depends upon what style appeals to you—some are smartly tailored in dark colors, others are spring-like with a pastel color scheme, some are modern, some antique. One of my favorites, mini-suite 29, has pale-yellow wallpaper, rich, natural-silk lemon-toned draperies, soft green carpet, and comfortable, off-white matching sofas. No matter what room you choose, you will find glamorous marble bathrooms, truly fit for a king. The Kronen Schlösschen has two excellent restaurants: one an elegant gourmet dining room, the other, The Bistro, a less formal, pub-like room enclosed on two sides with windows. It is less than an hour's drive from the Frankfurt airport, a convenient distance after a tiring transatlantic flight. Hattenheim is on the Rhine just west of Eltville.

KRONEN SCHLÖSSCHEN
Owner: Family Hufnagel-Ullrich
Rheinallee
65347 Hattenheim-Eltville, Germany
Tel: (06723) 640 Fax: (06723) 7663
8 rooms, 10 suites
Double: DM 294–368 Suite: DM 404–728
Open all year
Credit cards: all major
Restaurant open daily
39 km NW of Frankfurt airport
12 km W of Wiesbaden

The Weinhaus "Zum Krug" is located in Hattenheim, a tiny wine town along the Rhine, just west of Eltville. The village has many very old buildings with character, but only a few of them have been restored to reflect their historic past. Happily, the Weinhaus "Zum Krug," dating back to 1720, is one of them. The first floor is painted white and has dark green shutters framing leaded windows. The timbered second floor has a fairy-tale quality: it is painted dark green, merrily set off by an intricate design of gold grape vines. To add the finishing touch to this quaint house, bright red geraniums overflow from green boxes below each of the windows. There is no doubt about what awaits the guest within—suspended over the entrance is a jug of wine, enclosed in a wreath of grapes (as might be guessed, the restaurant has its own winery). Inside, the decor is appropriately rustic with a beamed ceiling, small tables with wooden chairs, Oriental throw rugs, and a dark-green tiled stove along the wall. This is not a deluxe hotel, nor is it meant to be. Upstairs there are eight guestrooms which, although simple, all have their own private bathrooms. For a reasonably priced place to stay along the Rhine, Weinhaus "Zum Krug" makes an attractive choice. It is less than an hour's drive from the Frankfurt airport, a convenient distance after a tiring transatlantic flight.

WEINHAUS "ZUM KRUG"
Owner: Josef Laufer
Hauptstrasse 34
65347 Hattenheim-Eltville, Germany
Tel: (06723) 99680 Fax: (06723) 996825
8 rooms
Double: DM 200–220
Closed January & last 2 weeks July
Credit cards: all major
Restaurant closed Sunday evenings & Mondays
39 km NW of Frankfurt airport
12 km W of Wiesbaden

The 300-year-old Zur Backmulde enjoys a quiet location just off the main pedestrian street of Heidelberg's picturesque "old town." This lovely small and atmospheric establishment offers an intimate restaurant and 13 bedrooms. From the street, guests pass under the old stone arched doorway to enter the softly lit restaurant filled with fresh flowers, antique pieces, old mirrors, photos, and paintings from Heidelberg. The restaurant, decorated in tones of red and green, offers excellent food in a cozy atmosphere. The hotel section faces its own quiet, enclosed courtyard (a convenient, free parking area for guests). A staircase, whose dark-blue walls are brightened by an overhead skylight, leads up one floor to the reception area and the breakfast room. With new ownership, the entire hotel has been totally renovated. A blue color scheme prevails throughout, including a patterned carpet of excellent quality. Each of the bedrooms is attractively decorated in pretty, blue floral draperies (with white sheer curtains beneath) and color-coordinating fabrics on the bedcovers (rooms 5 and 12 are special favorites). The bathrooms are not large, but each is brand new and spotlessly clean. With its recent face-lift, the Zur Backmulde has emerged as our favorite small hotel in Heidelberg.

ZUR BACKMULDE
Owners: Bernhard Zepf & Alex Schneider
Schiffgasse 11
69117 Heidelberg, Germany
Tel: (06221) 53660 Fax: (06221) 536660
13 rooms
Double: DM 155–165
Open all year
Credit cards: all major
Restaurant closed Sundays
80 km S of Frankfurt

Heidelberg is a romantic, beguiling old university town with one pedestrian street, the Hauptstrasse, the dynamic heart of the action. It is here that you will find the Romantik Hotel Zum Ritter St. Georg occupying one of the best locations in town. The hotel's stately façade dates from 1592 when the master builder, Carolus Belier, imprinted the gold sign still hanging above the door. Official records show the building served as a town hall for a decade before it became the Hotel Zum Ritter. Because of its impressive façade and central location, the lovely paneled dining room is popular with the throngs of tourists that flock to Heidelberg-this gives the hotel a very bustling atmosphere in the evenings. The hotel has been extended to the rear and in the newer wing you find ten spacious, modern bedrooms with fitted furniture and floor-to-ceiling draperies. The remainder of the rooms vary from little single rooms to large bedrooms overlooking the busy main street—room 100 stands out as a favorite amongst the larger bedrooms. Like several of the bedrooms, it has a not-too-charming old-world decor (stay here for the location, not for the decor). If you are driving, follow signs to Parkhaus 12. From there it is only a few blocks to the hotel.

ROMANTIK HOTEL ZUM RITTER ST. GEORG
Owners: Margaret & Georg Kuchelmeister
Hauptstrasse 178
69117 Heidelberg, Germany
Tel: (06221) 24272 Fax: (06221) 12683
39 rooms
Double: DM 245–325 Suite: DM 350–385
Open all year
Credit cards: all major
Restaurant open daily
80 km S of Frankfurt

Staying in a castle almost always guarantees an adventure, but not always a comfortable night's accommodation. All too often the knights in armor are ever present, but not the firm mattress and the welcome hot and cold running water. Near the Neckar River there are numerous castle hotels. One of these, Schloss Heinsheim (in the von Racknitz family for over 350 years), is especially appealing because of its excellent accommodations and outstanding cuisine. The hotel is surrounded by a forest and has all the ambiance of a large country estate. Horses frequently frolic in the fields visible from your bedroom window, enhancing the "country mood." There is a small circular pool that is favored by children and a lovely terraced area set with tables for enjoying meals outside in warm weather. There are two attractive restaurants: one is in a rustic decor and one is a bit more modern. The bedrooms are beautifully furnished with fine fabrics and many antiques—one of my favorites, room 15, is especially attractive. There is a small, baroque chapel on the grounds and on weekends you might well have the fun of witnessing a wedding celebration. Note: The town of Heinsheim is quite small and not on many maps. From Bad Rappenau (which you can find on most maps) go east for 5 kilometers to Heinsheim (signposted to Gundelsheim, a town beyond Heinsheim).

SCHLOSS HEINSHEIM
Owner: Monica Freifrau von Racknitz
Gundelsheimer Strasse 36
74906 Heinsheim, Bad-Rappenau, Germany
Tel: (07264) 1045 Fax: (07264) 4208
42 rooms, 1 suite
Double: DM 160–300 Suite: DM 480
Closed December 21 to end of February
Credit cards: all major
Restaurant closed Mondays & Tuesdays
74 km N of Stuttgart, 55 km E of Heidelberg
Gast im Schloss

Overlooking the village green in the center of Hinterzarten, two traditional chalet homes form the core of the luxurious Hotel Reppert. This small resort, run by dedicated brothers, Thomas and Volker Reppert, typifies the very best of small luxury German hotels. Volker ensures that guests are well taken care of while Thomas is in charge of the kitchen, making sure that guests are well fed. Plan your day's activities in the luxurious lobby lounge where elegant chairs are arranged into little groups facing the room-wide view of a little lake and pastoral countryside. Bedrooms are traditionally furnished and each is accompanied by a spacious bathroom. The most impressive feature of the hotel is its luxurious health club. Beyond the saunas, Jacuzzis, and small swimming pool lies the elegant salt-water swimming pool. After aquatic disportment, soak up the soothing warmth of the surrounding heated tile benches or relax in an aromatherapy room. I suggest you choose your room by temperature rather that scent—the 60°C lemon room was too hot for me while the cooler herb room was just perfect. Most European guests come for a week—after a day you will wish you had. Volker offers escorted tours of the Black Forest byways in his eight-seater mini-bus—perfect if you want to take a break from driving or have traveled here by train.

HOTEL REPPERT   **NEW**
Owners: Annette, Thomas & Volker Reppert
Am Adlerweg 21–23
79856 Hinterzarten, Germany
Tel: (07652) 12080 Fax: (07652) 120811
34 rooms, 5 suites
Double: DM 238–334 Suite: DM 360–450
Open all year
Credit cards: all major
Restaurant open daily
161 km SW of Stuttgart, 26 km SE of Freiburg

Hinterzarten is a small Black Forest resort famous for its healthy air where people come for family holidays with long country walks or cross-country skiing. Set beside the village green you find the Sassenhof. If your arrival is in the early afternoon, you will most likely find Irmgard Pfeiffer supervising the cleaning and presentation of each of her guestrooms. Everything is spic-and-span and well cared for. An extremely dynamic woman, Irmgard Pfeiffer strives to achieve the atmosphere of a private home with the advantages of very personalized service. From the attractive breakfast room you can see Hinterzarten's ski jump. Breakfast is the only meal served but you can enjoy tea in the afternoons and each room is thoughtfully provided with dishes and freshly pressed linen. Drinks and bread are conveniently available upon request and guests are encouraged to buy their own meats and cheeses to prepare their own light suppers or lunches. The halls that lead to the bedrooms are warmed by soft lighting, handsome prints, red carpet covered in Oriental throw rugs, and heavy wooden doors and doorways. Each room is individual in its decor but all are tastefully decorated. For relaxation there is an attractive indoor swimming pool.

SASSENHOF
Owner: Irmgard Pfeiffer
Alderweg 17
79856 Hinterzarten, Germany
Tel: (07652) 1515 Fax: (07652) 484
16 rooms, 6 suites
Double: DM 148–188 Suite: DM 196–206
Closed November to mid-December
Credit cards: none accepted
No restaurant: breakfast only
161 km SW of Stuttgart, 26 km SE of Freiburg

High above the beautiful Mosel valley is one of those rare, perfect hideaways—the Historische Schlossmühle. The Historische Schlossmühle was once an old mill. Bedrooms in the old mill (named after country animals) are stocked with thoughtful little extras that make a stay memorable—proper sewing kits and hair spray. The four new rooms in the granary are equally as lovely. There is no need to splurge on a suite—standard doubles (especially those overlooking the back pond) are most appealing. Rüdiger and Anneliese Liller are your charming hosts—Anneliese is responsible for the creative decor. A little corner room honors Napoleon who, so the story goes, sold the mill in 1804 to raise money. The enterprising new owner had the foresight to realize that once Napoleon had left, the original owner would reclaim his property, so to guard against this happening, he had the mill taken apart and erected 25 kilometers away in this quiet green valley outside the village of Horbruch. It is a little complicated getting to the hotel: a detailed map will certainly aid you in finding the Rhaunen turnoff from road 327 that runs to the south of the Mosel. You will find the Historische Schlossmühle a short drive from the junction, about half a mile beyond the tiny village of Horbruch. (In 1996 the Lillers plan to convert a nearby farmhouse into country-style accommodation.)

HOTEL HISTORISCHE SCHLOSSMÜHLE
Owners: Anneliese & Rüdiger Liller
55483 Horbruch-Hunsruck, Germany
Tel: (06543) 4041 Fax: (06543) 3178
10 rooms, 1 suite
Double: DM 198–265 Suite: DM 295
Open all year
Credit cards: all major
Restaurant closed Mondays
63 km NE of Trier, 20 km E of Bernkastel-Kues
Gast im Schloss

Just 30 kilometers from the fascinating city of Würzburg, the Zehntkeller, Romantik Hotel and wine house, is also convenient to the wine region at the foot of the Schwan mountains. Once a tax-collection point for the church, and hence a most unpopular building, the Zehntkeller (made into a hotel in 1910) is now the chosen destination of many. Iphofen is a small quiet village and it is amazing to find the traffic coming and going from the inn: the specialties of the menu attract diners from outlying regions. The restaurant is actually a number of rooms on the first floor and serviced by gracious girls dressed in attractive dirndls. The hotel rooms found in the main building above the restaurant are all lovely and well appointed with modern bathrooms. Single rooms are found on the top floor. A new wing of rooms has been added in an annex that backs onto a walled garden to accommodate guests who want to linger for a stay of more than a few days.

ROMANTIK HOTEL ZEHNTKELLER
Owner: Heinrich Seufert
Bahnhofstrasse 12
97346 Iphofen, Germany
Tel: (09323) 3062 Fax: (09323) 1519
47 rooms
Double: DM 150–230 Suite: DM 300
Closed last 2 weeks of January
Credit cards: all major
Restaurant open daily
72 km NW of Nürnberg, 30 km SE of Würzburg

Zum Goldenen Pflug (the golden plough) began life as the village hotel: now the hotel is larger than the village. Zum Goldenen Pflug encompasses the original inn with vast extensions, an adjacent farmhouse and farm buildings, and several contemporary buildings set in grassy grounds with underground tunnels connecting the whole complex together. The charms of the old inn with its adorable little country-style restaurants remain but now you have all the facilities of a first-class resort with the most glamorous indoor swimming pool (complete with rocky waterfall and exotic murals) and facilities for massages, facials, saunas, and the like. For the more active, tennis, golf, riding, and exhilarating sailing on Bavaria's largest lake, the Chiemsee, are close at hand. Bedrooms range from smartly contemporary (in the new wings) to luxuriously country (in the old inn and farmhouse). Ising is perfectly located for making forays into the mountains, taking a day trip to Salzburg, or visiting Ludwig's decadent palace, the unfinished Schloss Herrenchiemsee. Ising is located on the northeastern shore of the Chiemsee between Seebruck and Chieming. Take the Grabenstätt exit from the Munich to Salzburg autobahn.

ZUM GOLDENEN PFLUG
Manager: Christian Glaser
Kirchberg 3, Ising
83339 Chieming, Germany
Tel: (08667) 790 Fax: (08667) 79432
94 rooms, 6 suites
Double: DM 244–394 Suite: DM 1,200
Open all year
Credit cards: AX, VS
Restaurant open daily
104 km SE of Munich, near the Chiemsee

If you admire dramatic settings, the Parkhotel Wasserburg Anholt will certainly impress you. At first glance, this huge red-brick castle appears to be floating in its own lake. The hotel entrance is, of course, over a proper drawbridge and through an arched tower. Inside, the castle has a sophisticated aura, somewhat commercial, but pleasing. There is a pretty lounge where light-pine furniture, floral-print chairs, and a fireplace provide an inviting refuge. Another cozy spot is found in the rustic "Pferdestall" bar. The formal dining room is decorated in pastel tones and offers refined dining illuminated by candlelight and glowing chandeliers. There is a less elegant, but still very inviting, restaurant on a lower level which has a sunny terrace where tables and umbrellas are set right out over the water. Guest bedrooms are contemporary in style, but tastefully decorated in muted colors. The tower suite has a canopy bed, pretty floral wallpaper, and a crystal chandelier. Part of the castle is open to the public as a museum and offers beautiful examples of German and Italian master painters from the 17th and 18th centuries, Chinese porcelains from the 18th and 19th centuries, and Flemish tapestries from the 18th and 19th centuries, all displayed in historic rooms among period furniture. Outdoors, a large park including an 18-hole golf course surrounds the lake and castle.

PARKHOTEL WASSERBURG ANHOLT
Manager: Heinz Brune
46419 Isselburg, Germany
Tel: (02874) 4590 Fax: (02874) 4035
28 rooms
Double: DM 220–290 Suite: DM 315–390
Open all year
Credit cards: MC, VS
Restaurant closed Mondays
Near Dutch border, 13 km SW of Bocholt
Gast im Schloss

The introduction to this marvelous castle hotel is first an expanse of lawn, intricate turrets, and then an old timbered courtyard. Up a flight of stairs, the hotel entrance is a majestic banquet hall. The dining room is very regal. Take notice of a handsome, intricately inlaid door, lovely flower arrangements, and the crest of the family above both entrances. The present family has lived in the castle as far back as 927. Herr Bircks, both manager and chef, is a charming man, exuding pride in the castle and offering a warm welcome for each guest. The breakfast room looks out through large windows onto the lush surrounding countryside. Climb a steep staircase in the direction of the bedchambers onto a terrace that also enjoys an expansive view and is used in warmer months for dining. Down a timbered hallway, the bedrooms are all named for renowned actors and many overlook either the valley or the weathered tiles of another castle wing. The least expensive rooms are those without a private bathroom. The highlight of the adjoining armaments museum is an iron hand, unique because of its moveable parts. In summer months the courtyard becomes a stage for afternoon and evening plays.

BURGHOTEL GÖTZENBURG
Owner: Family von Berlichingen
Manager: Jüngen Bircks
74249 Jagsthausen, Germany
Tel: (07943) 2222 Fax: (07943) 8200
16 rooms, 1 suite
Double: DM 100–175 Suite: DM 260
Open March to November
Credit cards: all major
Restaurant open daily
82 km N of Stuttgart

Ambling from village to village on Die Deutsche Weinstrasse (The German Wine Road), with stops for wine-tasting at taverns and vineyards, is great fun. A most appropriate place for such pursuits is the Weinkastell "Zum Weissen Ross" that dates back to 1553, though most of what you see today as a lovely traditional building dates only from 1958. I particularly admired the timbered exterior where each vertical timber is supported by a colorfully painted carved figure and the beams are carved and painted with flowers. The same traditional craftsmanship continues in the interior where the dining room has a fan-vaulted ceiling set above a traditional tiled stove. The hunters' corner with its almost circular seating beneath an intricate wood ceiling is a snug place to dine. Jutta has added her own touches—over 900 ducks of all shapes and sizes. The bedrooms all have oak furniture in either a rustic modern or a traditional style—several have four-poster beds and one has two single alcove beds head to toe. All have modern white-tile bathrooms or shower rooms. Brother Philippi carries on the family tradition of winemaking across the courtyard. He is one of 35 vintners in the village whom you can visit to sample their produce. Other popular activities include bike riding on paved paths through the vineyards and walking on miles of well marked footpaths in the Pfälzer Wald (forest).

WEINKASTELL "ZUM WEISSEN ROSS"   **NEW**
Owners: Jutta & Norbert Kohnke
Weinstrasse 80/82
67169 Kallstadt, Germany
Tel: (06322) 5033 Fax: (06322) 8640
13 rooms, 1 suite
Double: DM 150–180 Suite: DM 180–200
Closed January to mid-February
Credit cards: AX, MC
Restaurant closed Mondays & Tuesdays
26 km W of Mannheim, 37 km E of Kaiserslautern

The lush Ruhr region is beautiful. Especially appealing is the landscape around Kettwig. Here, far from the smokestacks of the industrial area, you find the Schloss Hugenpoet, an imposing fortress surrounded by a water-filled moat where large carp swim lazily. There has been a fortification on this site for over one thousand years, and during violent periods of history several castles on the site were destroyed. The present structure has existed since 1650. The interior, rich in tradition, presents a castle in tiptop condition. The lobby is dominated by an impressive black-marble staircase; a grouping of fine furniture stands in front of the huge carved fireplace, while the surrounding walls host a picture gallery of fine oil paintings. This is a grand castle where the bedchambers were given spacious proportions. Many are furnished with authentic 17th-century furniture. Downstairs, the dining rooms are baronial in their size, each dominated by a grand carved fireplace. Boasting famous chefs and gourmet cuisine, the dining rooms command a large loyal, local following while still giving impeccable service to the hotel residents. The Schloss Hugenpoet is a member of the prestigious Relais & Chateaux group of outstanding hotels.

SCHLOSS HUGENPOET
Owner: Jürgen Neumann
August-Thyssen Strasse 51
45219 Essen (Kettwig), Germany
Tel: (02054) 12040 Fax: (02054) 120450
19 rooms
Double: DM 330–490 Suite: DM 790
Closed first week in January
Credit cards: AX, MC
Restaurant open daily
Between Wuppertal & Mülheim, 11 km SW of Essen
Relais & Chateaux

Our visit to the Schloss Hotel Kronberg coincided with that of visiting delegates and bedrooms were closed off for security reasons. However, based on the few rooms I saw and the sumptuous sophistication of the public rooms, I feel comfortable in recommending the Schloss Hotel Kronberg as an excellent choice for a hotel. Northwest of Frankfurt, a convenient half-hour drive by the autobahn from Frankfurt airport, this was once a gathering place for European royalty and most of the ruling monarchs were at one time guests here. Today it is a member of the prestigious Relais & Chateaux group, an indication of its outstanding attributes. The Schloss Hotel Kronberg has a number of grand halls, impressive with their high ceilings and adorning tapestries. A typical English afternoon tea is served on weekends in the stately library in front of its large stone fireplace (it is advisable to book a table in advance). The adjoining Blue Parlor is frequently reserved for private functions and luncheons. At the end of the hall a beautiful, wood-paneled dining room achieves intimacy and grandeur in its decor. The Schloss Hotel Kronberg was built originally in 1888 as a private home and has been offering rooms to guests for over 50 years.

SCHLOSS HOTEL KRONBERG
Manager: Hartmut Althoff
Hainstrasse 25
61476 Kronberg in Taunus, Germany
Tel: (06173) 70101 Fax: (06173) 701267
58 rooms
Double: DM 493–708 Suite: DM 948–2,028
Open all year
Credit cards: all major
Restaurant open daily
17 km NW of Frankfurt
Relais & Chateaux

If you are a castle connoisseur, the Schlosshotel Lembeck is worth a detour—it is a real winner. This 12th-century, moated castle is awesome in size yet not in the least foreboding as some German castles tend to be. Somehow, as you approach over the moat and through the gate, this massive building of mellow, cut stone and dark-gray slate roof with perky, pointed, cap-like domed towers is irresistible. The castle is also a sightseeing attraction—the museum and grounds are open to the public, but at the gate just say you are a guest of the hotel and there is no charge to enter. A door in the gate leads down to the small restaurant which is also where you register. The restaurant is informal and very inviting with a vaulted brick ceiling, wooden chairs and tables, soft lighting from rustic chandeliers, and a cozy fireplace. In the summertime, snacks are also served outside on the lawn overlooking the moat. The guestrooms are located in the rear wing of the castle. Splurge on one of the best rooms and you will be treated to antique furniture and an ambiance of days gone by. The bridal suite (Hochzeitszimmer mit Himmelbett) has a large canopied bed, tapestry chairs, and windows looking out over the countryside. The Schlosshotel Lembeck is surrounded with lovely grounds and woods where kilometers of footpaths meander beneath the trees.

SCHLOSSHOTEL LEMBECK
Owner: Josef Selting
46286 Dorsten, Lembeck, Germany
Tel: (02369) 7213 Fax: (02369) 77370
10 rooms
Double: DM 118–198
Open all year
Credit cards: MC, VS
Restaurant open daily
10 km N of Dorsten, 29 km N of Essen

Just inside Bavaria, this delightful island is the Bodensee's (Lake Constance) most scenic resort, joined to the mainland by railway and road. The Hotel Lindauer Hof, sitting right on the harbor—a perfect location—began life in the 1600s as two granaries for storing oats awaiting transportation across the Bodensee. It is owned by the energetic Wimpissinger family and Claudia Wimpissinger is responsible for the smart modern decor which gives a welcoming feeling to the public rooms and a restful one to the bedrooms. Pale-lemon walls contrast with cool-gray terrazzo floors in the appealing ground-floor lounge and bar where little tables and chairs spill out on to the quayside. Up the broad staircase you come to the restaurant which specializes in locally caught fish. If it's a warm evening, dine on the terrace overlooking the harbor and distant shore. While all the bedrooms are most attractive, two special rooms command the highest tariff. Santis (room 207), decorated in jade green, has a lovely paneled pine ceiling with a large crest in the center and a separate sitting room with views to the lake. Augustin (room 401) is set under the eaves and its French windows open up to a large terrace, perfect for sitting and watching the activity of the harbor below. If traveling by car, make a reservation for a parking space and have the hotel's brochure in hand as a map directs you to the hotel's back entrance.

HOTEL LINDAUER HOF   **NEW**
Owners: Gert, Karin & Claudia Wimpissinger
Seepromenade
88131 Lindau, Germany
Tel: (08382) 4064 Fax: (08382) 24203
25 rooms
Double: DM 205–325
Open all year
Credit cards: all major
Restaurant open daily March 1 to January 6
Island on N shore of the Bodensee

An absolutely fascinating niche in Germany is the Spreewald, an area midway between Dresden and Berlin where the River Spree fans out into a spider web of waterways bordered by quaint houses, many accessible only by boat. If you plan to overnight in the area, we heartily recommend a small castle which has been converted into a deluxe hotel. When we stayed at Schloss Lübbenau in 1990, it was a drab, dismal hotel with rooms so bedraggled we felt we could not include it in our guide. However, with the reunification, the Lynar family reclaimed the property which has belonged to their family since 1621 but which had been taken out of their hands in World War II. During their absence, the castle became dilapidated, being used as a school then later a cheap hotel, but now it has resumed its former glory. The restoration is complete and guestrooms which were quite dismal are now bright and cheerful. Italian, antique-style furniture gives a pleasing traditional look, enhanced by fine-quality carpets and drapes in restful tones of green. The most expensive bedrooms are very spacious (request one like room 210) while the least expensive rooms appear small and boxy by comparison. Countess Lynar's hobby is dried-flower arranging, and she is personally responsible for the pretty floral displays in the hotel.

SCHLOSS LÜBBENAU
Owner: Graf zu Lynar
Manager: Eckhard Laabs
Schlossbezirk 6
03222 Lübbenau, Germany
Tel: (03542) 8730 Fax: (03542) 873666
46 rooms, 6 suites
Double: DM 200–270 Suite: DM 290
Open all year
Credit cards: all major
Restaurant open daily
Midway between Berlin & Dresden

Hotels

Base yourself here for explorations of the Spreewald, an intriguing area criss-crossed by canals leading to traditional Slavic Sorb villages. Erica and Irvine Kuck have done a masterful job of converting what was for over 150 years the town's apostolic church into a lovely little hotel. With a craftsman's eye, Irvine has chosen warm cherry wood inlaid with white bird's-eye maple for all the hotel's woodwork, even the little circular dining-room tables and the art-deco-style bar. While neither Erica nor Irvine speaks English, their welcoming smiles and warm personalities transcend language barriers and their manager Kathrin Schwertfeger speaks excellent English. Up the broad staircase you find the 12 delightful bedrooms. The one with most character (room 14) contains lovely, delicate, French style furniture. However, the remaining bedrooms are equally delightful, with white walls, blue carpet, and Italian-style, white-wood furniture. All the bath or shower rooms are in gray marble. In the basement you find a sauna, Turkish bath, solarium, and relaxing room where the floor is heated and you lie on wooden slat beds while listening to a tumbling waterfall. On warm evenings enjoy a beer and dinner on the sheltered patio. The hotel is signposted from the autobahn, but if you miss the signs, you will find the back entrance to the hotel just down Bahnhofstrasse from the train station.

TURM HOTEL   **NEW**
Owner: Family Kuck
Nach Stottoff 1
03222 Lübbenau, Germany
Tel: (03542) 89100 Fax: (03542) 891047
12 rooms
Double: DM 200
Open all year
Credit cards: all major
Restaurant open daily
Midway between Berlin & Dresden

The Hotel Jensen enjoys a choice location just across the river from the dramatic walled entrance to the town of Lübeck. The hotel is one of many tall, narrow buildings lining the canal, and, like its neighbors, this slim and appealing structure has the characteristic steep roof that forms a "stair step" gabled effect in the front. The main thrust of the Jensen seems to be the dining rooms: there are "The Cabin," the "Yacht Room," the "Fireside Room" and the "Patrician's Room," each with its own personality. The bedrooms are located up a stairway leading from the reception area. They are small and do not exhibit much character in their decor, yet they are clean and adequately furnished. The rooms in the front of the building overlook the canal and the twin-towered Holstentor (Holsten Gate), affording good views of the boats and quayside activity. Although these front rooms face the busy street, they are very quiet due to well insulated windows. Handily, the pier for the ferry excursion boats (a must for enjoying the colorful town of Lübeck) is located just across the street from the hotel. Recommended mainly for travelers seeking a convenient location from which to enjoy Lübeck, the Jensen is a very modest hotel offering friendly management and a fun place to stay.

HOTEL JENSEN
Owner: Wilfried Rahlff-Petersson
Manager: Dietrich Bergmann
Am der Obertrave 4–5
23552 Lübeck, Germany
Tel: (0451) 71646 Fax: (0451) 73386
42 rooms
Double: DM 170–195 Suite: DM 250–300
Open all year
Credit cards: all major
Restaurant open daily
66 km NE of Hamburg, 92 km SE of Kiel

The Hotel Kaiserhof is located just across the canal and a short walk from the historic old city of Lübeck. The hotel is a clever combination of two stately 19th-century homes that have been joined with a central core serving as lobby and reception area. The hotel has grown over the years and now has amenities such as a large indoor swimming pool and sauna, yet it still retains the homespun ambiance and warmth of a small hotel. This homey feeling is undoubtedly due to the owner, Ruth Klemm, who cares deeply about the comfort of each guest. Her staff is carefully chosen and taught to give "service with a heart," thus making this a hotel with a special level of service. The reception area is light and airy with Oriental carpets setting off the polished marble floor. The intimate lounge has a magnificent sculpted ceiling, fully restored including the 24-carat gilt paint, yet this room's pièce de résistance is a superb, intricately formed Meissen porcelain fireplace. Each of the bedrooms is individually decorated and the ones I saw were spacious and filled with light from large windows. The Hotel Kaiserhof is not a showplace of antique furniture or a decorator's dream, yet these two lovely old buildings are beautiful and Frau Klemm has gone to great efforts to restore all of the architectural details to their original elegance.

HOTEL KAISERHOF
Owner: Ruth Klemm
Kronsforder Allee 11–13
23560 Lübeck, Germany
Tel: (0451) 791011 Fax: (0451) 795083
70 rooms
Double: DM 185–235 Suite: DM 350–400
Open all year
Credit cards: all major
No restaurant: breakfast only
66 km NE of Hamburg, 92 km SE of Kiel

The tiny village of Marienthal is little more than the Haus Elmer, an antique shop, and a craft shop clustered around what was once a thriving Augustinian monastery. The hotel is a clever blend of an old and a new building. Bedrooms in the old house are smaller and exude country charm, while those in the new section are larger and decorated with new, country-style furniture. There are two especially romantic rooms with old, four-poster beds making them favorites with honeymooners. There are several dining rooms: one is on the upper story of the new wing and has delightful views of the surrounding countryside through its large picture windows, another is paneled and cozy. The surrounding sky-wide landscapes are perfect for cycling: cyclists pedal easily along, enjoying the country sounds and smells lost to speeding motorists. The hotel has plenty of bicycles for you to use during your stay. If you prefer to venture farther afield, the hotel offers a four-night cycling holiday in conjunction with two other hotels in the area. The package includes bicycles, maps, accommodations, and the transportation of your luggage from hotel to hotel.

ROMANTIK HOTEL HAUS ELMER
Owners: Marlies & Karl-Heinz Elmer
An der Klosterkirche 12
46499 Hamminkeln-Marienthal, Germany
Tel: (02856) 2041 Fax: (02856) 2061
31 rooms
Double: DM 190–240 Suite: DM 200–260
Open all year
Credit cards: MC, VS
Restaurant open daily
100 km NW of Cologne, near Wesel

Michael Gilowsky is especially proud that the Gasthof Zum Bären, a picture-perfect, 15th-century inn, appears on the DM 20 note. The hotel is in the heart of Meersburg, an absolutely stunning little medieval town hugging the shore of Lake Constance. In the Gilowsky family for five generations, the Zum Bären is now run smoothly by Michael (who is also the chef). Upstairs, a treasure chest of bedrooms awaits: our room had a beautifully carved wooden ceiling, country-pine furniture, dainty print wallpaper, and lace curtains. Some rooms have old painted furniture and all have antique touches and pretty wallpapers. We were pleased to find that—unusual in a *gasthof*—every bedroom came equipped with telephone and color television as well as a snug shower or bathroom. Downstairs, the two cozy dining rooms are decorated with pewter plates and typical blue stoneware filling shelves above carved wooden furniture, fresh flowers, and comfy window benches with pretty print pillows. A wood parquet floor, low, beamed ceiling, and white tiled stove add to the pervading feeling of *gemütlichkeit*. Both dining rooms contain only large tables for six to eight persons. This is purposely done to encourage guests to share a table, perhaps some wine, and certainly good conversation. The gasthof has its own parking garage nearby.

GASTHOF ZUM BÄREN
Owner: Michael Gilowsky
Marktplatz 11
88709 Meersburg, Germany
Tel: (07532) 43220 Fax: (07532) 432244
17 rooms
Double: DM 140–150
Closed December, January & February
Credit cards: none accepted
Restaurant closed Mondays
170 km SE of Stuttgart, 31 km SW of Ravensburg

The Hotel Weinstube Löwen, located in the heart of the pedestrian section of the fairy-tale-like walled town of Meersburg, sits across the street from one of our favorite small inns, the Hotel Bären. Both adorable hotels are similar in ambiance: dining rooms filled with charm and guestrooms which are simple, but very comfortable. The Hotel Löwen's appeal is immediate: you are captivated by the wisteria-laden, deep-salmon-colored façade, green shutters, and steep gabled roof. You step inside to an attractive reception area where you will probably be greeted warmly by the pretty and ever-so-gracious Frau Bauer, the front desk manager. The owner, Sigfrid Fischer, is also exceptionally friendly, and although he speaks little English, his warmth of welcome crosses all language barriers. The romantic dining room with its low, beamed ceiling and cozy tables set with fresh flowers serves marvelous food, including many fish specialties from adjacent Lake Constance. The guestrooms are modern in decor. The one with the most personality is number 36, tucked up under the eaves with the gears of an antique hoist (used in former days to bring up goods from the street) incorporated into the design. The hotel will give you an entry permit for the nearby public parking garage.

HOTEL WEINSTUBE LÖWEN
Owner: Sigfrid Fischer
Manager: Frau Bauer
Am Marktplatz 2
88709 Meersburg, Germany
Tel: (07532) 43040 Fax: (07532) 430410
21 rooms
Double: DM 150–190
Open all year
Credit cards: MC, VS
Restaurant closed Wednesdays November to April
191 km SE of Stuttgart, on Lake Constance

On the left bend of the Main river, Miltenberg is a charming mix of cobblestoned streets and sloping slate and tile roofs. Much of the darling timbered façade with the hotel's name emblazoned upon it belongs to the adjacent restaurant—the actual hotel is two or three doors away. A small reception area is found on the ground floor with a wide, marble spiral staircase leading up to the bedrooms. All of the old-world characteristics of the 400-year-old building have been preserved and Cilly and Werner Jost have done a very nice job of adding snug bath/shower rooms to each bedroom. Beds are topped by plump down comforters and many of the bedrooms contain some very nice antique furniture. The country decor is further enhanced by handsome antiques and Oriental rugs cover the hardwood floors. Breakfast is served on the third floor. Easter morning we were greeted with a stunning breakfast setting: tables were laid with fresh linens, candles, and flowers, and thoughtfully wrapped Easter gifts were set out for all. Fresh jams, rolls, meats, cheese, juice, and eggs were served and Frau Jost was there to welcome and seat her guests. Hauptstrasse is the narrow, cobbled street that runs parallel to the river frontage road: hotel guests can drive their car to the front door to unload their luggage.

HOTEL ZUM RIESEN
Owners: Cilly & Werner Jost
Hauptstrasse 97
63897 Miltenberg, Germany
Tel: (09371) 3644
15 rooms
Double: DM 115–185
Closed December to mid-March
Credit cards: none
No restaurant: breakfast only
160 km SE of Frankfurt, 41 km S of Aschaffenburg

The Acanthus Hotel was a nondescript, commercial hotel (formerly called the Sendlinger Tor) until Carola Günther, a retired Lufthansa stewardess, and her husband Jörg took over. Under their loving care, the hotel has developed real heart and is now a wonderful option for those looking for a not-too-expensive place to stay in Munich's inner ring. You enter into an intimate reception area where the front desk is managed by a warm, gracious staff. There is no restaurant, but just off the lobby a cozy bar opens into a breakfast room. Each morning a bountiful buffet is set up in the bar and guests can help themselves to a delicious array of tempting foods. A tiny elevator takes guests to the upper floors where the bedrooms are located. The least expensive rooms are decorated in *Rustikana* style using attractive, pastel-colored fabrics and modern furniture. Costing just a little bit more are the guestrooms displaying the *Alba-Rose* theme: these are ever-so-prettily decorated and have an English-country look. In the *Alba-Rose* rooms there are accents of antiques (such as desks or tables), pretty wallpapers, and country fabrics. All the rooms have modern bathrooms, good lighting, comfortable mattresses, and down pillows. The Acanthus is not a luxury hotel, but for an especially friendly, well located place to stay with charm, it can't be beat. The hotel has a garage.

ACANTHUS HOTEL
Owners: Carola & Jörg Günther
Manager: Carola Günther
Blumenstrasse 40
80331 Munich, Germany
Tel: (089) 231880 Fax: (089) 2607364
36 rooms
Double: DM 190
Open all year
Credit cards: all major
No restaurant: breakfast only
U-bahn Sendlinger-Tor 50m

If money is no object and you are looking for an intimate, small deluxe
of historic old Munich, the Hotel Rafael makes a superb choice. It is tuc
side street, catty-corner from a tiny park and near the famous Hoffbrauhaus
into a two-story lobby with a registration desk of cherry wood with inlaid ebo
the reception area a sweeping staircase of pewter-toned marble imported from I
leads up to the mezzanine to "Mark's," the hotel's gourmet restaurant. A pianist pla
background music in the lounge in the evenings. Throughout the hotel there are authentic
antiques plus a treasured art collection of original prints and etchings which even
includes some by Raphael. The ambiance throughout is one of subdued elegance. This
refined mood extends to the guestrooms that are decorated in tones of parchment and
blue. Complementing the luxurious decor, every extra has been provided: each room has
four telephones, a fax/computer outlet, color television with VCR, mini-bar, and
electronic safe. Several of the rooms are either junior or executive suites. In summer,
guests enjoy the swimming pool on the roof terrace. Although definitely a posh, deluxe
establishment, the Rafael prides itself on its warmth of welcome.

HOTEL RAFAEL
Manager: Karl-Heinz Zimmermann
Neuturmstrasse 1
80331 Munich, Germany
Tel: (089) 290980 Fax: (089) 222539
74 rooms, 20 suites
Double: DM 540–690 Suite: DM 790–2,000
Open all year
Credit cards: all major
Restaurant open daily
U-bahn Marienplatz 500m
Relais & Chateaux

licitously under her wing at the Pension Schubert and
kfasts and comfortable, spotless rooms. Located on a
hubert's atmosphere is not at all hotel-like. There is no
of, but if you are looking for homey comfort and an
head at night, this is a reasonably priced choice. The
floor of a former villa, so the rooms are all high-ceilinged
are a mixture of antiques and contemporary pieces,
s and Oriental rugs. Only three of the six rooms have
additional charge for taking a shower if you do not have
one in your room). The foyer displays plants and a jumble of family knickknacks and
mementos that create a cluttered atmosphere. The tiny breakfast room has lace-covered
tables and antique furnishings and is an agreeable place to meet other guests and plan
sightseeing excursions for the day. The Pension Schubert is a good choice for travelers
who prefer to spend their time and money outside of their hotel, appreciate a home-like
ambiance, and do not require all the services offered in a hotel. However, the pension
seems to be constantly booked, so early reservations are advised.

PENSION SCHUBERT
Owner: Frau Fürholzner
1 Schubertstrasse
80336 Munich, Germany
Tel: (089) 535087
6 rooms
Double: DM 95
Open all year
Credit cards: none accepted
No restaurant: breakfast only
U-bahn Goetheplatz 500m

A somewhat sterile city façade hides this traditional and cozy hotel. Set at the quieter end of Maximilianstrasse (Munich's most elegant street) just a few blocks from the river, the Splendid is an ideally located treasure. The entrance and downstairs salon are inviting, giving only a glimpse of the mood of furnishings to be found in the individualized bedrooms. Oriental carpets enhance hardwood floors, lovely antiques grace the hallways, and clusters of tables and chairs upholstered in tones of pink make the salon an inviting place to rest after the inevitable city wandering. An outside terrace is a treat on warm days and an ideal spot for tea or an afternoon refreshment. The Splendid does not have a restaurant and a buffet breakfast is the only meal served. This is a small hotel with only 40 bedrooms and 1 suite, but each is delightful: some have painted armoires, traditional to the region of Bavaria, lovely wooden beds, and sitting areas. Everything is spotless. This hotel is an extremely convenient and comfortable place to reside in Munich and very pleasing to the eye as well. Traditional decor permeates every room—a surprise and unexpected discovery in a large city. A delight.

SPLENDID HOTEL
Owner: Klaus Lieboldt
Maximilianstrasse 54
80538 Munich, Germany
Tel: (089) 296606 Fax: (089) 2913176
40 rooms, 1 suite
Double DM 265–325 Suite: DM 450–680
Open all year
Credit cards: all major
No restaurant: breakfast only
U-bahn Lehel 200m

For years our friend Judi extolled the merits of her favorite hotel in Munich, the Torbräu. Now that we have had the opportunity to inspect it, we agree—the Torbräu (whose history dates back to 1490) has much to offer. For location, it can't be surpassed: a short walk down the Tal from Marienplatz, the attractive, five-story, ocher-colored building with red-tiled roof sits on a corner in the heart of Munich at the historic Isator (originally one of Munich's main tower gates). The lobby has a tiled floor, Oriental scatter rugs, mirrored panels on the walls, recessed lighting, and formal groupings of fancy, French-style chairs in light wood. From first impression, one might think this is a staid, rather impersonal hotel. But, in fact, one of the nicest aspects of the Hotel Torbräu is the warmth and friendliness of its staff. The guestrooms are found off the main street so you are guaranteed a quiet night's repose. They vary from having a somewhat staid ambiance with built-in beds and old-fashioned wallpaper to a more modern, traditional, hotel look. No matter what the decor, all the rooms have modern bathrooms. Breakfast is served each morning in an especially attractive dining room that has a balcony overlooking the street. At 11 am (when breakfast is over) this room converts to a tea room where a stunning selection of scrumptious pastries, fresh from the hotel's own bakery, is served. There is also an outstanding Italian restaurant located below the hotel.

HOTEL TORBRÄU
Owners: Werner & Walter Kirchlechner
Tal 41
80331 Munich, Germany
Tel: (089) 225016 Fax: (089) 225019
100 rooms, 3 suites
Double: DM 265–370 Suite: DM 320–370
Open all year
Credit cards: all major
Restaurant open daily
U-bahn Isator 50m

The Hotel Schloss Wilkinghege is located just 6 kilometers from Münster (with regular bus service available to the city). Although considered a castle, the handsome, red-brick building with red-tiled roof is really more reminiscent of a country estate. A pretty moat and lots of trees and gardens surround the castle, and it has an 18-hole golf course in the rear. The castle has changed hands many times and undergone several architectural alterations in the years since being built in 1719. Lubert Winnecken bought the property in 1955 and turned it into a hotel and restaurant, preserving the style and feeling of this romantic home's former grandeur. The restaurant at Schloss Wilkinghege is well-known for the quality of its nouvelle cuisine. Reservations are needed to dine in this atmospheric restaurant which has been completely renovated, reflecting the authentic mood of the late Renaissance period. There are some guestrooms in the main house with lofty ceilings and fancy decor. Especially dramatic is one new suite, resembling the style of 1759 with original furniture of the epoch of the commander General d'Armentier. There are also some apartments furnished in modern style in the annex. Note: the Hotel Schloss Wilkinghege is not located in the heart of town, but just on the outskirts, signposted off road 54.

HOTEL SCHLOSS WILKINGHEGE
Owner: Lubert Winnecken
Steinfurter Strasse 374
48159 Münster, Germany
Tel: (0251) 213045 Fax: (0251) 212898
33 rooms
Double: DM 260–285 Suite: DM 335–420
Open all year
Credit cards: all major
Restaurant open daily
70 km N of Dortmund, 164 km N of Cologne
Relais & Chateaux

Situated in the little village of Handorf just outside the town of Münster, the Hof Zur Linde is as lovely inside and out as the brochure depicts. It is a complex of old farm buildings connected by courtyards and surrounded by grassy lawns and woodlands leading down to a river. At dinner time you can choose from a selection of dining rooms. These are all actually adjoining, but each has been done in a totally different style so that you move from a light-pine-paneled room with gay red-gingham curtains where you dine in cozy booths to one with stucco walls and beams, a huge walk-in fireplace, flagstone floors, and hams hung from the ceiling. The main dining room is more formal with its tapestry-covered chairs and starched white linens. The menu is extensive, the food delicious, and the service friendly and efficient. Bedrooms are upstairs in the main building or in a lovely old farmhouse just a few steps away. You may find yourself sleeping in a bed that was made for British royalty or in a rustic pine bed beneath a curtained canopy. Summer mornings find Herr Löfken, the hotel owner, busy adjusting bicycles and providing maps for guests setting off to explore the area.

ROMANTIK HOTEL HOF ZUR LINDE
Owner: Otto Löfken
Handorfer Werseufer 1
48157 Münster-Handorf, Germany
Tel: (0251) 32750 Fax: (0251) 328209
30 rooms, 14 suites
Double: DM 200–250 Suite: DM 260–330
Closed Christmas
Credit cards: all major
Restaurant open daily
70 km N of Dortmund, 7 km NE of Münster

From the moment you step through the front door of the Spielweg Romantik Hotel you are surrounded by the warmth of a wonderful old farmhouse, lovingly converted into a small luxury hotel. To the left of the reception is a comfortable sitting area with chairs set around small tables for afternoon tea. An added bonus is an open fireplace to add warmth on a chilly day. To the right of the lobby is a series of dining rooms, each a masterpiece of country-cozy with antique paneling covering the walls and low ceilings, ceramic plates and pictures, hunting trophies, tiled stove, and pretty hanging lamps. All the dining rooms look like settings for *Gourmet* magazine. As the hotel has grown, the bedrooms have expanded from the original home to two additional wings. The rooms in the older part are smaller and more old-fashioned in decor, but very good value for the money. The rooms in the newer wings are larger and have more modern furnishings, but are more costly. None of the bedrooms has the same antique, country ambiance of the public rooms. If you are traveling with children, there is an enormous playroom for your little ones with all kinds of toys to keep them happy on a rainy day. Connected to the hotel by an underground passage is an indoor swimming pool and just beyond, in the garden, you'll find an outdoor pool.

SPIELWEG ROMANTIK HOTEL
Owner: Hansjörg Fuchs
Spielweg 61
79244 Münstertal, Germany
Tel: (07636) 7090 Fax: (07636) 70966
39 rooms, 2 suites
Double: DM 190–380 Suite: DM 400–480
Open all year
Credit cards: all major
Restaurant open daily
Located 65 km N of Basel, 27 km S of Freiburg

Most of the hotels in Oberammergau are irresistible outside with intricately painted façades and windowboxes overflowing with brightly colored geraniums, but unfortunately, on the inside most of the cozy ambiance usually evaporates. An exception is the Hotel Turmwirt where, from the moment you enter, a rustic mood is established by the use of pine paneling, antique trunks, Oriental carpets, colorful draperies, and carefully selected fabrics on comfortable chairs. There are two dining rooms, both very attractive. Especially cozy is one with 200-year-old paneled ceiling and walls. The Glas family has owned and operated the Hotel Turmwirt for over 60 years. Georg Glas now manages the hotel, but his mother does the baking—don't miss the impressive, mouth-watering display of cakes and marvelous pastries that she prepares each morning. Some of the guestrooms are located in the original house, others in a newer wing. The bedroom decor is hotel-like with built-in beds and modern, Danish-style chairs. All have every amenity: mini-bar, television, telephone, and radio. The rooms with the best views are those in the new wing, with balconies that look out to the mountains. I think, though, that perhaps my favorite is number 11, a front-facing room which, instead of a modern decor, has lovely, hand-painted Bavarian-style furniture dating back to the turn of the century.

HOTEL TURMWIRT
Owner: Georg Glas
Ettaler Strasse 2
82483 Oberammergau, Germany
Tel: (08822) 3091 Fax: (08822) 1437
22 rooms
Double: DM 145–85
Open all year
Credit cards: all major
Restaurant closed Wednesdays November to April
92 km SW of Munich, 19 km N of Garmisch

A hallway full of family antiques leads to a reception desk brightened by a bouquet of fresh flowers at the charming Gasthof Zur Rose, well located on a quiet street one block from the central square. Formerly a farmer's stable, the gasthof is almost 200 years old and has been in the Stückl family for many years—Renata is the third generation of her family to welcome guests here and is assisted by her husband, Ludwig, and her parents, Roswitha and Peter. All the family members are experts on local sights and history (Renata's brother, Christian, is currently the youngest-ever director of the famous Passion Play). Artistic touches are found throughout the Zur Rose, from colorful dried-flower arrangements and strategically placed paintings to pleasing combinations of fabrics. The two dining rooms are bright and cheerful, filled with pretty fabrics, rustic furniture, and green plants and offer many Bavarian specialties. Some of the simple guestrooms have antique accent pieces: my favorite room, number 3, has an antique bed and chairs and more of an old-world ambiance than some of the others. All the bedrooms have small shower cabinets neatly incorporated into them. For longer rentals, the Stückl family offers three Bavarian houses, with apartments for up to six persons. For warmth of reception and super-caring hosts, the Gasthof Zur Rose is a real winner.

GASTHOF ZUR ROSE
Owners: Renata & Ludwig Frank
Dedlerstrasse 9
82487 Oberammergau, Germany
Tel: (08822) 4706 Fax: (08822) 6753
22 rooms
Double: DM 100–120
Closed November
Credit cards: all major
Restaurant closed Mondays
92 km SW of Munich, 19 km N of Garmisch

The Auf Schönburg is the perfect castle hotel. High atop a rocky bluff, the façade is a fairy-tale picture of towers and battlements reached by crossing a narrow wooden bridge. Cobbles worn smooth by feet through the ages wind through the castle to the hotel at the summit. The terrace view is superb, dropping steeply to the Rhine below. The bedrooms are shaped by the unusual castle buildings—tower rooms sit atop steep winding staircases and several rooms have balconies (one leads to a long drop). Through tiny lead-paned windows you catch glimpses of the Rhine or vineyards far below. While several rooms have views to the Rhine you are assured a quieter night's sleep if you have a vineyard view but be aware that, whichever room you select, you will hear the trains rushing along beside the river. Some of the castle's most beautiful accommodations do not have river views (I prefer the more spacious rooms with window seats and balconies to those in the tower). The romance extends to the intimate dining rooms where you dine by candlelight. The terrace restaurant has lovely views to the vineyards while the tower dining room with its displays of pewter and weapons has medieval charm. Come spin yourself a dream or two in this fairy-tale castle above the Rhine.

AUF SCHÖNBURG
Owners: Barbara & Wolfgang Hüttl
55430 Oberwesel, Germany
Tel: (06744) 7027 Fax: (06744) 1613
20 rooms, 2 suites
Double: DM 235–320 Suite: DM 360–380
Closed January to March
Credit cards: all major
Restaurant closed Mondays
On the Rhine, 21 km NW of Bingen

A picturesque drive past green meadows and flower-bedecked chalets leads to the Gasthof Hirschen, located about 6 kilometers beyond Wolfach in the tiny hamlet of Oberwolfach-Walke. Colorful geraniums adorn the Hirschen's many windowboxes and a small stream flows by across the street. This inn is one of the oldest in the Black Forest, dating from 1609. Its lovely restaurant has been recently remodeled into a series of cozy rooms each decked out in an inviting, old-fashioned style. The menu is enticing, offering a delicious variety of local dishes. Follow the Oriental rug runners up the old staircase to a small lobby area which displays an antique clock and a cabinet filled with antique dolls. There are 17 guestrooms in the main building, all with private baths. These bedrooms are not overly large, but are pleasantly furnished. My favorite rooms are found in the lovely new wing of more modern rooms, many of which have balconies overlooking the lovely garden. You can enjoy sunny days on the flower-filled terrace or in the tranquil garden, the only audible sound the birds in surrounding trees. In winter cross-country skiing is a popular sport in this region of forests and rolling hills. The quiet rural location and warm welcome of the Junghanns family make it easy to see why the Gasthof Hirschen is a popular country inn for travelers "in the know."

GASTHOF HIRSCHEN
Owner: Family Junghanns
Schwarzwaldstrasse 2
77709 Oberwolfach-Walke, Germany
Tel: (07834) 366 Fax: (07834) 6775
42 rooms
Double: DM 112–160
Closed January
Credit cards: all major
Restaurant open daily
6 km N of Wolfach, 40 km NE of Freiburg

The Hotel Schwan, with its gray-tile roof and timbered façade, has been around since 1628 when it was a travelers' inn along the River Rhine. Today both the road and the river in front of the hotel are a lot busier than in the days of carriages and river barges. Fortunately, the hotel is saved from being overwhelmed by the busy Rhineside road by a broad band of garden that separates it from the highway. The Wenckstern family has owned and managed the inn for many generations. They produce their own wine which you can sample with dinner in the dignified dining room or sip on the outdoor terrace while watching the river. From a small hostelry, the Schwan has grown to a substantial hotel, and the joy of staying here is that you can obtain a Rhine-facing room. All the bedrooms are decorated in a rather unmemorable pastel-modern decor. Quite the nicest room (also the most expensive) is the tower room whose seven little windows command lovely river views. Incidentally, the Hotel Schwan is only about an hour's drive from the Frankfurt airport, a convenient distance after a tiring transatlantic flight. Its location on the Rheingau Reisling Road makes it an ideal base for touring the region.

HOTEL SCHWAN
Owners: Martina & Klaus Wenckstern
Rheinallee 5-7
65375 Oestrich-Winkel, Germany
Tel: (06723) 8090 Fax: (06723) 7820
37 rooms, 5 suites
Double: DM 149–225 Suite: DM 279
Closed December 20 to January 15
Credit cards: all major
Restaurant open daily
55 km W of Frankfurt, 21 km W of Wiesbaden

King Ludwig II looked out of his bedroom in Neuschwanstein castle at the distant ruin of Falkenstein castle and decided to replace the medieval ruins with his third and most fanciful castle. The plans were drawn up and workmen laid the narrow road that winds back and forth through the forest to the rocky precipice. But before construction could begin, Ludwig died and the castle was left as a romantic ruin. Living halfway down the mountain, in a high Alpine meadow at the Schlossanger Alp hotel, the Schlachter family decided to build a traditional chalet hotel for their son Toni (the talented chef), his gracious wife Hertha, and their young children. While everything is sparkling-new the theme is decidedly old-world with traditional Bavarian light-pine found throughout the hotel. I adored the lovely dining room, longed to dine on a warm summer evening on the narrow terrace that overhangs a sheer precipice dropping to the Austrian-German border post far below, and loved all the bedrooms, though a particular favorite was room 3 with its covered verandah. A small fitness room offers a sauna, solarium, and laundry room—very handy if you've been on the road for a while. Pfronten is a perfect location for visiting Ludwig's more famous castles Neuschwanstein, Hohenschwangau, and Linderhof.

BURGHOTEL FALKENSTEIN   **NEW**
Owners: Toni & Hertha Schlachter
87459 Pfronten-Obermeilingen, Germany
Tel: (08363) 309 Fax: (08363) 73390
9 rooms
Double from DM 180
Closed Christmas & New Year
Credit cards: all major
Restaurant closed Thursdays in winter
131 km SW of Munich, 30 km W of Garmisch

Arriving at the base of Falkenstein mountain, a right-hand turn winds you ever-upward to Burghotel Falkenstein while a left turn takes you up through the forest to a broad, green, high Alpine meadow and the Burghotel Schlossanger Alp. Muck and Toni Schlachter, who have been offering a traditonal Bavarian welcome for over 30 years, have been joined by their daughter Barbara and her husband Bernhard Ebert. When I visited in the summer of 1995 the final touches were being put to a complete refurbishment and construction was under way on 16 lovely suites, many of which have an extra bedroom. I especially admired the lovely furniture newly crafted from old pine. These spacious rooms are absolutely ideal for families—the hotel also has a playground, playroom, and small indoor swimming pool. However, whether you are traveling with or without children, you cannot help being captivated by the hotel's glorious setting at the edge of the pines overlooking the rolling green meadow and distant mountain peaks. Sit on your verandah in the evening and watch the deer grazing in the meadow.

BURGHOTEL SCHLOSSANGER ALP **NEW**
Owners: Barbara & Berhnard Ebert
87459 Pfronten-Obermeilingen, Germany
Tel: (08363) 6086 Fax: (08363) 6667
10 rooms, 20 suites
Double: DM 160–230 Suite: DM 170–300
Closed mid-January to mid-February
Credit cards: all major
Restaurant open daily
131 km SW of Munich, 30 km W of Garmisch

No sightseeing excursion to the Berlin area would be complete without a visit to the nearby town of Potsdam to see the sensational palaces and gardens of Sanssouci and Schloss Cecilienhof. Most tourists linger along the paths of the Schloss Cecilienhof, never realizing that if they had planned ahead, they could have spent the night there. This historic manor house, the very place where Truman, Churchill, and Stalin signed the Potsdam Agreement in 1945, now takes overnight guests. The setting of this large timbered, English-country-house-style hotel is magnificent—not one, but two lakes are on the property plus beautiful forests laced with walking paths. Only a part of the castle is operated as a hotel—the remainder and the surrounding park are open to the public. Most of the guestrooms are alike, very nicely decorated in a traditional decor. Room 49 is an especially attractive larger room. There is also an old-fashioned bridal suite (room 50) with heavy wooden furniture and a canopied, king-size bed. What makes all the bedrooms appealing are the views to the park and gardens. The paneled dining room is very attractive, especially in the evening when the cozy room glows from the candles on each table. On warm days, lunch is served on a pretty garden terrace. This is a serene, pleasant hotel that offers a wonderful alternative to staying in nearby Berlin.

SCHLOSSHOTEL CECILIENHOF
Manager: Petra Lubasch
Neuer Garten
14469 Potsdam, Germany
Tel: (0331) 37050 Fax: (0331) 292498
37 rooms, 5 suites
Double: DM 280–450 Suite: DM 500–800
Open all year
Credit cards: all major
Restaurant open daily
24 km SW of Berlin

Nestled at the foot of the Harz mountains, Quedlinburg is one of our favorite German towns: an enticing mixture of restored and time-weathered timber-framed houses giving a decidedly authentic medieval atmosphere. The Hotel Zur Goldenen Sonne faces a little fountain on a small square just a two-minute walk from the heart of the town. The hotel was built in 1671 and completely renovated in 1992. Enter through the ancient, heavy, studded doorway into a covered cobbled courtyard where rough-hewn benches and tables have been set up as a beer garden. Up a few steps and you are in the comfortable restaurant and bar which also serves as the hotel's reception. Bedrooms are found on the other side of the courtyard and your room key gives you access to this wing, the corridor on which your room is located, and your room—it seems like an awful lot of manipulating locks as you come and go. Everything about the bedrooms is smartly modern, all are very nicely kitted out with light-pine furniture, TV, and telephone, and each is accompanied by a spotless white-tile-with-red-accent shower room. Several rooms have the luxury of separate sitting and sleeping rooms. You reach the hotel by turning into the Altstadt (old town) opposite the Bahnhof (train station) and then turning right on the Pölken Street which brings you to the square.

HOTEL ZUR GOLDENEN SONNE   **NEW**
Manager: Kathrin Knauth
Steinweg 11
06493 Quedlinburg, Germany
Tel: (03946) 96250 Fax: (03946) 922530
14 rooms
Double: from DM 140
Open all year
Credit cards: all major
Restaurant closed Sundays
71 SW of Magdeburg, 133 km N of Erfurt

If you are using Hamburg airport and have a car, the Jagdhaus Waldfrieden is a splendid choice for your first or last night in Germany. Although the hotel is set peacefully in a lovely wooded park, the highway is conveniently close. During his career as the manager of large hotels, Siegmund Baierle formulated his plans for a small hotel with a first-rate restaurant—the result is the delightful Jagdhaus Waldfrieden. The latest renovation has added a glass-enclosed, greenhouse-style restaurant where you dine elegantly, yet feel as if you are in the garden. Just beyond the intimate bar there is a second high-ceilinged dining room with gleaming polished wood, Oriental carpets, and groupings of tables laid with crisp white linen before a roaring log fire. Dinner is an event where guests linger at their tables after a splendid meal before retiring for a contented night's sleep. A few bedrooms are found in the main building. The remainder are across the courtyard in what were once the stables. All the rooms have been lovingly decorated with a traditional look of comfortable sophistication achieved through the use of beautiful, color-coordinated fabrics and fine furniture. My favorite, room 45, is especially fantastic—a corner room on the ground floor of the stables with French doors leading out to the garden, and just beyond to the forest.

ROMANTIK HOTEL JAGDHAUS WALDFRIEDEN
Owner: Siegmund Baierle
Kieler Strasse B4
25451 Quickborn, Germany
Tel: (04106) 3771 Fax: (04106) 69196
24 rooms
Double: DM 215–235
Open all year
Credit cards: all major
Restaurant closed Mondays at lunch
23 km N of Hamburg

The Burg Hotel is a winning combination: a lovely hotel with an awesome view in a "must-visit" town. The Burg Hotel peers over Rothenburg's ramparts to a sky-wide vista of the meandering River Tauber and a cluster of timber-framed cottages in a wooded valley. Enjoy this lovely view from the sunny breakfast room. Breakfast is the only meal served but this is not a problem as there are a great many restaurants within easy strolling distance. Guests can relax in the attractive little parlor with its 150-year-old mini-grand piano and lovely grandfather clock. The ground floor Constantine Suite has a piano in the sitting room, a lovely bedroom, and doors opening to the battlement terrace that leads to one of the ancient watchtowers along the town's walls. Whether bedrooms face out to "the view" or to the monastery garden towards town, all are absolutely delightful and stylishly decorated by Gabriele Berger. Gabriele grew up at the nearby Markusturm hotel and being a gracious hotelier is certainly in her blood, though she admits to having wanted to be a librarian when growing up—but one look at the Burg Hotel and she was hooked on being a hotelier. Gabriele has converted the adjacent 14th-century hay barn into her home and an indoor parking garage for guests—very handy as you will not need your car for the duration of your stay in Rothenburg.

BURG HOTEL   **NEW**
Owner: Gabriele Berger
Klostergasse 1–3
91541 Rothenburg ob der Tauber, Germany
Tel: (09861) 94890 Fax: (09861) 948940
15 rooms, 5 suites
Double: DM 210–300 Suite: DM 300–320
Open all year
Credit cards: all major
No restaurant: breakfast only
62 km SE of Würzburg, 134 km NE of Stuttgart

The Hotel Eisenhut is Rothenburg's most deluxe hotel but with rooms very competitively priced when compared to other hotels in this "must-visit" town. The promise of a special experience is created as you walk into the spacious reception hall which has a hearty, German-castle look with beamed ceiling, Oriental carpets, massive, wrought-iron chandeliers, weaponry, large oil paintings, and a sweeping wooden staircase. Beyond the stately entrance there are comfortable lounges and several dining rooms opening onto a garden terrace, a wonderful retreat to escape the throng of daytime visitors. The high-ceilinged breakfast room, once a courtyard, is full of lovely, country-style tables and chairs. Throughout the hotel there is a fascinating collection of large, mural-like oil paintings depicting scenes of the Thirty Years' War. Because the Eisenhut was created out of four 15th- to 16th-century patrician mansions, the guestrooms are intriguingly tucked along a maze of corridors. While bedrooms at the front of the hotel are larger, we preferred the smaller back rooms with their peaceful countryside views. The hotel has not changed hands since established four generations ago by the Eisenhut family.

HOTEL EISENHUT
Owner: Hans Pirner
Manager: Karl Prüsse
Herrngasse 3–7
91541 Rothenburg ob der Tauber, Germany
Tel: (09861) 7050 Fax: (09861) 70545
77 rooms, 2 suites
Double: DM 285–380 Suite: to DM 640
Closed January & February
Credit cards: all major
Restaurant open daily
62 km SE of Würzburg, 134 km NE of Stuttgart
Gast im Schloss

The Gasthof Hotel Kloster-Stüble is a perfect little inn, combining reasonable prices with history, charm, and a good location. Just two blocks from the central market square, the Kloster-Stüble is tucked away on a quiet side street behind an old church and has pretty views of the surrounding countryside from many bedroom windows. There are 13 comfortable rooms, all with private shower and toilet and furnished in beautiful, country-pine reproductions. Most of the bedrooms are snug in size though a couple are larger. A large apartment, set under the eaves, is perfect for families or longer stays. Downstairs, the dining room and stube are cozily rustic. Murals depicting life in days gone by decorate the stube walls and in the evenings regulars gather at the *Stammtisch,* a special table reserved only for those who come every day. In the adjoining dining room pretty rose-colored walls and tablecloths set a romantic tone. Tables are dressed with gleaming silver, china, and glassware, topped off with pink candles and fresh flowers. A sense of history prevails in this inn dating from 1300. Jutta Hammel, who speaks excellent English, is your energetic young hostess. Her husband, Rudolf, is the chef and you meet his charming mother at breakfast-time. Enjoy a typical Franconian meal before setting out to join the nightwatchman on his nightly tour of the town.

GASTHOF HOTEL KLOSTER-STÜBLE
Owners: Jutta & Rudolf Hammel
Heringsbronnengassechen 5
91541 Rothenburg ob der Tauber, Germany
Tel: (09861) 6774 Fax: (09861) 6474
13 rooms, 1 suite
Double: DM 130–150 Suite: DM 160
Open all year
Credit cards: VS
Restaurant closed Tuesdays
62 km SE of Würzburg, 134 km NE of Stuttgart

Rothenburg, a fairy-tale medieval town completely enclosed by ramparts, walls, and turrets, is a popular daytime destination. Plan to overnight here so that you can enjoy the town's cobblestoned streets and timbered façades after the throngs have departed. The Markusturm, built in 1264 as a tollhouse, commands one of the town's best locations, on a main street, just a block or two from the main square and famous clock. Stephan and Marianne are the fourth generation of the Berger family to run the Markusturm since it became a hotel in 1902. The entry and restaurant are charmingly decorated with antiques. You can choose to dine in the lovely pine restaurant or in the more casual country stube next to it—consider enjoying a main course before the 8 pm nightwatchman tour of the city and return for a leisurely dessert and coffee. As you climb the stairs to the various bedrooms, the carpets appear a bit worn but everything is polished and spotlessly clean. The bedrooms are a very mixed bunch: some are delightfully old-fashioned and furnished with antiques while others have bleached pine furniture and modern, pastel decor. The rooms come in all shapes and sizes for the hotel has been extended over the years. Drive through the pedestrian streets to unload your luggage and you will be directed to the hotel's parking.

ROMANTIK HOTEL MARKUSTURM
Owners: Marianne & Stephan Berger
Rodergasse 1
91541 Rothenburg ob der Tauber, Germany
Tel: (09861) 2098 Fax: (09861) 2692
26 rooms, 2 suites
Double: DM 295–320 Suite: DM 350
Open all year
Credit cards: all major
Restaurant closed January to mid-February
62 km SE of Würzburg, 134 km NE of Stuttgart

Rottweil, an attractive town perched on a plateau looped by the Neckar river, reflects its medieval past in streets lined with colorfully painted buildings, many with ornate oriel windows. One of the oldest of these buildings is a patrician house, "Zum Sternen," dating back to 1278. Rottweil has not been discovered by tourists and there are no fancy boutiques or quaint pedestrian streets, so it is a marvelous surprise to discover here such an outstanding small inn as the "Zum Sternen," which not only is an excellent place to stay, but also features an intimate gourmet restaurant on the ground level. Steps from the foyer lead up to the reception and another stunningly decorated dining room where breakfast is served each morning. More steps lead to the beautifully furnished guestrooms. My favorite rooms were 35, a bright and cheerful corner room with a handsome, painted canopy bed, and room 37, a spacious room with antique brass bed, rich matching fabrics for the dust ruffle and draperies, and a small balcony. The view from the balcony is not perfect due to railroad tracks and some commercial buildings, but, even so, the outlook over the river to the rolling green hills is very pretty. All the rooms are exceptionally well decorated and antique furniture is used throughout.

ROMANTIK HOTEL "HAUS ZUM STERNEN"
Owner: Dorothee Ehrenberger
Manager: Markus Berns
Hauptstrasse 60
78628 Rottweil, Germany
Tel: (0741) 53300 Fax: (0741) 7008
12 rooms
Double: DM 185–250 Suite: DM 250–290
Open all year
Credit cards: all major
Restaurant open daily
98 km SW of Stuttgart

This is it—Sleeping Beauty's castle where, deep within the "enchanted" Reinhard forest, Jacob and Wilhelm Grimm set their famous fairy tale. The once-proud fortress is now largely a romantic ruin but, fortunately, part of the castle has been restored as a hotel. The romance of staying in Sleeping Beauty's castle cannot be denied, but be aware that it has a very isolated location. You must also realize that this is not Walt Disney's Sleeping Beauty castle—he chose the ethereal towers and turrets of Neuschwanstein Castle in Bavaria as his model. Tables in the dining room are assigned by management: the only way to ensure a lovely countryside view is to request a window table as you check in. Traditional bedrooms are found in a new wing. A walk through the ruined castle (the center of which is used for theatrical performances) brings you to the tower where you find six more romantic bedrooms up the broad spiral staircase. These are the hotel's most expensive rooms and have lots of charm and sparkling modern bathrooms. In honor of the Brothers Grimm and their world-famous tales, the German Tourist Office has outlined a fairy-tale route, the *Deutsche Marchen Strasse*, signposted by a smiling good fairy and accompanied by a colorful picture map. The Dornröschenschloss Sababurg is included on this routing and as a consequence is a popular tourist attraction.

DORNRÖSCHENSCHLOSS SABABURG
Owners: Sabine, Karl & Günther Koseck
34369 Hofgeismar-Sababurg, Germany
Tel: (05671) 8080 Fax: (05671) 808200
18 rooms
Double: DM 245–345
Closed mid-January to mid-February
Credit cards: all major
Restaurant open daily
23 km N of Kassel, 14 km NE of Hofgeismar
Gast im Schloss

The Romantik Hotel Josthof is located less than an hour's drive south of Hamburg in a lovely, peaceful region where spacious fields are dotted with handsome old thatched-roofed farmhouses. These large buildings are often constructed using exposed red brick between the wooden framework instead of the more commonplace stucco and half-timber combination. This unusual, and very attractive, architectural style is typified by the Romantik Hotel Josthof. Happily, the interior is as charming as the exterior. The first floor houses a gourmet restaurant which is well-known and frequented by diners from far and wide. Decorated in typical German-country style, the several dining rooms of the restaurant are all very cozy; each with its own personality. Ceilings are laced with massive beams, candlelight reflects off mellow, paneled walls, and beautiful tiled ceramic ovens and cheerful fireplaces warm the rooms on cold evenings. Antiques galore —grandfather clocks, cradles, pewter plates, copper pans—enhance the old-fashioned ambiance. Upstairs and in an adjacent building, reflecting the same style of architecture, there are 16 rooms available for overnight guests. These bedrooms, although not decorated with antiques, are modern and pretty and each has a private bathroom.

ROMANTIK HOTEL JOSTHOF
Owners: Martina & Jörg Hansen
Am Lindenberg 1
21376 Salzhausen, Germany
Tel: (04172) 90980 Fax: (04172) 6225
16 rooms
Double: DM 175–190 Suite: DM 215–235
Open all year
Credit cards: all major
Restaurant open daily in summer
45 km SE of Hamburg, 18 km SW of Lüneburg

In the Black Forest, on a hillside in the town of Schluchsee, is a delightful, modern hotel. Constructed in 1969 with a new wing added in 1984, Heger's Parkhotel Flora is beautiful in its decor and in the views it affords down to the Schluchsee. Each room is pleasant in decor with modern furniture, built-in headboards, and good lights for reading. Each also has a modern, tiled bathroom. All the bedrooms overlook the lake: views can be enjoyed from either a private balcony or terrace. The hallways are beamed, spacious, and airy, with floor-to-ceiling windows. The public rooms are attractive with colorful prints on the walls, wrought-iron fixtures, plants, and pink and green fabrics. Herr Heger, dressed impeccably in chef's attire, is frequently found in the lobby greeting guests and is as eager to make you comfortable as he is to please and tempt your palate. The St. Georgstube and the café-terrace restaurant are delightful—it is especially romantic to eat outside when the weather permits. The entry hall with its open fireplace is a cozy place to settle in inclement weather. In warm summer weather the Schluchsee comes alive with the sails of gaily colored sailing boats and windsurfers.

HEGER'S PARKHOTEL FLORA
Owner: Hugo Heger
Sonnhalde 22
79857 Schluchsee, Germany
Tel: (07656) 452 or 521 Fax: (07656) 1433
34 rooms
Double: DM 180–210
Closed November to Christmas
Credit cards: AX
Restaurant for guests only
172 km SW of Stuttgart, 47 km SE of Freiburg

The Romantik Hotel Goldener Adler, an exceptionally attractive building facing the Marktplatz in Schwäbisch Hall, was built in 1500 as the manor house of the Lords of Mückheim. Today the colorful, timbered Goldener Adler is owned by the Rapp family (Peter Rapp is the chef and his wife, Marion, is in charge of the day-to-day operation of the hotel). The entrance is through a gigantic archway, a reminder of the colorful past when horse-drawn coaches would come clomping through the portals. Inside, the hotel has been refurbished and is rather fussily decorated in pastels. Schwäbisch Hall is special—a well-preserved, medieval town built on a steep hillside sloping down to the Kocher river. The Marktplatz is one of the prettiest in Germany and always teeming with activity—a real town center with women carefully selecting their produce for the evening meal from small stalls in the square (market days Saturday and Wednesday) and children neatly dressed in uniforms chatting gaily on their way to school. Dominating the square (impressively set at the top of a wide flight of 53 steps) is St. Michael's Church. The prime objective in coming to Schwäbisch Hall should be to soak in the wonderful ambiance of this lovely old city—and for this, the Hotel Goldener Adler could not be more ideally located.

ROMANTIK HOTEL GOLDENER ADLER
Owners: Marion & Peter Rapp
Am Marktplatz 11
74523 Schwäbisch Hall, Germany
Tel: (0791) 6168 Fax: (0791) 7315
21 rooms
Double: DM 176–220 Suite: DM 270
Open all year
Credit cards: all major
Restaurant closed Wednesdays
68 km NE of Stuttgart

The friendly Heim family has been receiving guests into their home since 1959 and Bettina Willer-Heim continues in the family tradition of offering guests a warm welcome. Many of the guests who came as children now return with their children and grandchildren. It is easy to see why the Pension Heim is such a success: the entire family is warm and genuine and the house spotless and homey. Cheerful house plants brighten all the rooms and hallways and a rustic feeling pervades the breakfast room. Upstairs, most of the comfortable bedrooms have balconies that overlook spectacularly unspoiled mountain scenery, even offering a glimpse of the famous Zugspitze on a clear day. The rolling hills and pastures of this region make it ideal for relaxed hiking in the summer and cross-country skiing in the winter. Pension Heim offers comforts such as private bath or shower in each room, direct-dial phones, and even a sauna. Just the right ending to a day of enjoying all the activities which this scenic area has to offer. Coming from Fussen, take the first left as you enter the village and you will find the Pension Heim on your right.

PENSION HEIM
Owner: Bettina Willer-Heim
Aufmberg 8
87637 Seeg, Germany
Tel: (08364) 258 Fax: (08364) 1051
16 rooms
Double: DM 124
Closed November to Christmas
Credit cards: none accepted
No restaurant: breakfast only
120 km SW of Munich, 10 km N of Füssen

The Schloss Sommersdorf, conveniently located near The Romantic Road, is a sensational small castle with all the ingredients of a proper fairy tale: keep, turrets, tall towers, spiral staircases, stone bridges, ramparts, and even a moat. This is a special place, not a standard hotel at all, but rather the elegant and historical home of Dr Manfred von Crailsheim, who welcomes guests on a bed-and-breakfast basis. Guests enter the castle through an outer gate (a pink house topped by a whimsical clock), over the moat, into the rose-filled courtyard, through a massive door, and up a spiral staircase. Each of the guestrooms and apartments varies in decor and size, but all have an old-world feel. Especially dramatic is the Gothic Room; an enormous corner bedroom with a canopied bed, Oriental carpets, an antique armoire, and an incredible carved wooden column in the center of the room that supports massive ceiling beams. The Schloss Sommersdorf is an ideal base for exploring The Romantic Road and the surrounding region, and would thus be a marvelous find simply on the merit of its location and accommodations, but the presence of host Manfred von Crailsheim makes this a very special place to stay. He lived in the castle as a boy, loves to share his home with guests, is a natural host and an absolute delight. Note: Sommersdorf is not on most maps: ask for directions when making reservations.

SCHLOSS SOMMERSDORF
Owner: Dr Manfred von Crailsheim
91595 Sommersdorf, Germany
Tel: (0981) 647 Fax: (0981) 9707950
3 rooms, 3 apartments (one week minimum stay)
Double DM 120–140 Suite: DM 140–170
Open all year
No restaurant: breakfast only*
*Dinner can be arranged by special request
50 km SW of Nürnberg, E of Dinkelsbühl

Come dream a romantic dream or two at one of our favorite castles, the idyllic Schloss Spangenberg. High atop a hill with the town of Spangenberg spread at its feet far below, this once-proud fortress is now a gem of a castle hotel. All the romantic castle ingredients are here—a deep, grassy moat, a tower keep, and thick fortified walls. After surviving a seven-century history of battles, this fortification was badly damaged by British bombers in the closing days of World War II. The exterior has been painstakingly reconstructed and the interior converted into an inviting hotel. A few steps away, where soldiers once guarded the ramparts, gay tables and chairs now provide a perfect place for afternoon coffee and cake. Gleaming polished floors lead you down the long hallways to extremely attractive, individually furnished guestrooms. Everything is meticulously maintained and the decor throughout is comfortable and welcoming—not in the least stiffly formal or hotel-like. Many of the guestrooms have a fabulous bird's-eye view over the dense forest to the charming town of Spangenberg nestled at the foot of the hill. My favorite room (number 16) has a romantic bay window—a perfect niche to sit and dream of knights and their ladies while gazing out over the castle walls. If you are traveling with your family, you might wish to stay in the dear little gatekeeper's house comprised of a doll-sized living room, sleeping loft, tiny bedroom, and two bathrooms.

SCHLOSS SPANGENBERG
Owners: Angela & Wilfried Wichmann
34286 Spangenberg, Germany
Tel: (05663) 866 Fax: (05663) 7567
25 rooms, 1 suite
Double: DM 160–260 Suite: DM 300
Closed January
Credit cards: all major
Restaurant closed Sunday evenings
210 km S of Hamburg, 36 km SE of Kassel
Gast im Schloss

The Romantik Hotel Traube, conveniently located across the expressway from the Stuttgart airport, is a beguiling little inn. Should you be flying into Stuttgart to visit the Mercedes factory and perhaps pick up a car, the Hotel Traube would be an excellent choice for a place to spend the night since the factory is only a short drive from the hotel. The contrast between this small inn and the modern industrial city of Stuttgart, only about a half-hour's drive away, is dramatic. Located on a small cobblestoned square, contained in a cluster of three timbered buildings, the Hotel Traube would stand out as a perfect inn regardless of its location. The most famous feature of the hotel is its restaurant. The food is exceptional and the decor worthy of multiple stars. Tables laid with soft pink cloths, flowers, and candles are tucked under beams into cozy corners paneled in rich wood. If you'd prefer less formal dining, consider the neighboring rotisserie, managed by the gracious son and daughter who maintain the same high standards set by their parents. The rotisserie has a welcoming bar and lighter fare on the menu, letting you select from different cuts of meat grilled on the open barbecue. The guestrooms, located far enough away from the street to be quiet, are most attractive with traditional decor and comfortable beds topped with fluffy down comforters.

ROMANTIK HOTEL TRAUBE
Owner: Family Recknagel
Brabandgasse 2
70599 Stuttgart-Plieningen, Germany
Tel: (0711) 458920 Fax: (0711) 4589220
22 rooms
Double: DM 198–290
Closed Christmas & New Year
Credit cards: all major
Restaurant closed Sundays
Near Stuttgart airport

Hotels

Sylt, a sand-dune island located in the northernmost tip of Germany, is reached by taking the car-train across the narrow causeway linking the island to the mainland—a 45-minute ride. The Benen Diken Hof is one of the island's loveliest hotels. The hotel is several squat, Friesian farmhouses joined into a complex by means of glass corridors that appear to bring the outdoors indoors. Decorated throughout in white and cream with accents of pale pink and blue, the hotel is decorator-perfect, warm, and welcoming. After a walk along the sand dunes in the bracing sea air, you return to the hotel to pamper yourself with a sauna and a massage or a relaxing swim. The hotel's greatest asset is its owner, Claas Johannsen. In the evening he can be found, surrounded by his collection of old model fire engines, hosting the hotel's cozy bar. His warmth and graciousness transcend the language barrier and make you feel at home. The restaurant serves breakfast and in the evening a short seafood menu—the small island abounds with restaurants for dining out. A particular recommendation goes to the restaurant Landhaus Stricker in the adjacent village of Tinnum, offering elegant gourmet dining in a Friesian farmhouse.

ROMANTIK HOTEL BENEN DIKEN HOF
Owner: Claas Johannsen
Süderstrasse
25985 Keitum-Sylt, Germany
Tel: (04651) 31035 Fax: (04651) 35835
38 rooms
Double: DM 240–410 Suite: DM 430–565
Open all year
Credit cards: all major
Light meals, no formal restaurant
Island of Sylt, 160 km NW of Hamburg

There are many restaurants on Germany's lovely Isle of Sylt and among the finest is the well-known Restaurant Jörg Müller, situated on one of the main roads into Westerland. The restaurant, which has earned a coveted Michelin star, also offers—luckily for the gourmet traveler—three pretty guestrooms upstairs for overnight guests. In keeping with the fairy-tale quality of most of the houses on the island, the Restaurant Jörg Müller is brimming with charm. The pretty, red-brick house with thick thatched roof is given even further romantic appeal by a lacing of climbing roses. A small lawn and garden in front complete the attractive picture. Inside, there is a sitting area for guests waiting for dinner. On the left are two subdued, pastel-colored dining rooms where French cuisine is served. To the right of the reception is, in my opinion, the most enchanting dining room, decorated entirely in white, blue, and light-toned woods. The walls are covered in white tiles whose blandness is relieved by interspersing tiles with blue designs which seem Dutch in origin. The ceiling is paneled in a light wood, and the chairs and floor are also of light wood. The cushions on the chairs and the draperies repeat the blue accents on the tiles. In this extraordinarily fresh and pretty room, regional specialties are served. Jörg Müller, the owner, is also the chef and dining at his restaurant is a memorable occasion.

RESTAURANT JÖRG MÜLLER
Owner: Jörg Müller
Süderstrasse 8
25980 Westerland-Sylt, Germany
Tel: (04651) 27788 Fax: (04651) 201471
1 room, 2 suites
Double: DM 250–290 Suite: DM 340–380
Closed December & mid-January to mid-February
Credit cards: all major
Restaurant closed Tuesdays
Island of Sylt, 160 km NW of Hamburg

Sylt, a tiny island in the north of Germany, is connected to the mainland by a narrow thread of land negotiable only by train. Although most of the island embraces a tranquil scene of windswept sand dunes, long stretches of beach, and picture-perfect thatched cottages, the principal town of Westerland, with its large hotels, designer boutiques, souvenir shops, ice cream parlors, and pizzerias, bustles with activity. In the midst of this touristy town, the Hotel Stadt Hamburg is an absolute oasis of charm and tranquility. The hotel, in the Hentzschel family for three generations, dates back to 1869. You will be enchanted from the moment you walk into the exquisite lounge where rich-red walls create the perfect background for comfortable sofas and chairs grouped in intimate settings. Fine English antiques abound, including many grandfather clocks, gorgeous tables, and chests whose woods gleam with the patina of age. The lounge is so home-like, so inviting, that guests must almost welcome dreary weather for an excuse to settle into a cozy corner with a good book. The guestrooms, some located in the original hotel and others in a new wing, are exquisitely furnished and resemble rooms in an English country estate. Although the Stadt Hamburg is an elegant Relais & Chateaux hotel, it happily maintains the exceptional warmth and sincere hospitality of a small inn.

HOTEL STADT HAMBURG
Owner: Harald Hentzschel
2, Strandstrasse
25980 Westerland-Sylt, Germany
Tel: (04651) 8580 Fax: (04651) 858220
72 rooms
Double: DM 370–490 Suite: DM 540–590
Open all year
Credit cards: all major
Restaurant open daily
Island of Sylt, 160 km NW of Hamburg
Relais & Chateaux

Cuckoo clocks and Triberg's location at the heart of the scenic Black Forest trails are the initial draw to this popular town: the Parkhotel Wehrle is the reason to return. This appealing, ivy-covered, yellow-stone inn occupies a prime corner position on the main street of Triberg. From the moment you enter, you will experience the outstanding warmth of welcome that makes this luxury hotel so very special. This is one of the friendliest, best-run small hotels in Germany. It has the incredible record of being owned by the same family every since it was built in 1707. There are several parts to the hotel: the reception counter, beautifully decorated dining rooms, and antique-filled lounges are in the original inn, as are some of the guestrooms. This main house is my first choice of where to stay because the rooms have such a comfortable, homey ambiance and old-world charm. One of my favorites (number 3) is a spacious room with fine antique furniture. There are also two romantic houses nestled in the garden with excellent accommodations. (The rooms with least character are those located in the modern annex where you find the indoor swimming pool.) The Parkhotel Wehrle, in conjunction with neighboring hotels, has a plan whereby you can walk between hotels carrying only your picnic lunch—your luggage is transferred to your next destination.

ROMANTIK HOTEL PARKHOTEL WEHRLE
Owner: Claus Blum
Gartenstrasse 24
78094 Triberg, Germany
Tel: (07722) 86020 Fax: (07722) 860290
54 rooms, 2 suites
Double: DM 188–298 Suite: DM 358–498
Open all year
Credit cards: all major
Restaurant open daily
130 km SW of Stuttgart, 51 km NE of Freiburg
Relais & Chateaux

The exterior of the Romantik Hotel Menzhausen is a 16th-century dazzler, with a half-timbered façade and painted decorations. Found on the pedestrian main street of this attractive town, the Hotel Menzhausen has been offering travelers lodging for over 400 years. The hotel has expanded by adding a wing of rooms behind the original building connected to it by a covered walkway over a cobbled lane. The restaurants are full of country charm and are in keeping with the historic core of the hotel. Herr Körber, the manager, takes special pride is his wine cellar and he will be happy to show you around. It is great fun to follow him down the low, narrow, dark, brick passage into the cellars lined with neat rows of bottles. The decor of the bedrooms improves as you move from the front of the hotel to the back: rooms in the old building are somewhat dated—behind them you find small, smart bedrooms, and in the garden wing the stylish rooms are larger and have peaceful views of the pretty garden. The garden wing also contains the delightful breakfast room whose arched windows overlook the luxurious indoor swimming pool. Uslar features on the *Deutsche Marchen Strasse* or Fairy-Tale Route. The hotel has lots of off-street parking and a parking garage.

ROMANTIK HOTEL MENZHAUSEN
Manager: Fritz Körber
Lange Strasse 12
37170 Uslar, Germany
Tel: (05571) 2051 Fax: (05571) 5820
34 rooms
Double: DM 185–250 Suite: DM 290–330
Open all year
Credit cards: all major
Restaurant open daily
133 km S of Hanover, 62 km N of Kassel

The little towns along the River Main, upstream from Würzburg, produce some of Germany's most delightful dry white wines. One of the most picturesque towns is Volkach with its town walls, lovely town hall, and pretty houses. Almost opposite the town hall, on Hauptstrasse, the town's main street, you find the 600-year old Zur Schwane, an inn and winery owned by the Pfaff family. Sit in the sheltered cobbled courtyard and sample their wines and enjoy dinner in one of the cozy, adorable restaurants with their old-fashioned tables and chairs set beneath low, paneled ceilings. The inn has been extended to the rear and quite the most delightful bedrooms are found in this new wing which has half-paneled walls and ceilings and dark-wood furniture to replicate the mood of the restaurants. An apartment has a sitting room with ceramic stove, tables, and chairs and a spacious bedroom. The Pfaffs produce their own wine and are happy to take those with an interest in wine production on a tour of their vast cellars. Daughter Eva is a wine taster and can arrange for tasting in the ancient barrel-vaulted cellar filled with oak wine casks—a special cask was made to celebrate the birth of her son Julius in 1992. The Zur Schwane makes an ideal base for wine-tasting along the River Main and visiting nearby Würzburg with its splendid baroque Residenz.

ROMANTIC HOTEL ZUR SCHWANE   **NEW**
Owners: Petra, Michael & Eva Pfaff
Hauptstrasse 12
97332 Volkach, Germany
Tel: (09381) 80660 Fax: (09381) 806666
23 rooms, 2 suites
Double: DM 160–270 Suite: DM 350–370
Open all year except Christmas & New Year
Credit cards: all major
Restaurant closed Mondays
25 km NE of Würzburg, 64 km NW of Bamburg

Schlosshotel Waldeck has a stunning hilltop location overlooking the Edersee. If you arrive midday, you might be surprised to see so many cars, but most of these belong to the day-tourists who have come to visit the museum located in one wing of the castle. (Be sure to go through the museum—it is well worth a visit, especially the foyer where life-size figures depict what peasant life must have been like 1,000 years ago.) As you enter the hotel, you find a large room with stone walls. The reception counter is to the left and sitting areas are tucked into cozy niches formed by the vaulted ceiling. Look carefully and you will see above the reception desk the chimney for the giant fireplace that warmed the room in days gone by. Although the castle-look is dominant, the hotel exudes a sleek, sophisticated air and offers all the amenities of a modern hotel with three dining rooms, various conference rooms, banquet facilities, outdoor terraces for dining, and even an indoor swimming pool nestled within stone walls with a skylight overhead. Some of the guestrooms are in the castle, others are in an impressive new wing. The rooms, which have a modern-hotel decor, look similar whatever section you are in, but my preference is for staying in the old castle. I especially like number 407, a spacious room with large windows that gives you a bird's-eye view of the evening sun setting over the lake.

SCHLOSSHOTEL WALDECK
Manager: K.F. Isenberg
34513 Waldeck am Edersee, Germany
Tel: (05623) 5890 Fax: (05623) 589289
37 rooms, 4 suites
Double: DM 250–270 Suite: DM 340–360
Open all year
Credit cards: all major
Restaurant open daily
200 km N of Frankfurt, 57 km SW of Kassel
Gast im Schloss

The main claim to fame of the Hotel Alte Post is its location in the very heart of Wangen, one of Germany's colorful medieval villages. The Alte Post was built in 1409 as a posting station and is now one of the oldest hotels in Germany. In days gone by horses were stabled below the existing building and exchanged to cover the next postal journey. You can easily spot the hotel (a boxy, three-story building with small gabled windows peeking out from a steeply pitched gray roof) as it sits in the center of town, opening onto a cobblestoned, pedestrian-only-square. Rooms on the first level are devoted to the hotel's restaurants. As in many German hotels, the dining rooms have more personality than the guestrooms whose decor varies from comfortable contemporary to traditional. From the third-floor guestrooms (tucked under beamed ceilings) you can hear the peal of the nearby church bells. The Veile family also owns the Romantik Hotel Postvilla located on the outskirts of Wangen.

ROMANTIK HOTEL ALTE POST
Owners: Gisela and Thomas Veile
Postplatz 2
88239 Wangen, Germany
Tel: (07522) 97560 Fax: (07522) 22604
19 rooms
Double: DM 180–250 Suite: DM 280–350
Open all year
Credit cards: all major
Restaurant closed Sundays
27 km N of Bregenz, 23 km SE of Ravensburg

Just on the edge of the quiet rural village of Wartmannsroth you find Sepp Halbritter's Landgasthaus, a delightful, very chic hotel and restaurant. While the exterior of the hotel is old, the interior is very modern. The lobby is decorated with colorful men's ties for Sepp Halbritter manufactures ties and waistcoats in nearby Fuchsstadt: guests can visit his tie museum and purchase ties from his factory shop. Enjoy a drink in the lively piano bar and dine at either the gourmet French restaurant or in the appealing casual restaurant specializing in Franconian food and serving regional beer and wine. Here you find large joyful murals of fanciful folk reveling in good food and wine. Upstairs the bedrooms are smart and modern, yet very tastefully decorated. My favorites were 24 and 25, spacious rooms at the front of the house, with uninterrupted views of rolling farmland. Two of the rooms which face an adjacent farmhouse have large balconies. A popular sightseeing venue is Würzburg where the Marienberg fortress, former home of the powerful prince bishops, looms over the city. The bishops felt their fortress was too small so moved across the river to the magnificent baroque Residenz. From Frankfurt exit the A3 at Weibersbrunn and travel via Lohr, Gemünden, and Hammelburg to Wartmannsroth.

SEPP HALBRITTER'S LANDGASTHAUS   **NEW**
Owner: Sepp Halbritter
Hauptstrasse 4
97797 Wartmannsroth, Germany
Tel: (09737) 890 Fax: (09737) 8940
7 rooms, 4 suites
Double: DM 190–250 Suite: DM 250
Closed January & February
Credit cards: all major
Restaurant open daily*
*Gourmet open Wednesdays to Sundays
10 km NW of Hammelburg, 53 km NW of Würzburg

Weimar is a magical city where you can still hear the haunting melodies of Bach and Liszt, who long ago called Weimar home. The town has so many cultural traditions that it prompted Germany's democrats to put Weimar's name on the new republic in 1919. The Hotel Elephant occupies a prize-winning location within the old town facing the large market square, enclosed by beautifully preserved medieval buildings, including a stunning, timbered, 16th-century Rathaus—one of Germany's finest. Although the hotel has been reconstructed, its history dates back hundreds of years and it lists many famous guests such as Johann Sebastian Bach, Franz Liszt, Richard Wagner, and Lilly Palmer. The lobby has a modern-hotel look with gray marble floor, black leather sofas, and black accent tables. There are two restaurants, my favorite being the Elephantenkeller, a pub-like restaurant serving regional specialties. A curved stairway with polished brass handrails leads to the floors above. The guestrooms have been completely renovated and now all have private bathrooms, mini-bars, and televisions. Instead of an old-world ambiance, the mood is modern and sophisticated. In 1996/7 the hotel is being extended into an adjacent house, giving 50 additional bedrooms.

HOTEL ELEPHANT
Manager: Norbert Henschel
Markt 19
99423 Weimar, Germany
Tel: (03643) 61471 Fax: (03643) 65310
116 rooms
Double: DM 300–380*
*Breakfast not included
Open all year
Credit cards: all major
Restaurant open daily
22 km E of Erfurt, in city center

If you cannot secure a room at the Hotel Elephant (where space is often unavailable), the Hilton is certainly a good alternative choice for accommodation in the lovely town of Weimar. Hiltons are a far cry from the small, intimate hotels we usually recommend, but the one in Weimar, although large and commercial, is very pleasant and not a concrete high-rise. The six-story hotel has a lovely setting overlooking the beautiful Ilm Park. The entry is glass-enclosed, like a greenhouse, creating a bright, cheerful atmosphere. A modern, brass-railed, double staircase spirals up from the lobby to the mezzanine where there are two restaurants, the Esplanade serving international cuisine and the Trattoria Esplanade with Italian specialties. At breakfast I was overwhelmed by the selection of food offered by the most extensive buffet I saw in Germany. On the same floor as the restaurants is a superb health club featuring a stunning indoor pool completely tiled in white with a domed skylight above. The guestrooms (60 designated non-smoking) are all similar in decor: modern, built-in furniture, top-notch mattresses, good lighting, pastel color schemes, mini-bars, international TV stations, and, of course, tiled bathrooms. There is ample parking and it is a pleasant 15-minute walk along the lovely tree-lined paths of Ilm Park to the center of town.

WEIMAR HILTON
Manager: Wolfgang Schack
Belvederer Allee 25
99425 Weimar, Germany
Tel: (03643) 7220 Fax: (03643) 722741
294 rooms
Double: DM 275–380 Suite: DM 580–1,010
 (weekend specials from DM 219)
Open all year
Credit cards: all major
Restaurant open daily
25 km E of Erfurt, overlooks Ilm park

Although built in 1993, the Hotel Schwartze has a traditional ambiance. Its exterior is reminiscent of a simple country home—very pretty, very appealing. The two-story hotel is painted a crisp white and has arched windows enhanced by boxes of colorful red geraniums. A traditional, red-tiled roof accented by gabled windows completes the picture. Inside everything is new and sparklingly fresh and clean. There is no antique decor, but for a relatively inexpensive place to stay, the accommodations are an excellent value. You enter into a reception-lobby with white marble floor and a doorway on the left leads to the cheerful breakfast room where a bountiful buffet is served each morning. Attractive watercolors decorate the white walls of the staircase leading up to the bedrooms which, although small, are sweet and attractive and have colored televisions and modern white-tiled bathrooms. It is fun to stay in the center of the old town of Weimar, but the Hotel Schwartze is certainly a most acceptable option if the Hotel Elephant is over your budget or booked to capacity. It is only about a 15-minute drive into the heart of the city, where you can park your car and delve into sightseeing. The Hotel Schwartze is very easy to find: take the Weimar exit from expressway 6, then in less than half a kilometer you will see the hotel on your left. It is not actually on the main road into Weimar, but if you are looking closely, you can see it.

HOTEL SCHWARTZE
Owner: Gerhard Schwartze
99428 Gelmeroda bei Weimar, Germany
Tel: (03643) 59950 Fax: (03643) 512614
30 rooms
Double: DM 160
Open all year
Credit cards: AX, MC
Restaurant open daily
Just off freeway exit, 6 km S of Weimar

The Schloss Weitenburg, dating back to the 11th century, is superbly positioned in the rolling, wooded hills south of Stuttgart. The castle has been in the von Rassler family since 1720 and the present Baron von Rassler still lives there. Once within the castle, you are thrust back to days gone by: small windows looking out through 4-foot-thick walls, massive stone floors, beamed ceilings, hunting trophies, and ancestors watching your every move from portraits on the walls. The dining room was formerly the kitchen as evidenced by the enormous metal flue in the ceiling where the smoke from the stove escaped. The bedrooms are scattered throughout the maze of hallways. Some are quite mediocre in decor with modern furnishings, but others have a marvelous antique flair. I especially like number 104, a paneled corner room with antique furniture and an exquisite panorama of rolling forest and the meandering Neckar river. Another favorite, number 110, is a bright and cheerful room overlooking the front courtyard. An old-fashioned, enclosed swimming pool lies just over a covered footbridge from the castle. Note: Weitenburg is not on most maps, but is easy to find. Driving south from Stuttgart on expressway 81, take the Rottenburg exit then turn right to Ergenzingen and follow the white Schloss Weitenburg signs which guide you back over the highway to the castle.

HOTEL SCHLOSS WEITENBURG
Owner: Max-Richard von Rassler
72181 Weitenburg, Germany
Tel: (07457) 9330 Fax: (07457) 933100
34 rooms
Double: DM 180–220 Suite: DM 295
Closed Christmas
Credit cards: all major
Restaurant open daily
40 km S of Stuttgart
Gast im Schloss

Set at the foot of the Harz mountains, Wernigerode is a beautiful town of timber-framed houses with an elaborately decorated, twin-spired town hall. On the pedestrian cobbled market square, facing the town hall, sits the Hotel Weisser Hirsch where you find a brand-spanking-new hotel behind its ancient, timbered façade. From the marketplace you enter directly into the lovely, old-world dining room all decked out in bleached oak. Center stage sits a large buffet whose tempting breakfast fare is replaced at lunchtime with a splendid array of salads. Reception lies at the back of the hotel, for guests usually arrive here via the elevator from the underground parking garage. All the bedrooms are decorated similarly in a fashionable, modern style with light-wood fitted furniture, soft pastel decor, and matching drapes and chairs. Each room is accompanied by a smart, white-tiled shower room with red accent tiles. All the rooms have the same tariff. If you prefer peace and quiet, request a back room but for views request a room overlooking the Marktplatz (marketplace) where a produce market is held every Saturday morning. Set off on foot to explore the cobbled streets full of very nice shops and delightful cafés. A little tractor-train will take you through the suburbs and up the hill to the castle which is more a grand 19th-century home than fortification. The tourist office can help you plan an excursion on the little steam train that chugs you high up into the Harz mountains.

HOTEL WEISSER HIRSCH   **NEW**
Owner: Jörg Wieland
Marktplatz 5
38855 Wernigerode, Germany
Tel: (03943) 632434 or 602020
Fax: (03943) 633139
47 rooms
Double: DM 190
Open all year
Credit cards: all major
Restaurant open daily
88 SW of Magdeburg, 145 km N of Erfurt

Wirsberg is a village just off the autobahn north of Bayreuth. The Romantik Posthotel, found on the village's main square, was once a posting station. Although part of the hotel appears modern, the reception area and hallway are set under heavy beams and there is a cozy little room tucked back into a corner with leaded glass windows where breakfast is served. For lunch or evening meals the hotel's Patrizier Salon is an elegantly set restaurant, while the Jagerstube affords an environment for a more casual rendezvous, beer, or supper. For overnight guests, the Herrmann family's wish is to see to all their comforts and create an atmosphere that will tempt them to linger: *Gastlichkeitmit Herz*, "hospitality with heart." The bedrooms range in decor from comfortable modern to an attractive traditional, but all are with private bath and superb in facilities and comfort. Also available to hotel guests is the use of a pool styled after a Roman bath, sauna, fitness room, solarium, and massage. Werner and Melitta Herrmann are the fifth generation of the Herrmann family to offer a warm welcome to guests at the Romantik Posthotel.

ROMANTIK POSTHOTEL
Owner: Family Herrmann
Marktplatz 11
95339 Wirsberg, Germany
Tel: (09227) 2080 Fax: (09227) 5860
48 rooms
Double: DM 188–330 Suite: DM 240–580
Open all year
Credit cards: all major
Restaurant open daily
100 km N of Nürnberg, 21 km N of Bayreuth

It is difficult to pinpoint the best feature of the Gasthof Hecht because you must choose between its country charm, wonderfully gracious, friendly hosts, and extremely reasonable rates. The 300-year-old gasthof is located on the picturesque pedestrian main street of Wolfach where its half-timbered façade, overflowing with vari-colored geraniums, has long been a welcome sight for travelers. The ground floor contains two atmospheric dining rooms with pewter and pottery collections, beamed ceilings, wood-paneled walls, and fresh flower bouquets. When I was visiting, a friendly neighborhood gathering occupied the tables and chairs that spill over into the cobblestoned street, adding to the convivial atmosphere. Leave your diet at home, as traditional, home-style meals are served here, including pork and veal dishes, plenty of vegetables, and mouthwatering tortes for dessert. On our last visit (1995) the bedrooms and bathrooms were in the midst of a complete refurbishment and, rather than actual rooms, we looked at swatches of fabric, tile, and architects' drawings. Even when the renovation is complete, the Gasthof Hecht will remain a simple hotel, not for those seeking sleek perfection, but a great choice for those wanting to stay in an inexpensive place with heart.

GASTHOF HECHT
Owners: Renate & Eberhard Sattler
Hauptstrasse 51
77709 Wolfach, Germany
Tel: (07834) 538 Fax: (07834) 47223
17 rooms
Double: DM 98
Closed mid-January to mid-February
Credit cards: all major
Restaurant closed Mondays & Tuesdays
40 km NE of Freiburg

Germany is chock-full of appealing walled villages: many are well-known tourist destinations; others, like the ever-so-tiny village of Wolframs-Eschenbach in the Romantic Road region, are tucked away off the beaten path, seldom discovered by the tourist. There are only two entrances to this medieval jewel, both through old watchtowers. The village's perimeter is formed by old stone walls, and the main street is lined with colorful, half-timbered houses. One of the prettiest of these houses is the Alte Vogtei, which was welcoming guests 100 years before Christopher Columbus discovered America. Its picturesque façade features an intricate pattern of timbered wood, white stucco, green shutters, and a profusion of geraniums spilling from the windowboxes. The main claim to fame of this small hotel is its restaurant, attracting guests from near and far. There are several intimate dining rooms, each brimming with antique charm. The food is excellent and reasonably priced. Upstairs in the old section of the inn is the best room, the Bridal Suite, with pretty painted furniture and a canopy bed. A corridor leads to the newer section of the hotel where the bedrooms are more motel-like and less charming. If the Bridal Suite is not available, ask for number 30, a large room decorated in a pleasant, contemporary style. Nine additional rooms are located in a nearby guesthouse.

ALTE VOGTEI
Owners: Monika & Georg Dörr
Hauptstrasse 21
91639 Wolframs-Eschenbach, Germany
Tel: (09875) 97000 Fax: (09875) 970070
18 rooms
Double: DM 108–120
Closed Christmas
Credit cards: MC, VS
Restaurant closed Mondays
48 km SW of Nürnberg, 16 km SE of Ansbach

Hann Munden

244

Key Map of Germany

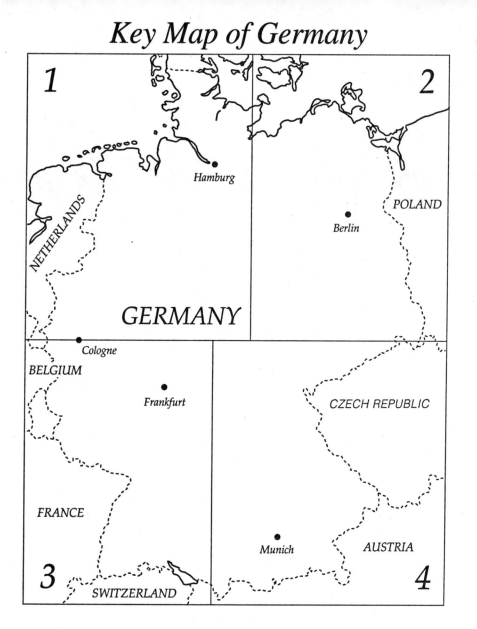

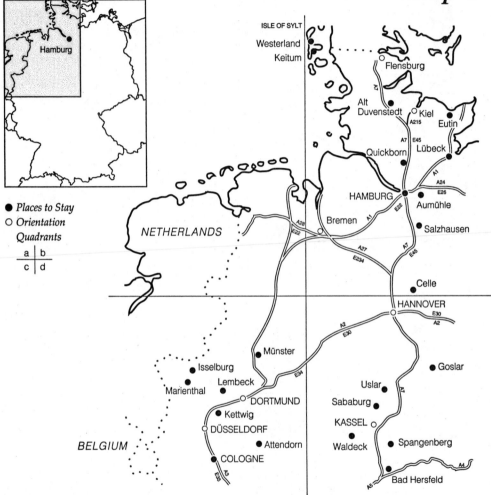

Map 1

ISLE OF SYLT
Westerland
Keitum

Flensburg

Alt
Duvenstedt

Kiel

Eutin

Quickborn

Lübeck

HAMBURG

Aumühle

Bremen

Salzhausen

NETHERLANDS

Celle

HANNOVER

Münster

Goslar

Isselburg

Uslar

Lembeck

Sababurg

Marienthal

DORTMUND

KASSEL

Kettwig

DÜSSELDORF

Spangenberg

BELGIUM

Attendorn

Waldeck

COLOGNE

Bad Hersfeld

● Places to Stay
○ Orientation
Quadrants

a	b
c	d

246

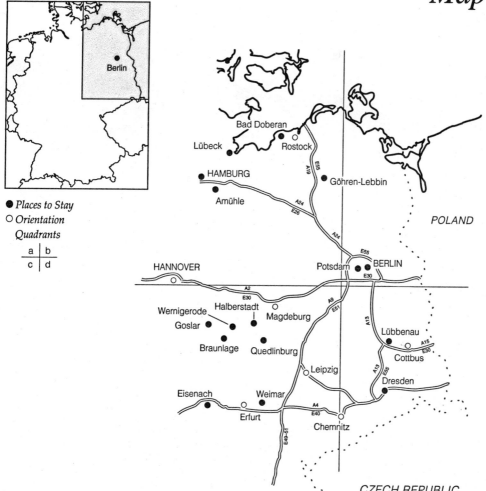

Map 2

Berlin

● *Places to Stay*
○ *Orientation*
  Quadrants

a	b
c	d

Bad Doberan

Lübeck

Rostock

HAMBURG

Göhren-Lebbin

A19

E55

A24

E26

A24

Amühle

POLAND

HANNOVER

E55

Potsdam

BERLIN

E30

A2

E30

E30

Wernigerode

Halberstadt

Magdeburg

A9

E51

A13

Lübbenau

Goslar

A15

E30

Braunlage

Quedlinburg

Cottbus

Leipzig

A13

E55

Eisenach

Weimar

Dresden

A4

Erfurt

E40

Chemnitz

E49-51

CZECH REPUBLIC

Map 3

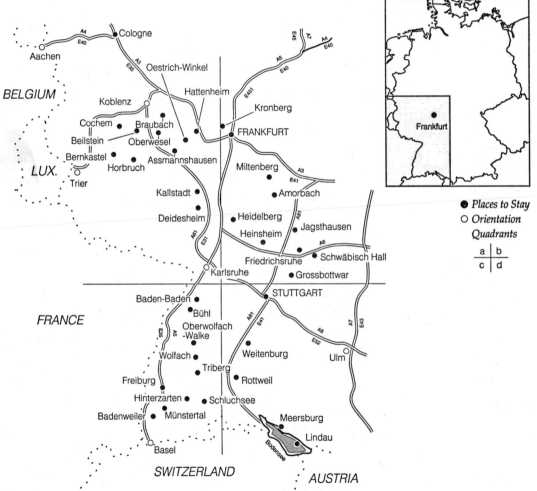

BELGIUM

Aachen

Cologne

Oestrich-Winkel

Hattenheim

Koblenz

Cochem

Braubach

Kronberg

Beilstein

Oberwesel

FRANKFURT

Bernkastel

Horbruch

Assmannshausen

LUX.

Trier

Miltenberg

Kallstadt

Amorbach

Deidesheim

Heidelberg

Heinsheim

Jagsthausen

Friedrichsruhe

Schwäbisch Hall

Karlsruhe

Grossbottwar

STUTTGART

Baden-Baden

Bühl

FRANCE

Oberwolfach
-Walke

Wolfach

Weitenburg

Ulm

Triberg

Freiburg

Rottweil

Hinterzarten

Schluchsee

Badenweiler

Münstertal

Meersburg

Basel

Lindau

Bodensee

SWITZERLAND

AUSTRIA

Frankfurt

● Places to Stay
○ Orientation
Quadrants

a	b
c	d

Map 4

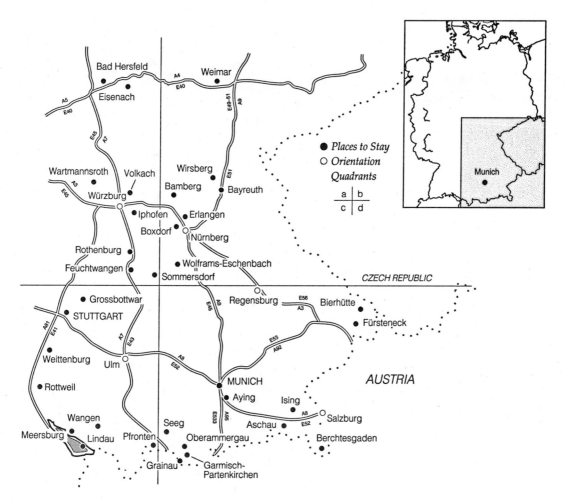

Bad Hersfeld
Weimar
A4
E40
Eisenach
A5
E40
E45
A7

Places to Stay
Orientation
Quadrants

a	b
c	d

Munich

Wartmannsroth
Volkach
Wirsberg
A3
E45
Bamberg
Bayreuth
Würzburg
E51
Iphofen
Erlangen
Boxdorf
Nürnberg
Rothenburg
Wolframs-Eschenbach
Feuchtwangen
Sommersdorf
CZECH REPUBLIC

Grossbottwar
Regensburg
E56
Bierhütte
A9
STUTTGART
E45
A3
Fürsteneck
A81
E41
A7
E43
E53
A92
Weittenburg
Ulm
A8
E52
Rottweil
MUNICH
AUSTRIA
Aying
Ising
Wangen
Seeg
E533
A95
Salzburg
A8
Meersburg
Lindau
Pfronten
Aschau
E52
Berchtesgaden
Oberammergau
Grainau
Garmisch-
Partenkirchen

249

Index

—I—

—L—

—M—

now that you've
DISCOVERED
these
CHARMING
HOTELS
who can you call to
BOOK THEM?

*Turn The Page To Discover
Your One Stop Connection!*

Euro-Connection

We Love to Hear from Karen Brown's Readers

ACCOLADES: We'd love to hear which accommodations you have especially enjoyed—even the shortest of notes is greatly appreciated. It is reassuring to know that places we recommend meet with your approval.

COMPLAINTS: Please let us know when a place we recommend fails to live up to the standards you have come to expect from Karen Brown. Constructive criticism is greatly appreciated. We sometimes make a mistake, places change, or go downhill. Your letters influence us to re-evaluate a listing.

RECOMMENDATIONS: If you have a favorite hideaway that you would like to recommend, please write to us. Give us a feel for the place, if possible send us a brochure and photographs (which we regret we cannot return). Convince us that on our next research trip, your discovery deserves a visit. All accommodations included in our guides are ones we have seen and enjoyed. Many of our finest selections are those that readers have discovered—wonderful places we would never have found on our own.

Please send information to:

KAREN BROWN'S GUIDES
Post Office Box 70
San Mateo, California 94401, USA
Telephone (415) 342-9117   Fax (415) 342-9153

SEAL COVE INN—LOCATED IN THE SAN FRANCISCO AREA

Karen Brown Herbert (best known as author of the Karen Brown's Guides) and her husband, Rick, have put nineteen years of experience into reality and opened their own superb hideaway, Seal Cove Inn. Spectacularly set amongst wild flowers and bordered by towering cypress trees, Seal Cove Inn looks out to the ocean over acres of county park: an oasis where you can enjoy secluded beaches, explore tidepools, watch frolicking seals, and follow the tree-lined path that traces the windswept ocean bluffs. Country antiques, original watercolors, flower-laden cradles, rich fabrics, and the gentle ticking of grandfather clocks create the perfect ambiance for a foggy day in front of the crackling log fire. Each bedroom is its own haven with a cozy sitting area before a wood-burning fireplace and doors opening onto a private balcony or patio with views to the distant ocean. Moss Beach is a 35-minute drive south of San Francisco, 6 miles north of the picturesque town of Half Moon Bay, and a few minutes from Princeton harbor with its colorful fishing boats and restaurants. Seal Cove Inn makes a perfect base for whale-watching, salmon-fishing excursions, day trips to San Francisco, exploring the coast, or, best of all, just a romantic interlude by the sea, time to relax and be pampered. Karen and Rick look forward to the pleasure of welcoming you to their hideaway by the sea.

Seal Cove Inn, 221 Cypress Avenue, Moss Beach, California, 94038, USA
Telephone: (415) 728-7325   Fax: (415) 728-4116

Be a Karen Brown's Preferred Reader

If you would like to be the first to know when new editions of Karen Brown's Guides go to press, and also to be included in any special promotions, simply send us your name and address. We encourage you to buy new editions and throw away the old ones so that you don't miss a wealth of wonderful new discoveries or run the risk of staying in places that no longer meet our standards—you'll be glad you did. We cover the miles searching for special places so that you don't have to spend your valuable vacation time doing so.

Name _____

Street _____

Town _____ State _____ Zip _____

Telephone: _____ Fax: _____

Please send information to:

KAREN BROWN'S GUIDES
Post Office Box 70
San Mateo, California 94401, USA
Telephone (415) 342-9117   Fax (415) 342-9153

CLARE BROWN has many years of experience in the field of travel and has earned the designation of Certified Travel Consultant. Since 1969 she has specialized in planning itineraries to Europe using charming small hotels in the countryside for her clients. The focus of her job remains unchanged, but now her expertise is available to a larger audience—the readers of her daughter's country inn guides. Clare lives in Hillsborough, California, with her husband, Bill.

JUNE BROWN, who hails from Sheffield, England, has an extensive background in travel, dating back to her school girl days when she "youth hosteled" throughout Europe. June lives in San Mateo, California, with her husband, Tony, and their children, Simon and Clare.

KAREN BROWN wrote her first travel guide in 1976. Her personalized travel series has grown to 12 titles and Karen and her small staff work diligently to keep all the guides updated. Karen, her husband, Rick, and their children, Alexandra and Richard, live on the coast south of San Francisco at their own country inn, Seal Cove Inn, in Moss Beach.

BARBARA TAPP, the talented artist who produces all of the hotel sketches and delightful illustrations in this guide, was raised in Australia where she studied in Sydney at the School of Interior Design. Although Barbara continues with freelance projects, she devotes much of her time to illustrating the Karen Brown guides. Barbara lives in Kensington, California, with her husband, Richard, their two sons, Jonothan and Alexander, and daughter, Georgia.

JANN POLLARD, the artist responsible for the beautiful painting on the cover of this guide, has studied art since childhood, and is well-known for her outstanding impressionistic-style watercolors which she has exhibited in numerous juried shows, winning many awards. Jann travels frequently to Europe (using Karen Brown's guides) where she loves to paint historical buildings. Jann lives in Burlingame, California, with her husband, Gene.

USA Order Form

Please ask in your local bookstore for KAREN BROWN'S GUIDES. If the books you want are unavailable, you may order directly from the publisher.

Austria: Charming Inns & Itineraries $16.95

California: Charming Inns & Itineraries $16.95

England: Charming Bed & Breakfasts $15.95

England, Wales & Scotland: Charming Hotels & Itineraries $16.95

French Country Bed & Breakfasts $15.95

France: Charming Inns & Itineraries $16.95

Germany: Charming Inns & Itineraries $16.95

Ireland: Charming Inns & Itineraries $16.95

Italy: Charming Bed & Breakfasts $15.95

Italy: Charming Inns & Itineraries $16.95

Spain: Charming Inns & Itineraries $16.95

Swiss Country Inns & Itineraries $16.95

Name _____ Street _____

Town _____ State _____ Zip _____ tel. _____

Credit Card [MasterCard or Visa] _____ Exp: _____

Add $4 for the first book and 50 cents for each additional book for postage & packing. California residents add 8.25% sales tax. Order form **only** for shipments within the USA. Indicate number of copies of each title; send form with check or credit card information to:

KAREN BROWN'S GUIDES
Post Office Box 70, San Mateo, California, 94401
Telephone: (415) 342-9117   Fax: (415) 342-9153